BUILDING TRUST

Advance Comments about *Building Trust*

Chief Executive Officers, regardless of their industry or company mission, share one common desire: To restore confidence in the integrity of American business by bringing the highest standard of ethics to their enterprise. They lead by example, and this book chronicles, with vivid detail, the simple truths and philosophies they and their employees live by — a refreshing look into the hearts and minds of America's business leaders.

> John J. Castellani
> *President*
> *Business Rountable*

Restoring trust in Corporate America will only happen with the strong leadership of CEOs. This book from the Arthur W. Page Society provides an invaluable blueprint to the basic principles essential to building trust. These principles come not from government or laws or regulations but from the experiences of CEOs who have a proven record for integrity and success. Learn from these lessons and you will understand the fundamental values of American business.

> Leon E. Panetta
> *Director*
> *The Panetta Institute for Public Policy*

This logically organized, tightly written and beautifully framed book demonstrates clearly that trust in Corporate America must be earned, first and foremost, by responsible, responsive, and values-based company performance — complemented by "open, honest, two-way communication" with key publics. Packed with principles and laced with lessons, it's a must read for practitioners and students.

> Douglas Anderson, *Dean*
> *College of Communications*
> *Penn State University*

ADVANCE COMMENTS ABOUT *BUILDING TRUST*

Building Trust offers practical and valuable perspectives — and real-life insights — on how to make trust, ethics, and customer focus the underpinnings of a corporate culture. It delivers an important message to all Americans about the integrity of corporations and the leaders who run them.

> John A. Thain
> *Chief Executive Officer*
> *New York Stock Exchange*

Building Trust examines the most salient issues facing CEOs today — building sustainable trust. Those who take leadership seriously will discover in its pages the invaluable advice of leading CEOs who have earned the trust of employees, the public, and the business community and who share with the reader their leadership philosophies and timeless lessons. This CEO wisdom creates ethical and enduring organizations built on bedrocks of integrity and forthright dialogue. It is well worth analyzing and makes *Building Trust* an indispensable tool and an engrossing read for the serious business and communications aficionado.

> Dr. Leslie Gaines-Ross
> *Author*
> *CEO Capital: A Guide to Building CEO*
> *Reputation and Company Success*

Finally a loud and articulate set of voices from the business community on the critical issues of building trust with stakeholders. *Building Trust* brings a fresh and honest view on the challenges and strategic value of restoring trust by a new generation of business leaders.

> Brad Googins, *Executive Director*
> *Center for Corporate Citizenship*
> *Boston College*

ADVANCE COMMENTS ABOUT *BUILDING TRUST*

Building Trust is an inspiring book, reminding us all that the vast majority of business executives are men and women of high integrity who work hard every day to uphold the reputation of their companies and perform honestly for their customers, investors, and employees. The CEOs who have contributed to this book represent the true face of American business, leaders who understand that honesty and trust are fundamental contributors to profitable companies and a vibrant free enterprise economy.

>Thomas J. Donohue
>*President & CEO*
>*U.S. Chamber of Commerce*

Building Trust is a must read collection of all the right reasons to do all the right things. From all the right people.

>Keith Reinhard
>*Chairman*
>*DDB Worldwide*

Building Trust is a sustained argument for public relations as the conscience of Corporate America. Testimony from 23 of the nation's leading CEOs is among the best case studies for business integrity I have ever read. It is a compelling account of how to conduct business in the private sector, even policy making, with the public at the table.

I cannot now imagine completing an undergraduate degree, or for that matter a graduate degree, in public relations or corporate communications without having read *Building Trust*. The academic community owes the Arthur W. Page Society a huge debt for demonstrating so fully how trust matters.

>E. Culpepper Clark, *Dean*
>*College of Communication and Information Sciences*
>*The University of Alabama*

> "TRUST, LIKE THE SOUL, NEVER RETURNS, ONCE IT IS GONE."
>
> – Publilius Syrus, *Sententiae* c.50 B.C.

BUILDING TRUST

LEADING CEOs SPEAK OUT:
HOW THEY CREATE IT,
STRENGTHEN IT, SUSTAIN IT.

©2004 BY THE ARTHUR W. PAGE SOCIETY, INC.

ALL RIGHTS RESERVED.
PRINTED IN THE UNITED STATES OF AMERICA.
EXCEPT AS PERMITTED UNDER
THE UNITED STATES COPYRIGHT ACT OF 1976,
NO PART OF THIS BOOK WHATSOEVER MAY BE USED,
REPRODUCED OR DISTRIBUTED IN ANY MANNER OR STORED
IN A DATA BASE OR RETRIEVAL SYSTEM
WITHOUT WRITTEN PERMISSION EXCEPT IN
BRIEF QUOTATIONS EMBODIED IN CRITICAL ARTICLES AND REVIEWS.
FOR INFORMATION ADDRESS THE ARTHUR W. PAGE SOCIETY
32 AVENUE OF THE AMERICAS, NEW YORK, NEW YORK 10013.

FIRST EDITION
LIBRARY OF CONGRESS CATALOGING-IN-PUBLICATION DATA
2004 115 888

BUILDING TRUST
LEADING CEOs SPEAK OUT
ISBN 974 47326 – 0 – 5

1. BUSINESS INTEGRITY 2. CORPORATE RESPONSIBILITY
3. EMPLOYEE MOTIVATION 4. MANAGING FOR TOMORROW 5. TELLING THE TRUTH
6. ARTHUR W. PAGE 7. PAGE PRINCIPLES.   I. TITLE

GRATEFUL ACKNOWLEDGMENT IS MADE TO
THE HISTORY FACTORY AND PIVOT DESIGN

PHOTO OF A.W. PAGE REPRINTED WITH PERMISSION OF AT&T

10 9 8 7 6 5 4 3 2 1 0

WWW.AWPAGESOCIETY.COM

ARTHUR W. PAGE SOCIETY

The Arthur W. Page Society is a membership organization for select senior corporate communications executives who seek to enrich and strengthen their profession. The Society is undergirded by management concepts articulated by Arthur W. Page that have been tested for more than half a century and have earned the respect and support of chief executive officers throughout the United States.

Since its incorporation in December 1983, the Society has sought to bring together senior communications executives representing a wide spectrum of industries who are interested in perpetuating the high professional standards set by Arthur Page. The Society draws on the experience and legacy of outstanding practitioners who have followed the Page philosophy.

Headquartered in New York City, the Arthur W. Page Society is a 501 (c) (3) organization.

THE HISTORY FACTORY

The History Factory is a heritage management firm that helps organizations discover, preserve and leverage their history to meet today's business challenges. Relying on its proven Start with the Future and Work Back™ methodology, The History Factory first gains an understanding of what each client is doing today to achieve its future goals, then systematically works back into the client's "experience inventory" to draw a continuous thread from yesterday to tomorrow.

In developing fully integrated heritage programs for leading organizations, The History Factory has published critically acclaimed books for Brooks Brothers, International Paper, Prudential, Schreiber Foods and many others. In addition, The History Factory leverages clients' heritage through anniversary planning, archives, documentaries, Heritage Servers, museums and exhibits, and oral histories.

Founded in 1979, The History Factory counts several of the world's biggest and most admired companies and organizations among its distinguished roster of clients.

The History Factory is headquartered in Chantilly, Va., a suburb of Washington, D.C., with offices in New York, Chicago, Atlanta and San Diego.

Contents

VII   **Acknowledgments**

XI   **Introduction**

XXIV   **Arthur W. Page**

The Page Principles

3   GUIDELINES FOR PROMOTING INTEGRITY AND BUILDING TRUST
Edward M. Block
Arthur W. Page Society

16   PRINCIPLED BEHAVIOR
Michael J. Birck
Tellabs, Inc.

Tell the Truth

28   BUSINESS INTEGRITY
Fred Hassan
Schering-Plough Corporation

42   THE CORPORATE NAVIGATION SYSTEM
Frederic M. Poses
American Standard Companies, Inc.

56   AFTER THE SPIN (OFF)
William T. Monahan
Imation Corporation

68   DOING BUSINESS RIGHT
Alexander M. Cutler
Eaton Corporation

80   PUTTING THE HEART BACK INTO BUSINESS
Rich DeVos
Amway Corporation

Prove it with Action

96   ETHICS IN ACTION
Ivan Seidenberg
Verizon Communications, Inc.

106   DRIVING INTEGRITY
Rick Wagoner
General Motors Corporation

118   LIVING THE MISSION
Art Collins
Medtronic, Inc.

130   RESPONDING TO THE WORST U.S. BLACKOUT
Dr. E. Linn Draper, Jr.
American Electric Power, Inc.

Listen to the Customer

144   ALL THE WAYS A BUSINESS SHOULD LEAD
Samuel J. Palmisano
IBM

160   SERVE CUSTOMERS BETTER, GROW FASTER
Louis J. Giuliano
ITT Industries, Inc.

172 PUTTING THE CLIENT FIRST
Michael H. Jordan
EDS Corporation

184 THE AETNA WAY
John W. Rowe, M.D.
Aetna Inc.

Manage for Tomorrow

200 RESTORING PUBLIC TRUST
Klaus Kleinfeld
Siemens Corporation

214 INTEGRITY:
KEY TO SUCCESS
Hank McKinnell
Pfizer, Inc.

226 REALITY AND INTEGRITY
John W. Rowe
Exelon Corporation

238 TRUSTED INNOVATION
Dr. Henning Kagermann
SAP AG

A Company's True Character is Expressed by its People

254 DELIVERING ON THE PROMISE
Michael L. Eskew
UPS

270 IMAGINE
J. Wayne Leonard
Entergy Corporation

284 INVEST IN TRUTHFUL
COMMUNICATIONS
Edward M. Liddy
The Allstate Corporation

296 OUR CREDO: WHO WE ARE
William C. Weldon
Johnson & Johnson

Coda

310 THE LONG VIEW
Marilyn Carlson Nelson
Carlson Companies

319 **Appendix**

Acknowledgments

In face of the current turmoil about the integrity of business, it is no surprise the Arthur W. Page Society's Board of Trustees readily agreed to undertake a project aimed at helping to restore confidence in business. Although 99 percent of corporate managers operate ethically, the actions of a few—fueled by media frenzy—were tarnishing the reputations of all.

When it was created, the Page Society set as an objective for itself to promote truth and honesty in matters of corporate governance. Among the ways it does this is by encouraging corporations to embrace a series of basic "principles" articulated by its namesake, Arthur W. Page. They are described in greater detail on the following pages.

At a meeting of the Heritage Committee in Ron Culp's office at Sears, Roebuck to plan activities to celebrate the Society's 20th anniversary in 2003, the idea of producing a book to counter the growing hostility towards business was first broached.

The Page Society's president, David Drobis, chairman of Ketchum, appointed a task force from the Heritage Committee to undertake the effort. The History Factory was asked to help bring the idea to fruition. The task force agreed the best way to reverse public perceptions would be to ask a cross-section of prominent CEOs representing a variety of industries to share their thoughts about integrity and how they built and sustained it in their companies. Thus *Building Trust* was launched.

To make this collection of essays by respected CEOs possible, the efforts of many people were required.

ACKNOWLEDGMENTS

David Drobis was of immeasurable help. His leadership was essential in getting the many pieces to fall into place properly. In addition to Ron Culp, board members Jim Arnold (Arnold Consultants), John Budd (The Omega Group), Jim Murphy (Accenture), and Kurt Stocker (Northwestern University) expressed encouragement from the outset. Board members volunteering to invite CEOs to participate were: Nick Ashooh (American Electric Power), Jack Bergen (Siemens), Kristen Bihary (Eaton), Roger Bolton (Aetna), Peter Debreceny (Allstate), Valerie Di Maria (GE Capital), Harvey Greisman (IBM), Steve Harris (General Motors), Anne McCarthy (SAP), and Bill Nielsen (Johnson & Johnson). Ed and Pat Nieder (Nieder & Nieder) offered valuable counsel.

Follow-through guidance by Tom Martin (ITT Industries), the Society's current president, enabled the production, promotion, and ultimate distribution of *Building Trust*. Executive director Paul Basista and administrative assistant Marjorie Brown supplied important backup support.

Leadership from The History Factory was provided by Founder and CEO Bruce Weindruch. He was assisted by Keir Walton, Kevin Manzel, Rod Thorn, and project manager India Perry.

In addition to the nearly two dozen CEOs who authored the essays, a host of people in the various companies contributed critical assistance. They included Page Society members: Brad Allen (Imation), Mark Bain (Alticor), Marybeth Barden (Verizon), Doug Cody (Carlson), John Iwata (IBM), Don Kirchoffner (Exelon), Shelly London (American Standard), Tom Mattia (EDS), George Stenitzer (Tellabs), Ken Sternad (UPS), Jessica Stoltenberg (Medtronic), and Art Wiese (Entergy).

Also assisting were: Bruce Brackett, Joellen Brown, Mike Calcina, Deborah Caldwell, Bruce Danielson, Christine Durica Orlowski, Amy Franklin, Tricia Geno, Kathleen Goldstein, David Hallisey, Marsha Hall-Jenkins, Chuck Hardwick, Steve Hiles, Meredith Hilt, Harriet DuVal Jones, Jason Loesche, Christine Campbell Loth, Stacie Prince, Thomas Pyden, Marianna Ricci, John Santoro, Adam Theodore, Mary Warner, Eileen Weber and Teresa Yoo.

But none of this would have been possible without the help, guidance and encouragement of the co-chair of the Society's Heritage Committee, Ed Block. Over the years, as a founding director of the Society, he has understood and interpreted the writings of Arthur Page in ways that keep them evergreen, as his essay on The Page Principles in this volume attests.

With so many people involved, it soon became obvious this undertaking would consume more time than originally forecast. That the pressure did not become unduly burdensome is a tribute to the patience and understanding of my wife, Catherine, without whose support my continued involvement would have been impossible.

> Jack Koten
> CHAIR
> *Heritage Committee*
> *January 2004*

TASK FORCE MEMBERS
Jim Arnold, Ed Block, Ron Culp, Ed Nieder

INTRODUCTION

The business environment at the turn of this century provides a sobering context for the publication of this book. For the last several years, stories about the malfeasance of corporations and corporate leadership have filled the news media.

Chief Executive Officers (CEOs) are frequently portrayed as arrogant, egregiously overcompensated, unrestrained in their greed, uncaring with respect to employees, disdainful of laws and regulations, and, in a few cases, as remarkably incompetent.

INTRODUCTION

Financial institutions stand accused of "puffing" stocks, self-dealing and "gaming" the markets. Auditors and lawyers are revealed as "enablers" of schemes to deceive investors as well as regulatory agencies.

Moreover, management, as a consequence of its actions to adjust to global competition and the speed of technological change, however necessary, is depicted as callous. Traditional white-collar as well as blue-collar employment has shrunk. Jobs are often moved to lower paying overseas locations. Workplace anxiety rules.

Loss of wages, taxes, and corporate philanthropy are squeezing the economies of many communities. New converts are joining traditional critics of "globalization" and the growing power of multinational corporations.

Given the flood of negative news, it is no wonder that corporate governance comes under heavy and continuing scrutiny. Government prosecutors, legislators, and regulators, along with consumer groups and media "investigators," are piling on. Many Americans, already harboring an innate mistrust of business—especially big corporations—accept the charges at face value. Congress, sensing the national mood, eagerly passed the Sarbanes-Oxley Act in near-record time. The legislation, signed promptly by the President, mandates stricter financial controls and reports and requires CEOs to personally sign off on their companies' financial statements. The already dismal reputation of business has sunk to new lows.

Concerned about the public's diminishing confidence in business and its impact on the nation's economy, President George W. Bush convened meetings with CEOs and others. He listened to their views and suggestions, but in the end he said Americans have lost faith in business's ability to govern itself. "I know the majority of those leading corporate America are good honorable people," he said, "[but] to help earn back public trust, it's up to you to speak for yourselves. I can't do it alone for you."

As American Standard's Fred Poses says (page 44), "[It's a] question of whether the well-publicized ethical lapses at some major corporations are the result of a few bad apples in the leadership ranks, or the product of a systemic fungus that infects the whole orchard of American business. Having spent 30 years working in that orchard, I am more convinced than ever that the overwhelming majority of corporations and the people who work for them value integrity."

Maintaining the public's confidence in corporations is important. Francis Fukuyama, in his book *Trust: The Social Virtues and the Creation of Prosperity,* observes that when a nation or society permits and supports a high level of trust, prosperity and high economic results usually follow.

Corporations are truly one of the greatest inventions of human beings. They are the tools that enable people to do great, constructive things. They organize human resources productively and empower people to achieve noble objectives and find fulfillment in doing so. Corporations are the most efficient institutions yet created to raise standards of living. In the process, they make the world a better place in which to live.

But if corporations are seen as abusing the privileges given to them by the public, sanctions can be imposed by government that severely hamper their effectiveness and efficiency. Moreover, companies

INTRODUCTION

perceived to be operating unethically or with tarnished reputations, discover people are reluctant to buy from, invest in, or work for them.

Especially alarming at the present time is the prospect that bright, able, conscientious young people, hesitant about entering an environment where respect and integrity are not present, may ultimately refuse to join the corporate work force, thereby avoiding the perception of being "bought" by enticing salaries and bonuses. If a company's talent pool is significantly diminished for this reason, its ability to be competitive in the global marketplace will be increasingly difficult.

As CEO Fred Hassan, who grew up in Pakistan, writes (page 38), "I never saw America as perfect. I never saw American business as perfect. However, I was absolutely convinced there was no better country and no business environment more welcoming to a young person with very big dreams and the heart to achieve them. I sincerely believe this is still true today."

Fred's opinion remains the majority view in the United States. By far, the preponderance of men and women who lead corporations are honorable. They believe honesty is a virtue. They respect employees. They are good citizens. They want to build shareowner value the old-fashioned way. They are eager to listen to customers and they recognize that in the long run, success will be measured by criteria imposed by customers. But awareness of these virtues must be rekindled with conviction and demonstrated by the actions of corporate leadership. That is the intent of this book.

To accomplish this objective, the Arthur W. Page Society invited a cross-section of the nation's leading CEOs to tell what they and their companies are doing to foster trust and integrity.

INTRODUCTION

Clearly the responsibility for managing a corporation's reputation belongs to the CEO. Under the leadership of former Page Society President Jim Murphy, global managing director of Accenture, the Public Relations Coalition (a partnership of 19 major communications organizations) issued a white paper on *Restoring Trust In Business: Models For Action*. It challenged CEOs to adopt ethical principles, pursue transparency, and make trust the basis for corporate governance.

The CEOs' willingness to participate in this project quickly became apparent. By sharing their efforts to assure accountability, openness, and ethical behavior within their organizations, they speak for the majority of CEOs. They demonstrate the fundamental soundness of American business and the ethical values that guide them. The companies they represent vary in size (both by market value and number of employees), age, industry, geographic location(s), and ownership.

The template for *Building Trust* already existed.

During the 1930s, another time of dismay about corporate performance and economic uncertainty, Arthur W. Page, the Society's namesake, articulated his postulates of what it takes to assure business longevity and build and sustain corporate reputation. Page was a vice president and member of the board of directors of AT&T.

Known familiarly as Ma Bell, it was a business that by definition had to be concerned about public trust. It was a monopoly and, at the time, the world's largest public corporation. Its operations were pervasively and continuously regulated by government agencies at the state and federal level. Consequently, the wisdom of Page's concepts was put to the test every single day—and thereby amply confirmed.

INTRODUCTION

What makes the Page concepts readily transferable to virtually every business is the fact that his admonitions are so remarkable in their simplicity:
- Tell the truth.
- Prove it with action.
- Listen to the customer.
- Manage for tomorrow.
- A company's true character is expressed by its people.
- Conduct public relations as if the whole company depends on it.

Page often suggested another precept: Remain, calm, patient and good-humored. In times of crisis, he advised, cool heads communicate best.

The CEOs were asked by the Society to write an essay about how they built and sustained trust in their companies using as a guideline one or more of the Page Principles. As a result, the essays are divided into sections corresponding to the principle closest to their content. Careful readers will find the authors frequently mention other principles helpful to them. Several companies, to emphasize their sincerity about the importance of this effort, provided copies of their credo, code of conduct, or values statement. These are included in the Appendix.

In the first section, Ed Block, a worthy successor to Arthur Page at AT&T, describes in greater detail how the Page Principles apply to business today—why they are as relevant now as they were 70 years ago—no matter how large or complex the business enterprise.

Following Ed's introduction, the 23 CEOs explain how these timeless principles impact their business and how they help to build trust among their constituencies. Though written over a period of several months, the concepts expressed by the CEOs are timeless.

In his overview, Michael Birck of Tellabs makes clear that CEOs must lead by example and that doing the right things in the right way is more important than anything "we preach." If you listen carefully enough, he adds, "your customers will tell you everything you need to know."

"Communication," he says, "just may be the most important element in business."

In the section on **Tell the Truth,** Schering-Plough's Fred Hassan says upfront that "business success is not about numbers, it is about trust." He goes on to explain, "Business integrity means living up to the intent, and not just the letter, of the laws and regulations wherever we operate." He amplifies this point saying "[This] means obeying the internal moral compass that we all have, so that in each situation we face in our business life, we consciously choose to do what we believe is right and reject what we believe to be wrong."

Eaton's Alexander Cutler says it a bit differently and more succinctly, "Decision-making, when faced with an ethical dilemma, is easy: Do the right thing. Always."

When a "spin-off" from an older, established, successful company creates a "new" company, it is not always easy to introduce a new culture into the new company. Bill Monahan of Imation describes some of the problems he encountered in getting employees who came from a perfectly good old culture (3M) to adapt to a new culture while resisting the temptation to be completely different. As he says, "Your reputation is your most valuable asset…hard won and built up over years, [it] can easily be destroyed in moments by a perceived betrayal of trust."

INTRODUCTION

Starting out by making soap in the family basement, Rich DeVos, with his partner Jay Van Andel, built giant Alticor (better known by its "Amway" branded products) from scratch. A lifelong optimist, he says "every challenge presents new opportunities—to learn, grow, gain strength, or reach a higher goal." He reminds us that "no matter what we make or distribute, we all exist to *help others*." In that connection he says, "we must always be straight about who we are and what we do as businesses." Trust in business, he believes, can be restored, "if we show more heart…[I]f we just treat others with greater respect, then there is no doubt…that business is going to earn new levels of trust and support."

The next section describes how companies **Prove it with Action**. Verizon's Ivan Seidenberg says, "The public is absolutely right to hold corporate executives to the highest standards of conduct." But he adds that while, "[T]he buck may stop at the CEO's desk, …it doesn't necessarily start there." In discussing ethical leadership from an institutional standpoint, he says it must be looked at "in terms of how it's exhibited in the everyday actions of the people." Expressing pride in the performance of his employees on 9/11, he says that when it comes to large organizations, "Leadership has less to do with any single individual…than it does with the culture, norms and values of the institution itself."

Discussing the importance of everyday workplace performance, General Motors' Rick Wagoner says quite clearly, "how we act as individuals has a profound effect on whether the organizations we represent achieve their full potential. Integrity has a direct impact on both the bottom line and the long-term viability of every company. Integrity transcends borders, language and culture. It's not something we can impose, but it is something we can influence and monitor…"

Agreeing that trust is built on the everyday actions of its employees, Art Collins of Medtronic says, "if we act responsibly and focus on meeting our customers' needs, strong financial performance will follow." He says that is why the company encourages "employees [to] do whatever is required to provide product and service whenever and wherever it's needed."

In discussing American Electric Power's response to the worst blackout in U.S. history, Linn Draper says, "Let me be clear—we did it right…Our protective systems performed as they were designed to perform, our operators performed and communicated as they should…" These actions were recognized by the industry and the company avoided the criticisms that were directed to many of its "partners" in the failure of the northeastern power grid.

The seemingly obvious principle **Listen to the Customer** is more easily stated than implemented. As Lou Guliano of ITT Industries expresses, "[Our customers] simply want us to look at the world through their eyes. To meet their expectations, we also have to take a pretty hard look at ourselves." IBM's Sam Palmisano takes it a step further, saying, "When technology and the nature of customer problems change, we do, too." That's a clear recipe for staying ahead of the competition and staying alive in the future.

Dr. John Rowe, responding to concerns expressed by Aetna's customers, takes a slightly different tack, offering, "When you ask the customer what they want, it boils down to more control over their

INTRODUCTION

health care decisions." The implication here is that to meet customer interests, often the support of other organizations or companies is necessary to achieve common goals. But in the end, EDS's Mike Jordan states it most explicitly, "Put the client first."

To **Manage for Tomorrow** takes a visionary leader capable of assessing the present and seeing the potential that lies in the future—and the possible pitfalls. Maintaining the status quo, though comfortable, is never an option. Managing just to survive has never demonstrated it can assure long-term financial success. Business history is littered with the names of top 50 companies that no longer exist. The CEOs whose essays appear in this section describe ways to assure that companies will have anniversaries beyond the century mark.

The importance of looking ahead can't be overemphasized, says Pfizer's Hank McKinnell, "[T]o think and plan long-term is particularly critical to [our] business of discovering and developing important medicines…Ultimately, shareholder interests are best served when management leads employees to think and act generation-to-generation, as well as quarter-to-quarter."

Just because something worked well in the past, doesn't mean it will continue to work well in the future. To Siemens' Klaus Kleinfeld, the formula for achieving success is plain: "Keeping all stakeholders in balance is [the] key to maintaining public trust." He elaborates, saying, "We strive constantly to overcome the temptation to let technology, rather than our customers and our market, drive the development of our products." Henning Kagermann would agree. In discussing SAP's approach he writes, "…trust and innovation…if you want to manage your business for tomorrow…you can't have one without the other."

INTRODUCTION

Exelon's John Rowe would add, "Meeting commitments to others is essential to long-term financial performance."

A Company's True Character is Expressed by its People. How true! Each of us tends to shape our strongest opinions about companies—good or bad—by what our friends say about them, or by the actions and/or words of the employees with whom we come in contact. Ed Liddy leaves no doubt in anyone's mind about the importance of employee actions, declaring, "Allstate people hold the success and reputation of the company in their hands." To gain employee support, he says, "Leaders must be held accountable by the people they lead." When it comes to developing an ethical culture, he states, an "Open, honest, two-way communication is the bedrock of ethical standards."

The importance of employee behavior is stressed by Mike Eskew when he states, "[W]hat really characterizes the UPS culture [is]—not rules or procedures—but—[the] fierce determination to do the right thing for the customer." The examples he cites of employees who went "an extra mile" in the performance of their jobs help explain the high regard in which UPS is held by its customers.

At Johnson & Johnson, a company often held up as a model for excellent reputation, Bill Weldon declares, "Values are everyone's job…Ethical decision-making requires more than integrity." Wayne Leonard of Entergy describes it this way: "Our word has to be as good as or better than any contract ever written." He goes on to say that the company tries to create "an environment where every employee [feels] respected, appreciated and that they [make] a difference."

xxi

INTRODUCTION

The final essay appears in the section entitled **Coda**. It is written by Marilyn Carlson Nelson, chairman and CEO of Carlson and daughter of the founder. She expresses what all CEOs, who are proud of their accomplishments and have an eye towards the future, would wish for *their* company.

Doesn't every ethical CEO aspire to leave for the next generation of managers a company imbued with the philosophy of "doing the right thing" for *each* of its major constituencies? Such a company would be looked upon favorably by the public. It would have loyal employees, satisfied customers, and supportive owners.

As Marilyn Nelson says, "In the end, doing the right thing will always triumph." She reminds the next generation that "the true value of a business leader cannot be judged until he or she has been gone at least ten years—only then can the world determine whether that person's judgment was sound." She asks, "Will the world say a company served as a positive link between the past and the future of their communities, that it added value, and helped society prosper?"

In the long run, there is no substitute for viewing business any way other than as a means to serve people. Being truthful and operating with integrity in all that is done, as elsewhere, has many rewards.

Companies that look to the future and serve the people can aspire to long lives and continue to do good works—thereby benefiting their primary constituencies: customers, employees, shareowners, and communities.

The CEOs whose essays appear in this book demonstrate that the key to building trust lies not only by operating with unquestionable integrity, but also by following easily understood fundamental principles in a focused manner.

By providing clear objectives that strive to bring out the best performance in employees and that are coupled with flawless execution, success in the marketplace and on the bottom line is virtually assured.

By taking the high ground, business not only will regain the public's confidence, but, with a minimum of sanctions, it will be permitted to continue to raise the standard of living and serve as a role model of ethical behavior for people everywhere on this earth.

Building Trust provides guidelines for achieving this noble purpose. Furthermore, as Arthur Page would suggest, by following the basic precepts of management outlined herein, business people will better be able to relax, remain calm and enjoy themselves.

John A. Koten
EDITOR
January 2004

Jack Koten is a founding director and first president of the Arthur W. Page Society. During his career he worked in a variety of operating, financial and corporate communications departments for Illinois Bell, AT&T, New Jersey Bell and Ameritech. During the course of his experience, he reported directly to seven different CEOs—"an experience all its own. Their personalities varied, but their expectations for ethical behavior were uniformly high."

Arthur W. Page

1883 – 1960

"All business in a democratic country begins with public permission and exists by public approval."

– Arthur W. Page

Arthur W. Page served as vice president of public relations for the American Telephone and Telegraph Company from 1927 to 1946. He was the first person in a public relations position to serve as an officer and member of the board of directors of a major public corporation. During the time he was at AT&T, it became the world's largest public corporation.

Page was distinguished as an outstanding public relations practitioner, churchman, educator and statesman. Both in belief and in practice he held that "all business in a democratic country begins with public permission and exists by public approval."

A graduate of Harvard, he was the son of Walter Hines Page, co-founder of the publishing house Doubleday & Page and later ambassador to Great Britain during World War I. Arthur served in France during the war as a member of G-2, a psychological war intelligence unit. After the war he became editor of the monthly magazine, *World's Work*, and a part owner of Doubleday Page.

Throughout his life, Page devoted himself to his avocation as a counselor to private and public sector executives. He was on the boards of numerous corporations, charities, colleges and civic groups.

He contributed his energy and inspiration to enterprises such as the Marshall Plan and Radio Free Europe. He was a special confidant of Henry L. Stimson, who served in the cabinets of William Howard Taft, Herbert Hoover, Franklin D. Roosevelt, and Harry S. Truman. Page is credited with writing, at Stimson's request, Truman's announcement of the dropping of the atomic bomb on Japan.

The principles of business conduct for which he became known have influenced thousands of American thought leaders during the past 70 years. He, more than any other individual, laid the foundation for the field of corporate public relations.

THE PAGE PRINCIPLES

"…these principles will build, strengthen, and sustain a corporate culture that assures integrity, inspires trust, and promotes an agreeable relationship with the consultancies whose opinions facilitate—or frustrate—management's goals."

– Edward M. Block

"Doing the right things, and doing them the right way, is more important than anything we preach."

– Michael J. Birck

GUIDELINES FOR PROMOTING INTEGRITY AND BUILDING TRUST

The Arthur W. Page Society was established 20 years ago to pursue what might be accurately characterized as an evangelical mission; namely, to reawaken and promote a concept of corporate governance that embodies the essential building blocks of trust and integrity.

Beginning in the 1920s and continuing until his death in 1960, Arthur Page articulated and demonstrated the usefulness of policies and practices that are as relevant and timely today as they were in his lifetime.

You will find the Page legacy implicit in every one of the commentaries by chief executive officers in the chapters that follow. You will also discover why his ideas are readily adaptable in endless ways to every business enterprise, regardless of its scale, business model or strategic direction.

From its inception, the Page Society has drawn from a bountiful body of work that is the legacy of Arthur W. Page. From that legacy we have distilled a set of what we choose to call "principles." These cryptic statements scarcely do justice to the rich legacy of a man who literally wrote the book on corporate governance. Even so, the unequivocal, enduring and proven guidelines we express as principles can be used to ensure the validity as well as the durability of management decisions. Big decisions for the long pull. Ordinary day-to-day decisions. These principles are not discrete "silos." Their boundaries overlap. They are integrated, all of a piece. Taken together and applied with consistency, these principles will build, strengthen, and sustain a corporate culture that assures integrity, inspires trust and promotes an agreeable relationship with the constituencies whose opinions facilitate—or frustrate—management's goals.

Arthur Page earnestly believed that policy-making is the cornerstone of effective management. He also believed—and demonstrated—that effective corporate governance is the product of wise policies wisely implemented.

Our Society's commitment to the Page legacy derives from its obvious relevancy to the practice of corporate public relations. But Page did not refer to himself as a public relations counselor. Rather, his focus was everlastingly on matters of fundamental policy that, in turn, shape the character of corporate behavior. In the language of business today, many authorities would call this approach the cornerstone of Reputation Management. And this is the context in which the implications can most readily be understood of what Page had in mind when he wrote: "...all business in a democratic country begins with public permission and exists by public approval."

THE PAGE PRINCIPLES IN BRIEF

Tell the truth. Taken at face value you wouldn't think this axiom requires elaboration. But many of the complex issues that confront management are seldom, if ever, framed as a simple choice between telling the truth, obscuring the truth or denying the truth.

At the highest levels of policy-making, the truth can be elusive. Inevitably, there are endless, sometimes bewildering, considerations to take into account when top management seeks consensus on the right policy, the right course of action or even a response to unanticipated events.

Getting at the truth isn't always easy in the context of policy deliberations. Nevertheless, management is obliged to be as forthcoming as possible, even in circumstances when all facts, in complete detail, may not be available. Many executives who have endured contentious deliberations in the absence of all the facts will nevertheless agree: You always know intuitively what the truth is.

Decision-making involves sorting through differing perceptions and alternative possibilities, especially when events require prompt action. A general counsel may advise caution as a means of limiting exposure to litigation. A marketing executive may seek to limit potential damage to a brand. An operations executive may seek to pin blame on an employee who didn't follow prescribed methods. But in the end, the CEO must make the decision, keeping in mind that the greatest of all risks is the damage that will result if the truth is obscured, ignored or denied. Employees, customers, shareowners and the news media easily recognize dissembling or spinning half-truths. When management's actions or statements don't pass the "smell test," credibility is the immediate casualty.

Truth-telling must also be a priority in all aspects of a company's routine activities. Product claims and guarantees. Internal information directed to employees. Speeches and presentations. News releases. Financial disclosure. Representations made to customers by sales people or intermediaries. These are only a few examples of the many, many communications channels or transactions that shape public perceptions and must therefore be continuously and scrupulously monitored by management.

In short, truth-telling is a habit of the mind in business enterprises no less than in individuals. And truth telling over time is the first line of defense in protecting a company's reputation.

Prove it with action. A company's reputation is a product of what it does, not what it says. This simple principle is an affirmation of the unassailable old adage, "Action speaks louder than words." Time and again, Page argued that building a durable relationship with the public is 90 percent doing and only 10 percent talking about it. Furthermore, the action ought to come first and taking credit for it should follow. If this homey truth is so obvious, why do businesses ignore it in so many different ways every day?

Most recently, an epidemic of almost unthinkable scandals has beset the top managements of several large corporations as well as financial institutions. Law firms and accountants have also been caught up in ethical lapses. Clearly, these kinds of actions speak loudly and destructively. Any semblance of integrity is lost, possibly forever.

Of course, Page wasn't thinking of headline-making scandals when he drew upon the common-sense notion that a company's reputation is based on what it does rather than what it says. He fully understood that public approval is created in large ways and small, day by day, through satisfactory interactions with key publics, internally as well as externally.

For example, top management too often gets it backward when promulgating policy. Its rhetoric may be earnest, but organizational follow-through is inconsistent or even nonexistent. A good policy that is ignored, countermanded or its purpose misunderstood by lower level managers or employees in the field will be taken as clear evidence that top management is insincere.

Another interface where action—or inaction—sullies reputations occurs when management fails to recognize that a company's reputation is mainly reinforced and enhanced—or not—by the impressions that result from ordinary, everyday interactions with customers. Decades of opinion research have consistently demonstrated that when a customer endures an unsatisfactory personal experience with a company, the loss of goodwill and loyalty is significant. Yet management often fails to intervene even when it is readily apparent that frequent and highly personal relationship-building opportunities are undermined by policies or business practices that are insensitive, out-of-sync with expectations or just plain wrongheaded. As a consequence, a company's reputation is needlessly diminished.

Communications programs designed to justify bad policies only make matters worse.

It is also accurate to say that reputation-building opportunities are wasted when management ignores or misreads the expectations of key publics.

A now familiar example is the degree to which the social contract with employees is ruptured by restructurings occasioned by downsizing, outsourcing and offshore investments.

The substitution of "savings plans" for the traditional pension trusts has also taken a toll. As employees see it, management is generously rewarded by bonuses, stock options, employment contracts and golden parachutes. Yet the rank and file too often discovers its benefits reduced and its retirement nest eggs diminished by the declining value of equities. Sometimes losses in the latter are the result of prior contributions of their own company's stock made in lieu of payments to a pension trust.

Other examples also derive from cost-cutting measures: Reductions in philanthropic programs and local community support activities. Resistance to desirable and reasonable environmental proposals and initiatives.

These actions are not unlawful. Indeed, cost-cutting may be a survival strategy for some corporations. Nonetheless, can it be surprising that so many influential publics and political leaders are concluding that corporate social responsibility is a cruel joke in the hands of a new generation of richly compensated chief executives and directors who do not feel compelled to explain their actions except in terms understood only by Wall Street? Have managements and boards of directors become so insular they no longer see a connection between their obligations as "stewards" and the discretionary authority delegated to them by shareowners and public policy?

Listen to the customer. Large enterprises are especially vulnerable if they fail to take account of the legitimate entitlements and preferences of consumers and non-government consumer advocates. How many companies today invest sufficiently in continuous, comprehensive opinion research to measure what customers approve or disapprove about the way they do business? How many assign management accountability for this function? How many provide timely assessments of these data to top-management or boards of directors as a means of ensuring oversight? How many companies track their competitors on these parameters? When business doesn't listen to customers in a systematic way or otherwise remain open to reasonable modification of policies or practices, small issues have a way of needlessly escalating into big, confrontational issues.

There is a second approach to "listening" that management must also employ to keep its ear closely tuned to what consumers are experiencing and feeling. Regrettably, it is precisely at this critical interface that so many large enterprises fail to translate their institutional strengths into opportunities for reputation building.

The best place to listen for negative feedback is at the consumer interface.

Just reading the daily newspapers and watching local television news can identify some of the most common complaints. News outlets would not devote so much space and time to consumer complaints if this "service" did not matter to consumers. Another rich source of consumer dissatisfaction can be found in the letters, phone calls and e-mails addressed to a business. Here are just a few "generic" examples:

Are individual consumers treated with the same courtesy and responsiveness as large accounts?

Can consumers navigate through automated telephone answering systems without losing their tempers? Can consumers actually talk to a human representative without undue delay? How are customer attitudes influenced when automated answering systems announce delays of 10 to 20 minutes?

Do customers have to be computer "geeks" to successfully complete transactions on Internet sites?

Do the employees or lower level managers have time to actually listen to customers? Do these employees and managers have the authority to handle routine customer complaints? Are they empowered to use common sense and good judgment when standard business practices are inappropriate? Are they encouraged or rewarded for doing so?

Are senior managers encouraged to spend a few hours each month with customers in order to get a feel for the company's everyday business practices and, also, seek input from front line employees?

If a company's sales offices are available evenings and weekends, why aren't its repair or billing services also available?

Many consumers eagerly offer suggestions that will reduce a company's expenses or suggest new applications for existing products and services. Shouldn't every company collect, evaluate or otherwise respond to these well-intentioned ideas?

It is hardly a secret that easily remedied complaints fester mainly because top-level corporate managers are insulated by "assistants" and impenetrable layers of subordinates. Yet, feedback and responsiveness at the consumer interface are absolutely essential to building trust and demonstrating integrity.

Who's watching the store?

Manage for tomorrow. Expediency is not a strategy. Organizational success over time requires a shared understanding of strategic goals as well as commitment to operational plans and financial targets. This approach encourages teamwork internally and builds approval externally. Few would challenge this doctrine. Nevertheless, distractions may arise. Short-term objectives may lead management to decisions that contravene policies or business objectives that otherwise sustain loyalty and trust. As we have so recently witnessed, too much emphasis on Wall Street's objectives at the expense of employees, consumers and other key constituencies have disgraced management and substantially compromised the integrity of some previously highly regarded corporations and financial institutions.

The concept of the "three-legged stool" may be an old idea but it surely remains a good guidepost for success over time.

In today's dynamic global marketplace it can be difficult to stay the course. But managing for the long pull does not—and never did— imply that management must stick doggedly to policies, strategies and operational plans despite threats from competitors, changing consumer preferences and demographics or the ever-increasing pace of technological changes. Rather, it means a business must remain faithful to its values and build upon its strengths in accommodating changes in its marketplace and in responding to new opportunities.

Management's policy decisions must clearly reflect long-term considerations, not transitory fads, whether in the realm of personnel matters or business practices. Change must always be accompanied by careful, thorough explanations that will make sense to employees, customers, shareowners and other important stakeholders. Investments in research or new lines of business, whether undertaken in a context of expansion or retrenchment, must meet these tests. Otherwise, a company may erode or destroy the reputation assets that once reassured customers and earned employee buy-in.

Employee commitment requires structure, predictability and continuous understanding of business plans as they unfold.

Customers expect a company to remain "in character" and reflect the values and the strengths they associate with its image, even as its products or services evolve over time.

Finally, this question: Is managing for the long pull a useless abstraction in a business environment that moves at an increasingly fast pace? Arthur Page would answer with an emphatic "No."

It was said of Mr. Page by a CEO to whom he reported, "He's the best executive I have. He thinks." This anecdote serves as a good reminder that virtually any issue or event that could conceivably confront a corporation can be anticipated if management periodically takes time to reflect on the possibilities. When policy decisions are under consideration, wouldn't it be useful to be equipped with a reasonable degree of insight and introspection about what the future may have in store? Wouldn't management's decisions more likely take account of the long pull if the implications were viewed through a long lens?

Conduct public relations as if the whole company depends on it. For a general business audience it may be helpful to restate this principle as follows: Employ all of the resources of a business to build public approval. And stay at the task everlastingly.

As Arthur Page saw it, every aspect of the business must be managed with public relations considerations in mind. He conceived public relations as an institutional mindset, not a staff department. His conception includes everything from fundamental policies fashioned by top management right down to the day-to-day competencies and behavior of employees in the field or on the shop floor. Actually, his concept can be summed up in the modern understanding of the term "corporate culture." Public relations is everyone's job and it's an imperative for ensuring effective constituency relationships. It's an attitude, a bias that strives always to fashion policies, actions and business practices that project integrity and build trust. It's a state of mind, a style of leadership that reflects genuine respect for the sensibilities of all constituencies all the time as a way of life in conducting everyday business activities.

A company's true character is expressed by its people—all of them. That's why Page urged management to provide training and education to continuously deepen employee understanding of the business and its goals and policies. He believed in employee empowerment. He urged management to support employee volunteerism in community activities and, in connection with those activities, to encourage employees to gather feedback and gauge customer attitudes toward the company's policies and business practices. Finally, he believed that well-trained, well-mannered and empowered employees represent an army of powerful ambassadors for the company — but only to the extent that management respected, valued and rewarded their contributions on the job and off.

These may seem like old-fashioned ideas. Perhaps even naive. But if every manager would only search the memories of their own personal experiences with the companies they do business with, it would be starkly obvious that well-trained, properly motivated employees decisively influence customer impressions. Once again, Page got it right. His advice is based on common sense and human experience. It's not a romanticized ideal. It's not an impossible goal in today's business environment. Treating others as you wish to be treated is still what counts if building trust is the objective.

Remain calm, patient and good-humored. This is Arthur Page's advice to CEOs and top-level managers. In today's world, in the U.S. as well as abroad, management is beset by litigation, critical media scrutiny, legislative and regulatory harassment.

Management also faces a thousand other kinds of unwelcome distractions, many of them seemingly unfair. And, now and again, political opportunists and non-government organizations may attack a business for no purpose other than to make self-serving news. It isn't easy, perhaps not even natural, for management to remain calm and good-humored in a contentious environment fed by 24-hour news cycles and endless numbers of so-called single-cause watchdog organizations.

When your business is a target, take a deep breath. Do not risk damage to the reputation of your company and its leadership by responding in words or actions that will be perceived as angry, arrogant or insensitive. Keep in mind that you have a reservoir of good will to draw upon. Initiate your own rejoinders at a time and place of your own choosing, presented credibly in words or actions that strengthen your position. You may also have credible third parties who will come forward to support you. To the extent possible, avoid being drawn into an arena that gives advantage to your adversaries.

Remain "in character." Every CEO and every business must strive to reflect a style of leadership that is "principled" and speak in a tone of voice that is reasoned and respectful. The objective is to earn respect and strengthen your reputation in the long run. Whatever the issue, your adversary's theatrics will have a short shelf life if you have a good story to tell and you tell it well. It's more important to win the war, not the opening skirmish.

In the chapters that follow, another precept that Arthur Page pioneered will be recognized. A company's goals, business strategies and policies must be articulated clearly and consistently. This is a continuing task of corporate communications in all of its forms. This will provide "context" for marketing communications, financial communications, and effective brand management. As Page would argue, communications programs must flow from and support goals and strategies. Any other purpose is a waste of resources and will only result in confusion and clutter.

—Edward M. Block

Ed Block is a founding director of the Arthur W. Page Society. Prior to his retirement in 1986, he was a senior vice president of AT&T responsible for public relations, employee information and advertising. His mentors included two senior executives who had reported to Arthur Page.

Michael J. Birck

CHAIRMAN AND CHIEF EXECUTIVE OFFICER
TELLABS, INC.

"Communication may be the most important element in our business."
– Michael J. Birck

PRINCIPLED BEHAVIOR

The telecommunications industry continues to endure the darkest period in its history.

Some call it "telecom winter."

A challenging regulatory environment, a glut in network capacity and a lack of needed consolidation beleaguer us. We're in the midst of an unprecedented period of debt, bankruptcies and reduced spending by telecom service providers, our customers. As our customers stagger under the weight of this burden, so does Tellabs.

But let's keep things in perspective. Tellabs started in 1975 and ended that first year with only 20 employees and $312,000 in sales. There was a recession going on then, too. No one knew that we would grow to employ 4,000 people and generate more than $1 billion in 2002 sales. We've come a very long way, and I'm confident that we will emerge from this frigid telecom winter more competitive than ever.

As we were in the early days of Tellabs, we're very much focused on the future. A lot of the strategic pieces are in place. We have one of the strongest balance sheets in the industry. We ended 2002 with more than $1 billion in cash and equivalents and zero debt. Even in the face of painful restructurings, our employees rise to meet challenges every day. The result: innovative solutions and products that help our customers efficiently move communications traffic worldwide.

In more than 40 years in the technology business, I've seen a lot of companies come and go. Successful companies are the ones who stick to the basics. While there might be several different schools of thought on how to capture those basic principles, the Page Principles, with which I have recently become familiar, seem to have them well defined.

TELL THE TRUTH.

It doesn't get any more basic than this. Unfortunately, there have been several recent examples of companies who strayed from the truth. Names like Enron, Global Crossing, WorldCom and Arthur Andersen are now and forever associated with lies, deceit and greed.

As the cult of highly paid CEOs began to evolve in the 1990s, they became celebrity-like household names. During this time, the seeds that destroy credibility were sown. And as greed replaced candor, exorbitant compensation for celebrity CEOs became commonplace. Our industry was part of that, and it now sports a black eye due partially to unethical, greedy leadership.

As a result, our task of recovery is more difficult than it might otherwise have been. A return to health will not occur until the industry's companies and executives earn back the respect that we as an industry have lost of late. That will not be easy. Respect is gained over a long period, but it is lost in just an instant. In my opinion, CEOs of corporations must lead by example, or that respect will be very elusive. At Tellabs, one of our core commitments is to open, honest and constructive communications.

A healthy telecom industry must have visible, vocal, ethical leaders willing to tell it like it is, and be sufficiently visionary to see beyond the next earnings report. Fortunately, I think they are out there, and we need to hear more from them.

PROVE IT WITH ACTION.

Doing the right things, and doing them the right way, is more important than anything we preach from a podium or say in a public statement. The public expects more than words, and rightfully so. Actions define a corporation's character.

In fact, the health of a business depends upon a bias for action, another one of our core commitments at Tellabs. As a young manager, I started my career at Bell Laboratories, which at that time was part of AT&T, and I lasted six years there. I was entranced by the technology and the access to the world's authority on almost anything technical. But I had problems with the bureaucracy. You had to wait your turn, and that took an eternity. And virtually all communication was vertical rather than horizontal, and that was wasteful.

Starting Tellabs was a breath of fresh air. We rolled up our sleeves and got things done, and we vowed never to add unnecessary layers to our work. Tellabs employees are expected to speak with their actions and results. We aren't punching time clocks; we don't have time clocks anywhere for that reason. I'm more interested in what people do while they are here. Our entrepreneurial roots continue to shape our culture and will hopefully do so far into the future.

LISTEN TO THE CUSTOMER.

If you listen closely enough, your customers will tell you absolutely everything you need to know. Tellabs spends considerable time developing close relationships with customers. As a result, we are better able to focus our product development on what they really need — products that help them increase revenues, reduce waste and inefficiency, and restrain operating expenses.

Listening is a continuous process, and one that requires constant attention. Our customers are highly satisfied, as evidenced by customer survey data, business ethics rankings and awards from customers such as Verizon, Sprint and TELUS. These are all good barometers, but we rely most on face-to-face communication to keep those important relationships alive and well.

Since we sell our products to other businesses and not directly to consumers, we need to listen to not only our direct customers, but also to our customers' customers. As an example, when cell phone users and wireless carriers demanded better sound quality, Tellabs listened and developed products to enhance the voice quality of our customers' networks.

MANAGE FOR TOMORROW.

My vocation is technology, and my avocation is higher education. Both fields require vision and a passion for the future.

Let me begin with technology. Living in the age of technology, we are used to some pretty remarkable advances in every aspect of our lives. For example, we have virtually limitless ability to communicate anywhere on earth by satellite, optical fiber and wireless services. We have become accustomed to hand-held devices that hold more computing capacity than a room full of mainframes did just a few short years ago. Each extraordinary advance is the end result of a complex journey—each one with its own set of painstaking steps.

What keeps each step heading in the right direction? Focusing on the future. Eliminating problems before they interfere with progress. Recognizing that all things are possible.

Most of these same strategies apply to the field of education. I've had the good fortune to be involved with many fine educational institutions—Purdue University, Benedictine University, the Illinois Mathematics & Science Academy and others. In their classrooms, I see the future.

Each student is about to embark upon his or her own complex journey, with its own set of painstaking steps. Today's students are tomorrow's employees, and they need to develop skills to approach, comprehend, analyze and use information effectively, regardless of the subject matter. Through internships and applied research relationships, such as the one we have with the Danish Technical University, Tellabs helps students do just that. It is our responsibility to help guide their steps and make an investment that will give unending returns to the community.

Enormous opportunity awaits us. I'm truly excited about the potential that is starting to unfold in fields such as biotechnology, nanotechnology and advanced manufacturing, including additional opportunities still ahead in communications.

CONDUCT PUBLIC RELATIONS AS IF THE
WHOLE COMPANY DEPENDS ON IT.

At Tellabs, we insist that our people, especially our managers, have the ability to communicate. To succinctly make a point, through the written or spoken word, is an important element of business. If someone enters the workforce without the ability to share thoughts and ideas, that's a problem. Communication just may be the most important element in business, because it is such a large part of our global business community today.

The age of technology has effectively shrunk our world into a community that acts much like a small town. Information is readily accessible and travels with great speed. Our constituents around the globe know our latest news almost as soon as it comes to light. We have a saying here to help put some perspective on this trend: "Don't say it or do it unless you want to see it on the front page of *The Wall Street Journal.*"

It is imperative that every corporate strategy be developed in concert with the priorities of our multiple publics. We at Tellabs consciously evaluate each strategy and how it will affect our customers, employees, investors, vendors, suppliers and communities where we live and work. In the end, these audiences will be the ones to judge whether or not our company stands or falls.

REMAIN CALM, PATIENT AND GOOD-HUMORED.

Recognizing that our employees are our best ambassadors to the public, we make every effort to keep open and consistent lines of communications with them. Once a month, the whole company gathers for our "Town Hall" meetings. Executives report on different aspects of business, and I end each meeting with an overview of the state of our company and of our industry. We all take questions from the floor to encourage employees to speak their mind and deal with any rumors that might be out there.

Needless to say, in telecom for the last couple of years we haven't had much good news to share. But that makes our presence all the more important. By getting up there and giving honest, reasoned responses to each question, we hope to convey our confidence in the future. We will eventually emerge from this telecom winter. In the meantime, we will best deal with things as they are, calmly and thoughtfully. It's also important to have a sense of humor, and to have a little fun along the way.

There's hope that telecom spring will soon appear. When it does, these practices will continue to guide our efforts. Through good times and bad, the Page Principles speak pretty well to appropriate corporate behavior.

Michael J. Birck
CHAIRMAN AND CHIEF EXECUTIVE OFFICER
TELLABS, INC.

Michael J. Birck, a founder of Tellabs, Inc., is currently its chairman and chief executive officer. Birck began his telecommunications career at AT&T's Bell Telephone Laboratories. He then managed the transmission system design department at Continental Telephone Laboratories. From 1968 to 1975 Birck was director of engineering at Wescom, Inc.

The Electronic Industries Alliance (EIA) presented Birck with the 2003 Medal of Honor for his achievements and leadership in the U.S. telecommunications industry. He was awarded an honorary doctorate of engineering by Purdue University in 1995. Birck has been inducted into the Chicago Business Hall of Fame and received the Chicago Area Entrepreneurship Hall of Fame Lifetime Achievement Award.

He serves as a director of the Purdue Research Foundation and is a member of the Dean's Advisory Council of the Krannert School of Management, and is a trustee of Purdue University. He is a member of the board of trustees of Benedictine University and of the Illinois Mathematics and Science Academy Fund Board. Birck also serves on the University of Illinois President's Advisory Council.

Birck is a member of the board of directors of the Lincoln Foundation for Business Excellence, the board of trustees of Hinsdale Hospital and the Chicago Museum of Science and Industry. He is a member of the Civic Leadership Committee of the Chicago Academy of Sciences and is vice chair and a director of The Economic Club of Chicago. Birck has served for a number of years on the United Way/Crusade of Mercy campaign.

Birck received a bachelor of science degree in electrical engineering from Purdue University and a master of science degree from New York University. He and his wife, Katherine, have three grown children.

PRINCIPLED BEHAVIOR

TELLABS, INC.

Tellabs provides innovative data switching and bandwidth management solutions to help carriers around the world move communications traffic efficiently, effectively and profitably. The world communicates through Tellabs™ more than two thirds of telephone calls and Internet sessions in several countries, including the United States, flows through the company's equipment. Tellabs customers include many of the world's largest and strongest carriers. Tellabs experts, including approximately 3,200 employees, design, develop, deploy and support our solutions throughout telecommunications networks in more than 100 countries worldwide.

Tellabs is the market share leader in North American bandwidth management, according to research firm RHK, as well as the No. 1 digital cross-connect provider in the United States, with more than 4,000 systems deployed. The company is also the world's leading provider of voice-quality-enhancement solutions, as well as the leading provider of cable telephony solutions in Europe and one of the top three worldwide.

Tellabs is focused on the future of data switching using IP/MPLS and helping its telecom service provider customers build the networks to meet these growing demands. Tellabs is the first vendor with a complete data solutions portfolio to integrate Layers 1, 2 and 3 of the network.

Giving back to the community is an integral part of Tellabs' commitment to good corporate citizenship. Since its creation in 1997, the Tellabs Foundation, a separate entity, has given more than $5.4 million. Tellabs is headquartered in Naperville, Illinois.

For more information, visit: www.tellabs.com.
Stock Symbol: TLAB

TELL THE TRUTH

"Business success is not about numbers. It is about trust"
– Fred Hassan

"Do nothing to compromise…personal integrity or…corporate integrity"
– Frederic M. Poses

*"We knew the only way to maintain credibility…
and to hold their trust was to come clean."*
– William T. Monahan

*"Decision-making when faced with an ethical dilemma is easy:
Do the right thing. Always."*
– Alexander M. Cutler

*"People today are very smart…
they can spot a corporate smoke screen miles away."*
– Rich DeVos

Fred Hassan

CHAIRMAN OF THE BOARD AND CHIEF EXECUTIVE OFFICER
SCHERING-PLOUGH CORPORATION

"Business integrity means living up to the intent, and not just the letter, of the laws and regulations wherever we operate."

– Fred Hassan

BUSINESS INTEGRITY

In my more than 30 years as an executive in the pharmaceutical industry, I have seen a simple but elusive truth proved many times over: By doing the right thing when it comes to business integrity, you will also be doing the right thing to grow your business for the long term.

The reason for this is also simple, but still can elude many people. In the end, business success is not about numbers. It is about building trust. You must develop mutual trust among the people in your organization for everyone to do his or her best. An essential element of trust is being truthful. And when you have the trust of your customers and shareowners, you have an exceptional competitive advantage.

I use the term "business integrity," rather than "business ethics," for a reason. In my experience working across many cultures, the language of "ethics" can unintentionally be divisive. It can imply that one culture's ethics are better or more profound than another's. By contrast, I have found that business integrity is something that people around the world can understand and own. In many ways, business integrity is also a broader concept than ethics. I explain it very simply to the people I lead in a complex, global industry. Business integrity means living up to the intent, and not just the letter, of the laws and regulations wherever we operate. It also means more. It means obeying the internal moral compass that we all have, so that in each situation we face in our business life, we consciously choose to do what we believe is right and reject what we believe is wrong. There will always be shades of gray in life, but we must evaluate them and make our choices in line with the direction of this internal compass.

Operating in this way builds trust. By building trust, you also build business success for the long term. Business integrity, and the trust it generates, is not merely a matter of words. It is about behavior. I see 80 percent of my role as a leader consisting of modeling the right behaviors—in other words, leading by example. The good news is that people are very quick to learn from example. They can change their behavior. They can learn that listening more intently to their moral compass is the right thing to do and see that by doing so they are not in conflict with business success. They are in fact enhancing business performance by building trust.

In my relatively new role leading Schering-Plough Corporation, a global science-based pharmaceutical company, I inherit an array of challenges. Among the biggest of these challenges are serious issues of compliance with manufacturing standards and the integrity of business practices. These issues have been featured repeatedly in media headlines and have undermined the trust of stakeholders interested in the success of Schering-Plough, most notably our employees, customers, and shareowners. They have also caused great disruption to business processes and the supply of medicines to our customers. At the same time, we confront major long-term challenges in the core business, including the need to enhance the flow of new medicines that are the lifeblood of our industry, sub-optimal business processes, and many other problems. To turn this downward spiral of poor performance into an upward spiral of success, we have set out to reinvent the company through a dramatic change process that will affect every person and every component of our organization.

Fundamental to this change process, and a cornerstone of Schering-Plough, is the expectation that everyone who works for the company, from the Chairman and CEO on down, will conduct all corporate activities with business integrity. A big part of this expectation is quite simple: Be honest with yourself and with other people.

Many times in my career I have found that decisions based on business integrity can catalyze positive and dramatic change. Six years ago, I was the new Chairman and CEO of another global pharmaceutical company. I had been on the job for just a few weeks. There was a meeting of the board of directors and, unfortunately, I had bad news to share. It was clear to me that the company was operating under a dysfunctional business model. Three separate units were each doing their own thing and not working together. The model had to change. If we were going to compete, we had to come together as one global unit.

Unfortunately, the business model had been carefully crafted by the previous CEO and board. Many of these people, including the former CEO, were now members of my board. For a moment I considered whether it might be smarter to let a few meetings go by before I "lowered the boom." After all, wouldn't it be easier to convince the board after they'd seen me in action for a few months? The answer, I quickly decided, was no. The truth is the truth, regardless of when it's delivered. And in this case, it needed to be delivered quickly. So I spoke my mind at the board meeting and waited for the board's reaction. I was actually surprised when they agreed with me. It was a reluctant agreement, but agreement nonetheless. In hindsight, I believe this decision saved the company. Had we waited another six months, the downward spiral would almost certainly have reached a point where we could not have rescued the company.

I soon shared another observation with the board. Our headquarters was overseas. It was in the wrong location. The United States was, and still is, the only free market for pharmaceuticals. If the company wanted to be a long-term global player, we had to make a transAtlantic move to the United States. This was simply the truth. But, again, this change would dismantle plans put in place by the previous administration and the board. Although shocked at my proposal, the board again agreed with my recommendation. We soon moved—lock, stock, and pharmaceutical barrel—to New Jersey. It was the right move. Innovation goes where you have free markets, as opposed to price controls. The United States was where pharmaceutical research and basic science was gravitating, and the move here allowed us to hire some of the brightest scientists and management professionals in the world.

Earlier in my career, I was faced with another challenge where business integrity could have taken a back seat to financial expediency. It concerned an important product in the business entity I was responsible for. The product was being made in a slightly different manner from the New Drug Application (NDA) that had originally been written on it. The issue was not product quality. But, because the NDA was poorly written, technically, an argument could have been made that we were not making the product to specifications. I was advised to ignore the discrepancy. Nobody would notice, they told me. I responded that if our company had high aspirations, we were going to disclose this information as a matter of integrity. We should file a report with the Food & Drug Administration (FDA) and, essentially, tell on ourselves. We did file the report. The FDA reviewed our notice, determined that the discrepancy was inconsequential, and did not penalize us. But, had the FDA discovered the discrepancy on its own, the trust between my company and a major regulatory body would have been damaged.

Within the first hours of my arrival on the Schering-Plough campus, I began to hear rumors about corporate layoffs and whether I would be bringing in new people. There is no question that I could have made loyal, hard-working employees feel a lot better if I had responded that, no, we would not be bringing in new people. I could have said that the best pharmaceutical people in the world were already working at Schering-Plough. I chose not to do that.

During my first Town Hall Meeting on the Schering-Plough campus (I had been CEO all of three days), I spoke what I felt about what I wanted to accomplish. I talked about building a successful environment where competent, hard-working professionals thrive, grow, and succeed. I said we were building a company where people would do these things and, believe it or not, have fun as they did them. I spoke about my belief that many very good people—some of the best people in our industry—were working at Schering-Plough. Then I asked the question that was on everybody's mind: "Will we bring in some new people?" I answered that, yes, we would. As we saw needs for specific skills and competencies to help make our company the best, yes, we would bring in some new people. I emphasized, however, that we would do it very carefully and with great respect for the people we currently had in the company.

H ad I been less than completely honest, the short-term results would have been smiling faces, relieved employees, and the vocal "attaboys" that come when people believe they have dodged a bullet. In the long-term, though, I would have undermined my credibility. I would have hurt my relationship with both my employees and my executive team.

During this same Town Hall Meeting, I was faced with another opportunity to avoid the truth. As expected, many employees were concerned about how much corporate restructuring would be required to achieve my vision of the new Schering-Plough. I could have sidestepped the issue by saying that I wasn't certain, I hadn't completed my analysis, I needed more time, etc. Again, I chose not to do that. I knew the truth, and my employees needed to hear it. To become the best, I said, we must reinvent the company. We must embrace change and, then, drive positive change. We could not focus simply on doing better than we had been doing. We had to change and adapt.

Change, as everyone knows, is one of the most terrifying words in the corporate lexicon. Yet, by telling the truth about changes that were coming, employees prepared for, and became accustomed to, their new future. Less than a month later, I disclosed some of the specifics of the changes to our corporate structure. They were not small changes. They were huge. And it was clear that they would result in the loss of some jobs. But because of my earlier candor, colleagues were now prepared for, accepting, and even anticipating change.

Also fundamental to the change process, which will affect every person and every component of Schering-Plough, is the dissemination of clear and frequent communication from the CEO. There is no such thing as spontaneous success. Success does not occur in a vacuum. Success is a direct result of thousands of interdependent actions that occur every day. A company's employees are clearly the creators, messengers, and recipients of these actions. In order to be fully engaged contributors to success, employees must understand the current state of their company and what their role is in moving the company forward.

In larger companies, communication from the CEO is even more important than it is for smaller companies. In very large companies, the CEO runs the danger of becoming too removed from his or her employees. Co-workers must not see the company as a faceless operation without a soul. Workers must relate emotionally to a company in order to give their best to the company. As CEO, I have found over and over again that if you try to share your thoughts with employees and keep them abreast of the general happenings in their company, it has a huge, positive impact on employees' emotional connection with both the company and the CEO. The consequence of ignoring this reality is excessive rumor. Misinformation via rumor can sap the enthusiasm of even the most dedicated employees and wound a company.

Since my arrival at Schering-Plough, I have traveled thousands of miles to meet with employees, observe production facilities, and review operational processes. I have attended dozens of meetings with cross-functional working groups, with my top executive team, with doctors, lawyers and scientists. I have held Town Hall Meetings with thousands of Schering-Plough colleagues.

Perhaps most important, I have personally written a continuous flow of e-mails to update employees on specific aspects of our corporate turnaround—and their roles in making it happen. This flow will continue. I often spend two or three hours on each of these messages. For any CEO that is an enormous time commitment. It is all the more so in our situation, where almost every aspect of our company requires urgent attention from me. I carve out this time and commitment for personal communication because I am convinced that it is absolutely critical to the transformation of our company that we are engineering, and to the long-term success we are working toward.

I also develop reports when I travel to a plant or to a foreign affiliate, or when I meet front-line people in "CEO dialog sessions." I share these reports with my management team. I relate what I heard, what I observed, what the local challenge is, and how it might be fixed. The purpose of these reports is not to attack individuals who may not be performing at the highest level, but to communicate procedures, processes, and perceptions that need attention, as well as those that can be considered first-rate and implemented elsewhere. I believe it's important for my executive management team to hear my thoughts about operational areas that directly impact the success of our company. This is another dimension of business integrity: listening to and learning from the people on the ground so that we keep getting better at what we do and stay committed to doing things right.

A final fundamental of the change process for Schering-Plough that I see as yet another dimension of business integrity is promoting and mirroring emotional intelligence. By emotional intelligence I mean the ability to lead with your heart, to maintain perspective and to listen to your moral compass. Leaders with strong emotional intelligence maintain intellectual and behavioral effectiveness even when things don't go their way. Emotional intelligence also means understanding how to be transparent and honest, while at the same time maintaining confidentiality when it is necessary. The honest and prudent response is sometimes "I cannot answer that question right now because we must keep this information confidential." I am very rigorous in rating myself on emotional intelligence, and I also rate my management team on it.

My own unforgettable experience with emotional intelligence—with maintaining intellectual and behavioral effectiveness when things aren't going well—concerned one of my previous company's most profitable new drugs. Soon after becoming CEO I learned that, due to some particularly sloppy oversight, the drug was in imminent danger of falling into a rival's hands. As I visualized the company disintegrating around me, I immediately set in motion plans to regain control of the product. I was patient and professional regarding the claims of the rival company. We worked out a settlement that was reasonable from their point of view, but also was very good for my company because the drug became an $800 million product. Although there were a few individuals whose management skills received additional attention, no one lost his or her job. Emotional intelligence demanded that we not resort to an emotional, knee-jerk reaction. This was the right thing to do for the business, and it was the right thing to do on a human level. Many, many colleagues were watching closely to see how I handled this situation while I was still early in my tenure as CEO. I believe that most of them would say that what they saw was business integrity in action.

Business integrity as I have defined it makes big demands on everyone in an organization. However, I believe it is very important that we recognize that no one is perfect in this dimension. Mistakes are inevitable where there are so many shades of gray. What we demand in our company is that all our people keep striving to become better and to learn from their mistakes.

In conclusion, I want to address Schering-Plough shareowners who, after reading this book, may still be suspicious of the present state of Corporate America. Growing up in Pakistan, I knew that to achieve my dreams I would one day follow the advice of the famous New York newspaperman Horace Greeley. He said, "Go West, young man!" And I did—enthusiastically. I went to London for a chemical engineering degree and, later, to Harvard for an M.B.A. During this time, I never saw America as perfect. I never saw American business as perfect. However, I was absolutely convinced that there was no better country and no business environment more welcoming to a young person with very big dreams and the heart to achieve them.

I sincerely believe this is still true today. To lead an American science-based pharmaceutical company is a proud and honorable profession. I am proud of the good things we do for patients and society. I am proud of our people. As we seek to transform Schering-Plough into a great global health company, I know that we must earn the trust of all of our stakeholders and, most especially, our shareowners. To do so will be an honor.

Fred Hassan
CHAIRMAN OF THE BOARD AND CHIEF EXECUTIVE OFFICER
SCHERING-PLOUGH CORPORATION

Fred Hassan is chairman of the board and chief executive officer of Schering-Plough Corporation. He joined Schering-Plough on April 20, 2003, as chief executive officer. He was elected a director and chairman of Schering-Plough's board of directors on April 22, 2003.

Prior to joining Schering-Plough, Hassan was chairman and chief executive officer of Pharmacia. He joined the former Pharmacia & Upjohn in May 1997 as chief executive officer and was elected to the board of directors. In February 2001, Hassan was named chairman of the board of Pharmacia, the company created through the merger of the former Monsanto and Pharmacia & Upjohn companies.

Previously, Hassan was executive vice president of Wyeth, formerly known as American Home Products, with responsibility for its pharmaceutical and medical products business. He was elected to Wyeth's board of directors in 1995. Earlier in his career, Hassan spent 17 years with Sandoz Pharmaceuticals (now Novartis) and headed its U.S. pharmaceuticals business.

Hassan received a bachelor of science degree in chemical engineering from the Imperial College of Science and Technology at the University of London and a master of business administration from Harvard Business School.

Hassan recently served as chairman of the board of directors of the Pharmaceutical Research and Manufacturers of America (PhRMA) and is chairman of the HealthCare Institute of New Jersey. In addition, he serves on the board of directors of Avon Products, Inc.

SCHERING-PLOUGH CORPORATION

Schering-Plough Corporation is a leading research-based pharmaceutical company dedicated to discovering and delivering products that can extend lives and improve the quality of life for people around the world. With over 30,000 employees worldwide, the company's products reach patients and caregivers in more than 125 countries. In 2002, sales totaled $10.2 billion.

Many of Schering-Plough's prescription products are recognized market leaders. In 2002, the company launched ZETIA™ (ezetimibe), a cholesterol-management product discovered by Schering-Plough scientists. In September 2003, Merck/Schering-Plough Pharmaceuticals submitted a New Drug Application for ezetimibe/simvastatin tablet, an investigational cholesterol-lowering medicine, along with diet, for the reduction of elevated cholesterol levels.

The company's other major products marketed in the United States include PEG-INTRON® Powder for Injection, a longer-acting form of INTRON® A Injection, as monotherapy and in combination with REBETOL® Capsules, for treating hepatitis C; INTRON A, as monotherapy and in combination with REBETOL for treating hepatitis C; CLARINEX®, a nonsedating antihistamine; NASONEX®, a corticosteroid nasal spray for allergies; TEMODAR®, an oral chemotherapeutic agent for certain types of brain tumors; INTEGRILIN®, for acute coronary syndromes and percutaneous coronary intervention; and LOTRISONE®, a topical antifungal.

Schering-Plough's consumer health care business includes leading consumer brands of foot care, over-the-counter and sun care products.

Schering-Plough's global animal health care business comprises pharmaceuticals, vaccines, growth promotants and parasiticides. Schering-Plough is headquartered in Kenilworth, New Jersey.

For more information, visit: www.schering-plough.com.
Stock Symbol: SGP

BUSINESS INTEGRITY

BUILDING TRUST

Frederic M. Poses

CHAIRMAN AND CHIEF EXECUTIVE OFFICER
AMERICAN STANDARD COMPANIES, INC.

"The overwhelming majority of corporations and the people who work for them value integrity."

– Frederic M. Poses

THE CORPORATE NAVIGATION SYSTEM

During the high-flying growth decade of the 1990s, annual spending on mergers and acquisitions went from $205 billion to more than $3.4 trillion in 2000.

Some of the acquisitions were painful mismatches, some were well-thought-out and successful, with others still awaiting long-term proof. Corporate assets were bought en masse, merged into new companies, spun off whole or sliced, diced and sold off in pieces for quick cash returns.

Yet in all this horse-trading, there is one corporate asset that has never been bought or sold and never will be. That asset is integrity.

As the corporate scandals that emerged in the wake of the Enron collapse have reminded us, integrity is a priceless and fragile asset. It is also essential to the survival of any business.

This is not a new revelation. It's been true since the beginning of recorded commerce and probably even earlier. Then why is corporate governance in America a bigger issue today than it was in the days of the "Robber Barons" a century ago? How is it that some very bright business leaders in the early 21st century apparently lost sight of the connection between integrity and the growth or even survival of their companies?

There are no glib answers to these questions, and before I share my views on them, I think it's important to make clear where I stand on what's sometimes called the "apple question." Basically, that's the question of whether the well-publicized ethical lapses at some major corporations are the result of a few bad apples in the leadership ranks, or the product of a systemic fungus that infects the whole orchard of American business.

Having spent 30 years working in that orchard, I am more convinced than ever that the overwhelming majority of corporations and the people who work for them value integrity. Most people who lead corporations and the people who follow their leadership would do nothing to compromise their personal integrity or the corporate integrity of the companies where they work.

Then why have we seen the discouraging example of corporate governance scandals at some highly respected companies? And what can we do to restore the public's confidence in business?

THE CORPORATE NAVIGATION SYSTEM

I think the answer lies in navigation systems.

Like many vehicles today, our family car is equipped with a satellite-based navigation system controlled from the dashboard. When our family goes on a road trip, the first thing we do is program the navigation system by telling it where we want to go. It's up to us to get there, but the navigation system will literally tell us the best route to follow. It's an audible system that tells us in advance when it's time to turn and warns us to turn around if we're heading in the wrong direction—a pretty nifty system.

Every one of us is born with a personal navigation system that isn't all that different from the satellite system in an automobile. We don't program our personal navigation system with a computer, but with the values we learn. Some of those values are taught to us formally and others are learned through experience, but they're all part of our personal navigation system.

Such a system is not optional equipment. We've all got one, and it's the one part of us that gets more effective as we get older. Like the satellite-based system in a car, our personal navigation system can be ignored, but doing that increases the danger of getting lost.

My own personal navigation system uses a simple litmus test I learned years ago for evaluating the ethics of potential decisions. I ask myself whether the course of action I'm contemplating would be something I would feel comfortable explaining to our employees, or to our board, or even to my own family. And finally, I ask myself if I would be proud or ashamed.

If I don't get the right answers to those questions, then I'm not going in that direction. This test is one I've applied to many decisions that, practically speaking, would not be of the slightest interest to most of our employees, our board or my family. Like most tests, of course, it's not foolproof. And the more complex an issue gets, the harder it can be to apply a simple test.

Yet such a litmus test, regularly applied, could have saved some corporate executives and their boards the shame of having their companies' names linked to accounting scandals and other forms of corporate greed. And I can only imagine the personal agony it could have saved the families of the executives involved.

The lapses in corporate integrity dominating the news today reflect situations where the personal navigation systems of individual business leaders failed. These systems, after all, don't come with a warranty. If they did, that warranty would have to include caveats that the effectiveness of the system can be impaired by excessive exposure to unrealistic financial targets, the ego of the executive star system, and to the plain truth that people's capacity for rationalization is infinite.

I'm not knowledgeable enough to diagnose the specific ethical failures at America's problem companies. I am absolutely certain, however, that the personal navigation systems of the top leadership at each of these companies broadcast an alarm signal which was ignored.

Why was it ignored? Part of that answer lies in the pressure to perform. It's pressure shared by most business leaders, and that pressure tends to be concentrated on numbers. With the stock price affected by a movement of one or two percentage points in sales or earnings, and with the compensation of many CEOs affected by the stock price, there is an ever-present pressure to produce the numbers rather than the results.

Some executives create artificial pressure by thinking they have to be perfect rather than human. They tend to forget that they, too, make mistakes like the rest of us. The important thing is not that you made a mistake but how you deal with it.

In truly great companies, though, CEOs have a sense of ownership that includes ownership of the pressure to perform. Those CEOs deal with reality. They acknowledge that they make mistakes, accept responsibility for disappointing results and rally their people to produce better results.

In the long run, companies with leadership like that produce the best results for investors and their own people.

While the headlines on corporate governance scandals usually feature the CEO, the foundation of a company's ethics is much broader and deeper. Most companies aren't directed by the personal navigation system of just one person, not even the CEO. Companies have corporate navigation systems made from the personal systems all employees bring to work with them each day. I know from experience that those people overwhelmingly want to be part of a company whose integrity and ethics are a comfortable fit with their own.

That's why so many companies, American Standard included, have adopted formal sets of values that employees can relate to and live by. These values are not a set of aphorisms designed to be framed and forgotten. In a successful company, the corporate values are the ethical navigation system that shapes the daily decisions and overall direction of the corporation and the people who give it life.

The set of values we have in place at the American Standard Companies unites a corporate community of people as diverse as any in the world. We are 60,000 people who work in three different businesses—Bath and Kitchen, Air Conditioning Systems and Services, and Vehicle Control Systems. We manufacture our products at 109 plants in 29 countries and market them in 50 countries.

American Standard people speak more than 20 different languages and represent all of the world's major religious faiths and ethnic groups.

Our common set of values helps link us together. In part, that's because the values we officially adopted in 2002 were drafted with participation from a broad cross-section of our people around the world. I personally believe our values are a good reflection of the personal values and priorities of most of our people. They reflect the way most of our people want their company to operate *(see Appendix)*.

Yet, in a company of 60,000 people, occasional problems are inevitable. Even with the best of navigation systems, some people will lose their way. It would be naïve to think otherwise.

At American Standard, we are enthusiastic practitioners of Six Sigma quality techniques. Six Sigma is essentially a search for perfection, but even Six Sigma-level quality allows for three imperfections out of every one million opportunities. If total perfection is impossible when you're dealing with processes and products, it's certainly not going to happen when you're dealing with people.

By adopting company-wide values, though, you provide clear expectations of how you expect the company and its people to operate. Most of our employees find those values both helpful and reassuring.

THE CORPORATE NAVIGATION SYSTEM

Readers familiar with the Principles of the Arthur W. Page Society will also recognize the comfortable fit our values have with those principles, especially the Page Principles that counsel companies to "Tell the truth" and "Listen to the customer." Since American Standard's five values are so critical to the direction of our company, I'd like to share them here.

We are driven by customers. We succeed by exceeding customers' expectations. Our commitment to premier customer service begins with understanding customer needs. It is realized through the design, manufacture and delivery of quality products and services, and the personal support we provide. Each contact with a customer is an opportunity to increase customer satisfaction and win new business.

We recognize the importance of our people. Our people built this business and are the key to its future. We are committed to creating a workplace that is safe, a workplace where diversity is valued, and a workplace that thrives on teamwork and leadership. We are committed to a workplace where individuals are treated fairly and with respect, where all people have the opportunity to expand their skills and take advantage of new opportunities, and where accomplishments are recognized.

We operate with integrity. As a company and as individuals, we do the right things and never compromise our values. We honor our agreements and are honest in our communications. Our relationships with co-workers, customers, suppliers, partners and the investor community are based on openness and opportunities for mutual gain. Our sense of responsibility extends to leadership in protecting the environment and good citizenship in the communities where we work.

We strive for excellence. No matter how good our products, services, processes and performance, we are dedicated to making them better. We strive for excellence in everything we do by being open to new ideas and better ways of working, and not being afraid to take risks. We recognize that each of us can add real value to our business. By approaching our daily work with a passion for innovation and a desire to learn and share that learning with colleagues, we all can make a difference.

We deliver on our promises. We set our goals high because we know we can do great things. We treat these goals as promises to our customers, our shareowners and ourselves. Our continued success depends on keeping our promises. Success is measured by the results we produce in customer satisfaction, sales, profitability, investor value and the scope of opportunities we provide for our people.

Our challenge is to use these values as guidelines on the job every day. We want to routinely shape our actions to conform to our values. Ideally, the values will keep us asking the right questions about how we're treating our customers, investors and our own people. We're still working on this, but I'm confident the effort will make us a better company.

While only one of the values mentions integrity specifically, they are all essential to the integrity of our business and its reputation.

The absence of scandal is not synonymous with integrity. True integrity means doing everything possible to live up to each of our values all the time. If we are not consistently trying to raise the level of what we can do for customers, investors and our own people, then we're not living up to the spirit of our values. That would be a lapse in our integrity.

THE CORPORATE NAVIGATION SYSTEM

Integrity is also the heart of a successful relationship with customers. Breaking implied or direct promises to customers is a lapse in integrity just as serious as overstating your quarterly revenues to boost your stock price. So we're spending more time and money listening to customers and trying to build our business around what they tell us about their needs.

Experience tells us that the responsibility of leadership is not to preach the corporate values to employees but to demonstrate their own commitment through action. We were reminded of that responsibility during the anxiety over the American invasion of Iraq. In the heat of the moment, two of our managers in America sent out e-mail messages expressing personal opinions that could be hurtful to our employees in the Middle East, Germany and France.

Our values say that we will treat all of our people fairly and with respect. So we tried to set an example by issuing a worldwide message taking issue with the offensive e-mails, apologizing to our international employees and advising them that the employees responsible had been counseled that their actions were not consistent with our values.

The positive side of that experience was the enthusiastic response our message generated from employees in the countries targeted by the offensive e-mail. These employees volunteered that our actions demonstrated that American Standard's values are taken seriously as a guide for operating the business.

Most people associate integrity with ethics and morality, especially after the revelations of ethics meltdowns in a few, now infamous companies. The fact that we are not one of those companies does not give American Standard or any other corporation in our position cause to be passive about issues of right and wrong.

Most people do, indeed, want to do the right thing. But the best intentions are no guarantee of the correct decision when it comes to ethics. In the complicated world of global business, people with high ethical standards and adherence to corporate values will find themselves with difficult decisions to make where the ethical choice is far from obvious.

At those times, a corporation has to provide the help people need. We have tried to do that through the creation of a company-wide ethics committee. Anyone with an ethical quandary can call a qualified member of the committee and get an expert opinion on what decision would be in keeping with our values. We also operate a 24-hour ethics hotline. All employees can call, anonymously if they wish, to share a concern about what they consider unethical behavior anywhere in the company. And that concern will get prompt attention.

Given the detailed corporate governance guidelines in recent legislation passed in the United States, corporations now have a full plate of legal requirements for assessing their behavior and reporting results. New rules and regulations were inevitable to help shore up public confidence in corporate America.

These rules and regulations raise the stakes for those who would compromise the integrity of their companies, but I'm not sure they resolve the problems of corporate governance. After all, speed limits don't stop speeding, do they?

Corporate integrity is preserved and expanded by the individual navigation systems of the people who work for a company. Their individual commitment gives meaning and energy to the corporation's collective values. Our people at American Standard are the ultimate guardians of our integrity. They, in turn, enjoy being part of a company where their personal integrity doesn't have to be left in the parking lot when they come to work.

I don't think our commitment to integrity and ethical behavior is unique or unusual among American companies. If the corporate scandals of the last several years have taught us anything, however, it is the lesson that integrity cannot be taken for granted. The navigation systems of individuals and corporations can't be left on automatic pilot and still be expected to keep us on course.

Frederic M. Poses
CHAIRMAN AND CHIEF EXECUTIVE OFFICER
AMERICAN STANDARD COMPANIES, INC.

Frederic M. Poses is the chairman and chief executive officer of American Standard Companies, Inc. He joined the company in November 1999.

Prior to joining American Standard, Poses was president and chief operating officer of AlliedSignal, Inc., which has since merged with Honeywell. He joined AlliedSignal as a financial analyst in 1969 and was named general manager of the company's Home Furnishings Division in 1977. He was subsequently promoted to positions with increasing responsibility and was named president of the Engineered Materials Sector and executive vice president of the corporation in 1988. In October 1997, he was elected to the board of directors and named vice chairman of AlliedSignal, Inc. Poses was appointed president and COO in June 1998.

Before joining AlliedSignal, Poses spent two years on assignment in Peru with the Peace Corps. Born in 1942, he holds a B.B.A. from New York University.

He serves on the board of directors of Centex Corporation, Raytheon Company, National Center for Learning Disabilities and the 92nd Street YMCA. He also serves on the Duke University board of visitors. Poses resides in Manhattan with his wife and two children.

THE CORPORATE NAVIGATION SYSTEM

AMERICAN STANDARD COMPANIES, INC.

American Standard is a global manufacturer with market-leading positions in three businesses: air conditioning systems and services, sold under the Trane® and American Standard® brands for commercial, institutional and residential buildings; bath and kitchen products, sold under such brands as American Standard® and Ideal Standard®; and vehicle control systems, including electronic braking and air suspension systems, sold under the WABCO® name to the world's leading manufacturers of heavy-duty trucks, buses, SUVs and luxury cars.

The mission at American Standard is to "Be the best in the eyes of our customers, employees and shareholders." To support this mission, in May 2002 the company launched a set of company-wide values. In December of 2002, as part of the company's values initiative, American Standard drafted an updated Code of Conduct and Ethics *(see Appendix)*, which applies to everyone in the company, including officers and members of the board of directors.

American Standard traces its roots back to 1872 when John B. Pierce opened a tinware shop in Ware, Massachusetts. He would later found the Pierce Steam Heating Company, one of three companies that would merge in 1892 to become the American Radiator Company, which merged with Standard Sanitaryware in 1929.

Today, American Standard is headquartered in Piscataway, New Jersey. It employs approximately 60,000 people and has manufacturing operations in 29 countries. American Standard is included in the S&P 500.

For more information, visit: www.americanstandard.com.
Stock Symbol: ASD

William T. Monahan

CHAIRMAN OF THE BOARD, PRESIDENT AND CHIEF EXECUTIVE OFFICER
IMATION CORPORATION

"Your reputation, hard won and built up over years…can easily be destroyed in moments by a perceived betrayal of trust."

– William T. Monahan

AFTER THE SPIN(OFF)

I'm privileged to serve as the CEO of Imation Corp., the data storage company. And I want to share a key element of what we have tried to build in this company that was created by the spin-off from 3M Company on July 1, 1996, of several businesses in the imaging and information technology industries.

Prior to the spin, I was heading up 3M's Austin, Texas, operations and the telecommunications and health care businesses. I was not involved in the businesses that were being spun off—though I had headed up the largest one, data storage, earlier in my career.

3M's CEO at the time, L.D. DeSimone—Desi to his friends and colleagues—called me to ask if I would consider becoming CEO of "NewCo," as it was called. After a twenty-three year career at 3M, I was being given the chance to lead a brand new company, with more than $2 billion in revenue and more than 10,000 employees. But it would mean I had to leave the company I had known my whole professional career.

I knew it was an opportunity I couldn't pass up. I also knew that it would be one of the biggest challenges of my career and would serve up surprises no one could fully anticipate or plan for.

At the start of any business endeavor, you never know exactly what obstacles you will encounter or the answers you will come up with. All that you can count on is that no matter how much you plan and anticipate, you should expect to be surprised. So it's critical to have a compass, a set of principles to help find a way through the challenges, problems, conflicts and confusion. The disciplines of finance and management have been developed and refined to provide that compass for many of the problems in business. But they cannot provide all the answers.

The surprises that business—and life—serve up are too unpredictable. People are involved, each with their differing needs and expectations. Sometimes, the only way you can bridge the gap between a problem and its resolution is by saying, "Trust me." Your reputation is your most valuable asset. The trust that all stakeholders are willing to extend to you, from employees and customers to shareholders, partners, suppliers and distributors, is often based on your reputation, hard won and built up over years. But it can easily be destroyed in moments by a perceived betrayal of trust. These are simple truths that every business person knows. Easy to say, not always easy to live up to.

Many of the businesses spun off into Imation were solid businesses, but in very competitive and fast-changing, technology-driven markets. For over 50 years, first as part of 3M, then as Imation, our Data Storage and Information Management business has been a worldwide leader in developing and manufacturing a full line of removable data storage products to help customers manage, store and share data for the desktop and mobile, network and data center environments. With more than 300 technology scientists and more than 300 data storage patents in the United States alone, Imation continues to pioneer today's proven magnetic and optical media technologies.

Imation's other businesses at "spin" included the world's leading supplier of color proofing materials for the graphic arts industry, as well a strong position in printing plates. Its medical imaging business was a leading supplier of laser imagers for medical diagnostics, with unique dry film technology just being introduced, and also was a supplier of conventional X-ray films. It had a private-label color photography film business for the consumer market, a microfilm document management business, an imaging equipment services business, a CD replication business and a carbonless paper business.

What these businesses all had in common was that they came from 3M. As valued as the 3M culture and heritage are, they also needed a new model, focused on their core, quick to respond to fast-changing digital technologies and competitive markets, with low operating costs and a lean corporate structure. In other words, a lot of change was ahead for this new company.

It was clear that we were going into new territory: creating a new company and shedding many of the 3M ways that would not work within this new, smaller entity. But we also realized that there were elements that we needed to bring with us. In addition to the significant product and patent portfolio, business agreements, skills, know-how and facilities, we needed to bring something else. Our success lay in the people, in our employees and customers, partners, suppliers and distributors sticking with us as we made this journey together. So we needed to preserve that part of our 3M legacy that would bridge our first days as a new, unknown company into one with a solid future. We did not know all the massive changes that the new company would go through, but knew that the values put in place at the outset would be critical to our success.

These values, which have remained unchanged since the first days of Imation, are:

- Delivering unsurpassed value to our customers, shareholders, employees and community;
- Maintaining the highest level of integrity and honesty;
- Valuing and respecting our people and their diversity;
- Protecting the environment, the safety of our people and the respect of our local communities;
- Providing the highest quality in everything we do.

So we launched ourselves into the world, confident and excited, and quickly got down to the hard work of establishing an independent company. We had to create a new company—a $2 billion start-up—not quite from scratch. We faced the immediate challenge of removing Imation from the 3M hierarchy, systems and processes. Every system, every process, every relationship had to be evaluated for who Imation was, and redesigned and re-established without interrupting our ongoing business of imagining, creating, manufacturing and selling products. We had to ensure that our customers experienced this transition seamlessly. At the same time, a new way of doing business—quicker-acting, leaner, more responsive—needed to be created. We were defining and cultivating a new culture for this new company.

Within 18 months of the spin, we realized that there was no synergy between our disparate businesses. Our success as a company depended on our ability to streamline our operations, focus on our core technologies and better position our various businesses for success in the future. That meant we had to rationalize our portfolio and restructure the entire company if Imation was going to survive.

We began to evaluate each business to find the highest-value home for each, recognizing the needs of customers, shareholders and employees alike. We evaluated the potential for each business by asking three questions: Is this a growth industry? Do we hold a strong technology position and intellectual property portfolio that differentiates us? Do we have a global market presence? If we could not answer yes to all three, then we had to find another home for that business, where it could succeed.

At the same time, we were faced with deteriorating financial results. We recognized that we had to aggressively reduce the cost structure and that meant taking significant restructuring actions.

Once the business decision was made to restructure the company, the management team faced a choice. We could announce just the restructuring and quietly continue the tough work on the portfolio, only announcing what we were doing as we went along. Or we could level with people and tell them as much as we could say publicly about what needed to be done: that we could not at that time precisely describe the endpoint to them, but that we would keep everyone updated.

We recognized how risky it can be to announce to the world that you are "reviewing strategic alternatives" without describing the endpoint in detail. We got plenty of opinions, both from within the management team and from outside advisors. Most of it was along the lines of, "Don't say anything, just announce to the world when you have a transaction. Employees will be paralyzed, customers will flee."

But there were other considerations as well. First, from a practical standpoint, we recognized that it could be more damaging for the inevitable rumors to circulate without any comments at all from management. More importantly, Imation was building its own identity and culture. While many employees had come with the spin, we were also bringing in people who had experiences with different companies. We had established a respect policy and encouraged openness and accountability, fostering an open exchange of ideas and the opportunity for all employees to personally impact the business. Personal accountability and responsibility became critical components of employee performance evaluation and development.

So how could we foster that atmosphere if we were not going to treat employees with honesty and openness? Similarly, we had made a commitment to deliver value to customers who were concerned that the business was going to provide long-term support. And many of our shareholders, as new to Imation as we were to them, needed to understand management plans and see results.

We knew the only way to maintain the credibility of the company with these various stakeholders and to hold their trust through an admittedly difficult time was to come clean. So that's what we did. We announced that we were going to restructure the company and we had hired an investment bank to help us in our portfolio review.

The reaction of employees was better than reasonably could have been expected. By and large, employees appreciated our full disclosure, acted with great maturity and redoubled their efforts to create value within their particular businesses, recognizing that the value in their business was the key to their individual success. We showed our customers that we valued their trust in Imation by being willing to take a chance—by asking them to come along on the journey with us, even if we could not precisely describe the destination. Customers stuck with us, based on the trusted relationships that had been established over the years and that remained unbroken. Shareholders by and large supported the moves, although they were impatient for results.

Imation's first divestiture was also its largest. The sale of our Medical Imaging Systems business was finalized in late 1998, and the people working in that division were given the opportunity to transfer to the acquiring company. That business has become one of the most successful with the new company.

A total of 16 transactions were completed, with the last one completed in August, 2002, enabling the company and its remaining 2,800 employees to focus on its core data storage business. About half these employees trace their careers back to 3M and half do not, so we truly have become our own company.

Over the course of this process, reported net sales went from $2.4 billion to a little more than $1 billion as a result of the divestitures, while the core data storage revenue continued to grow. From 1998 to the end of 2002, we generated significant earnings growth and a financial turnaround of nearly $1 billion in increased cash, reduced debt and stock buyback.

What have the results been for customers, employees and shareholders? Customers of divested businesses were protected as the products and services they relied upon were transferred to organizations better focused and equipped to meet their long-term needs. With our sharpened focus and financial strength, we have been able to invest more than $600 million in data storage R&D and capital since the spin. Imation's data storage customers continue to rely on us and we now have the broadest portfolio of products in the industry.

Employees of the divested businesses were considered as part of every negotiation, and most were taken into the acquiring company. Where jobs were eliminated, we sought to ensure that employees were treated fairly and with respect. Shareholders were rewarded for their patience, as Imation's stock was one of the best performing stocks in 2001 and 2002, up 39 percent and 62 percent, respectively.

There has been other recognition, as well. Imation was named by *Business Ethics* magazine as one of the "100 Best Corporate Citizens." In this blind evaluation, we ranked 39 out of 1,000 employers in 2002. The company has received top recognition from *Working Mother* magazine as one of "100 Best Companies for Working Mothers" and was recognized as one of the "10 Great Places to Work" in Minnesota by a regional business publication. Readers of *Fortune* magazine have voted Imation one of "America's Most Admired Companies" in its industry category. While the recognition is gratifying, particularly for such a young company, I know that everyone who has worn an Imation badge really has earned that recognition through their dedication, sacrifice, passion — and the values we brought forth.

Today, Imation is focused on data storage. The advantage we gain from that focus will be proven in our future results. But as important as that is, the reputation of Imation has been built and enhanced throughout all our change. We have been constant in our core values of integrity and honesty, respect for employees and focus on delivering value to customers and shareholders, building for the long-term success.

The future is always uncertain, but we're confident in the future because of where we've been before.

William T. (Bill) Monahan
CHAIRMAN OF THE BOARD, PRESIDENT AND CHIEF EXECUTIVE OFFICER
IMATION CORPORATION.

Bill Monahan is chairman of the board of directors and chief executive officer of Imation. He was named to the position in November 1995 and since then has led the development and creation of the company, its structure and management team.

Prior to leading the Imation team, Monahan was group vice president of 3M's Electro and Communication Systems Group in Austin, Texas. He joined 3M in 1972, and has held numerous management positions, including group vice president of Electronics, Electrical and Telecommunications Group, division vice president of Data Storage Products and senior managing director of 3M Italy.

Monahan serves on the board of directors of Hutchinson Technology, Inc. and Pentair, Inc. He is also on the board of directors of the Greater Twin Cities United Way and on the board of overseers of the Carlson School of Management, University of Minnesota.

Born in Scranton, Pennsylvania, Monahan spent most of his youth in New York and New Jersey. He holds a bachelor of science degree in economics from St. Peter's College and a master's in business administration from Rutgers University.

AFTER THE SPIN (OFF)

IMATION CORPORATION

Imation Corp. is a global company that develops, manufactures and markets the broadest portfolio of magnetic and optical removable data storage media products for both business and consumers. Imation's product portfolio includes diskettes, optical discs and tape cartridges that provide a wide spectrum of storage capacities. These products span major application areas from enterprise data centers to the network server environment, mobile and professional desktops to the personal consumer electronics user. Removable data storage media provide the benefits of easily expanded capacity, data transportability, high reliability, convenient access, long-term storage and data security.

Imation's roots in the data storage industry go back half a century. In 1952, the first commercial magnetic tape for computers was introduced by Minnesota Mining and Manufacturing Company (3M). Imation was created in 1996 as a result of the spin-off of several separate businesses that comprised the data storage and imaging systems groups of 3M. Since the spin-off, Imation has divested non-strategic business segments and readjusted the basic operational infrastructure to compete profitably as a focused data storage company. Today, Imation leverages 50 years of experience to deliver value to customers and to remain their trusted partner for removable data storage media.

The name Imation combines the essence of the company's core business-information management, with its core values of imagination and innovation. Pronounce it with a short "i," just as the words that generated the name are said. Imation is headquartered in Oakdale, Minnesota.

For more information, visit: www.imation.com.
Stock Symbol: IMN

Alexander M. Cutler

CHAIRMAN AND CHIEF EXECUTIVE OFFICER
EATON CORPORATION

*"There is no pride in ill-gotten gains.
Just as any victory won through dubious means is hollow,
so too are business results achieved
through unethical behavior."*

– Alexander M. Cutler

DOING BUSINESS RIGHT

The broad subject of "doing business right" is the essence of corporate governance and ethics. It is all about a higher standard, a standard that is, in fact, the soul of any values-based enterprise. It is this soul that defines and differentiates an enterprise, and so often is the very reason employees want to dedicate themselves to that organization.

I am proud that Eaton Corporation is a values-based enterprise. We all want to be proud of where we work, just as we want to be proud of our families, proud of our communities and proud of our personal and collective accomplishments. We also want to be winners, or part of a winning organization. But winning alone is not enough. We want to be proud of how we have won.

Eaton employees have heard me say repeatedly that I want us to achieve great results. And I always say in the next breath that we must care about how we get those results. There is no pride in ill-gotten gains. Just as any victory won through dubious means is hollow, so too are business results achieved through unethical behavior.

Any conversation about doing business right has to be grounded in the values and beliefs of the organization, or it can easily turn into a series of statements about policies, expectations and guidelines. It's impossible for any corporation to write a rule book comprehensive enough to cover every conceivable situation where integrity might be put at risk. In a values-based organization, your values establish the boundaries. Decision-making when faced with an ethical dilemma is easy: Do the right thing. Always. It is the practical application of the company's values and beliefs every day that makes a real difference to the success of the enterprise.

Reflecting on our own history, we have had more than a few opportunities to test our beliefs. And I know that our convictions have been strengthened by having experienced and dealt with these situations.

We had an issue many years ago where we were doing some advanced product development work for a significant global OEM (original equipment manufacturer) customer. There were established timetables for development, testing and shipment, and our customer was expecting the fully tested product to be shipped at the end of a particular quarter. When it came to the end of that quarter, not all of the testing had been accomplished. Two senior operating managers in the United States falsified the test results and thereby misrepresented the product's readiness for shipment. Both signed the reports willingly.

Upon investigation, we learned that they felt they should do this in order to meet the targeted shipment timetable, because they thought this was what both Eaton and the customer wanted. Yet, clearly, this was a violation of Eaton's quality and ethics policies. We terminated the two managers. Both had been high-potential, highly promotable people.

We learned a lesson from this incident — that integrity can break down at any level, no matter how much you preach and teach ethics. These were respected managers who had performed well for years, but they made a serious, serious mistake in judgment.

The safety of Eaton products is often critical to the safe performance of other products. If our products don't perform properly, people may be put at substantial risk. Our overarching concern is always to meet the highest levels of expectation and scrutiny. We will not tolerate any compromise of our standards for quality.

Nor will we knowingly violate any laws or regulations in any country. I say "knowingly," because mistakes sometimes do happen. What's important is that we act immediately to correct the situation. For example, in 1999, we unknowingly violated a U.S. Department of the Treasury regulation. One of our U. S. divisions shipped products, valued at less than $17,000, to a distributor in Switzerland for eventual delivery to a customer in Serbia. At the time, U.S. export-control laws restricted U.S. sales to Serbia.

Before shipping the products, our business unit followed established corporate procedures to determine whether the sale was permissible under America's export-control laws, and was incorrectly advised by a member of Eaton's corporate staff that the shipment was appropriate. We identified the mistake following additional internal review and Eaton submitted a voluntary detailed disclosure, with supporting documents, to the Department of the Treasury's Office of Foreign Assets Control. Even though the company faced a possible fine for the improper export, we made the voluntary disclosure because it was the right thing to do.

This is one small example of the many challenges that companies confront while doing business in today's global marketplace. At Eaton, we do not practice what I call "geographic" ethics. We have one set of ethics worldwide. And if the laws and regulations of a given country differ from our own company standards, we comply with whatever requirement represents the higher standard of behavior in that situation.

It's common knowledge that governments in certain parts of the world demand substantial payments in exchange for the conduct of business. This is unacceptable geographic ethics, which is not tolerated at Eaton. I'll give you an example. Several years ago, we had a facility that encountered piracy of our technology, theft of other intellectual property and the sale of our products into gray markets. Additionally, local businessmen made copycat versions of Eaton products and threatened to label them with Eaton brand names unless we paid them not to. The local government repeatedly approached us for payments, without which it would not pursue or prosecute these matters. It became clear that we were not going to be able to do business in an environment where the ethics of the local officials were so different from our own. So we abandoned the facility and our business in that country, at a not-insignificant cost.

I firmly believe that operating under a single code of ethics not only strengthens our own organization, but also those organizations that do business with Eaton. When "a rising tide lifts all boats," the situation changes. Can one company change the world? No, but it *can* chart its own ethical destiny.

In conflict-of-interest situations, I think a company clearly controls its own destiny. Conflicts of interest can arise in any aspect of business life and therefore present multiple opportunities to choose the ethical course. Such conflicts may involve everything from personal knowledge, to relationships, to business decisions and everything in between. Problems in this area often result from an unwillingness to acknowledge the conflict of interest, rather than a lack of recognition of the potential for a conflict. On the other hand, occasionally an individual fails to understand that a potential conflict even exists. That lack of sensitivity is truly problematic when you're trying to run an ethical enterprise. And sometimes what we would consider conflicts of interest are ordinary business dealings in other cultures.

China, for example, is a country where some people may see conflict-of-interest issues differently than how these matters are viewed in other countries. We've learned a lot about operating in that region and are very explicit about our expectations. Eaton had a plant manager in China, a Chinese national, who fell afoul of our prohibition against conflicts of interest. Although his actions may have been acceptable to some in that country, they were not acceptable to Eaton. He replaced the supplier that was providing a commodity to our plant with a supplier in which his wife had a financial interest. It was quite clear that his decision had not been based on quality or price issues with the previous supplier.

Until then, we had been very pleased with this executive's performance. He was a highly valued employee in whom we'd invested considerable training, including almost four years of cumulative operations experience in the United States and China. Despite our investment in this employee, we had to let him go. We simply could not allow his action to stand or to appear to be endorsed when it was so clearly a violation of our conflict-of-interest standards.

We also expect our business partners and suppliers to uphold Eaton's standards of ethical conduct. Doing business right is not a subject that any of us can delegate, nor can we outsource ethics. I cannot conceive that we could ever be comfortable doing business with a supplier that employs child labor, or with a business partner that bribes government officials. Our Code of Ethics *(see Appendix)* transcends all we do, and we should expect it to have a positive influence on all our interactions.

In a diversified industrial manufacturing company like Eaton, we have thousands of business relationships around the world that touch every part of our enterprise. When a supplier or business partner acts without integrity, we trust that our employees will make it clear that if the unethical action does not stop, the business relationship with Eaton will. When acting within the scope of our employment, every single one of us *is* Eaton.

Of course, we have had our share of ethical lapses since Eaton's founding in 1911. Like that of every company, our workforce comprises human beings, and people make mistakes and sometimes do bad things. Over the years we have become aware of situations where employees have defrauded the company through the use of a variety of different accounts, through receiving cash and not depositing it, by stealing company property and selling it for their own benefit, and by committing other serious transgressions. In these cases, we have acted very directly and very quickly to terminate the employee, sometimes filing criminal charges. At Eaton there are no one-, two- and three-strike offenses in situations like these. One strike and you're out.

Like Eaton, there are many other companies that hold to high standards of integrity. Years ago, the strategic planning book for one of our businesses was stolen and sold to a competitor. To that company's credit, its chief executive officer, upon receiving the book, immediately put it in an envelope, sealed it and sent it back to us. He said that neither he, nor any of his associates, had looked at it, and I trust his representation. I would expect the same of any Eaton employee in similar circumstances.

There is absolutely nothing wrong with seeking competitive information that is in the public arena. Rigorous competitive assessment is good business. If you work at it, you can put piece one and piece three of public information together and figure out what piece two is. But at Eaton, we absolutely do not steal data, and we do not take or use data that has been inappropriately or illegally procured. There is everything wrong with paying for illegal access to confidential information, just like there is everything wrong with debriefing employees you hire from another company to gain confidential information about that company, or to appropriate that company's intellectual property.

There are as many ways to violate a company's integrity as there are people and circumstances to do it. All the ethics codes and governance charters in the world cannot overcome the actions of a single misguided individual. But our company's set of beliefs and values do form the basis for establishing expectations, evaluating situations and taking immediate actions in order to address ethical issues. Reinforcement of the company's beliefs is critical to ensure that our values-based culture remains vibrant, and that Eaton remains an enterprise about which we all can be proud.

Yes, we care about results, but not at the expense of integrity. We run Eaton as an integrated operating company that uses the standardized tools and processes of the Eaton Business System, such as the Eaton Lean System and PROLaunch, to achieve breakthrough results. Our Code of Ethics, the Eaton Philosophy and Values, our Mission and Vision, all comprise the foundation of the Eaton Business System. It is that foundation of beliefs, that ethical expectation of how business will be conducted, that makes the operational "how," operational.

I believe every business leader—whether in Eaton or any other company—needs to emphasize the expectation of "doing business right," and to act quickly and decisively when ethical values are violated. In a values-based enterprise, ethics and governance are daily considerations that permeate decision-making and action. Few, if any, principles are more important to the long-term viability of an organization. And there is no truer window into a corporation's soul.

———

Alexander M. Cutler
CHAIRMAN AND CHIEF EXECUTIVE OFFICER
EATON CORPORATION

Alexander M. Cutler is chairman and chief executive officer of Eaton Corporation, and a member of its board of directors.

Cutler, who has 28 years of service with the company, began his career with Cutler-Hammer in 1975. After the acquisition of Cutler-Hammer by Eaton, he served in a variety of progressively responsible management positions. In 1989, he was named president of Eaton's Controls Group. He was elected executive vice president of Operations in 1991, executive vice president and chief operating officer of Controls in 1993, president and chief operating officer of Eaton Corporation in 1995, and assumed his current position in September 2000.

He received his B.A. from Yale University and an M.B.A. from the Amos Tuck School of Business Administration at Dartmouth College.

Cutler is a board member of KeyCorp, Axcelis Technologies, Inc., the Amos Tuck School of Business Administration at Dartmouth College, The Loomis-Chaffee School, the Greater Cleveland Roundtable, Cleveland Tomorrow, The Electrical Manufacturers Club, and the Musical Arts Association. He is the 2003 Campaign Chairman of United Way Services, Co-Chairman of The Cleveland Commission on Economic Partnerships & Inclusion and a member of the Yale University Development Board.

Cutler has served as a board member for a number of organizations, including the Yale University Alumni Fund, the National Electrical Manufacturers Association (where he also served as past chairman), the Visiting Committee of the Weatherhead School of Management, and the Greater Cleveland Growth Association.

ALEXANDER M. CUTLER | EATON

EATON CORPORATION

Eaton Corporation is a global diversified industrial manufacturer that is a leader in fluid power systems; electrical power quality, distribution and control; automotive engine air management and fuel economy; and intelligent drivetrain systems for fuel economy and safety in trucks. Eaton has 51,000 employees and sells products in more than 50 countries. Eaton's businesses comprise four distinct segments. These are, by size: Fluid Power, Electrical, Automotive and Truck.

The Fluid Power business is a worldwide leader in the design, manufacture and marketing of a comprehensive line of reliable, high-efficiency hydraulic systems and components for use in mobile, industrial and aerospace applications. Mobile and industrial markets include earth-moving, agriculture, construction, mining, forestry, utility and material handling.

The Electrical segment is a leader in electrical control, power distribution, and industrial automation products and services. It provides customer-driven solutions that serve the changing needs of the industrial, utility, light-commercial, residential and original equipment markets.

Eaton's Automotive segment is a partner to the passenger car and light-truck industry. Principal products include superchargers, engine valves, valve train components, cylinder heads, locking and limited slip differentials, sensors, actuators, intelligent cruise control systems, tire valves, fluid connectors, decorative body moldings and spoilers.

The Truck segment is a leader in the design, manufacture and marketing of drivetrain systems and components for medium-duty and heavy-duty commercial vehicles. Eaton markets the "Roadranger System"—a complete line of drivetrain components and truck systems, including manual and automatic transmissions, clutches, driveshafts, steer and drive axles, trailer axles, tire pressure control systems and collision warning systems. Eaton is headquartered in Cleveland, Ohio.

For more information, visit: www.eaton.com.
Stock Symbol: ETN

BUILDING TRUST

Rich DeVos

CO-FOUNDER AND FORMER PRESIDENT
AMWAY CORPORATION

"We must always be straight about who we are and what we do as a business."

– Rich DeVos

PUTTING THE HEART BACK INTO BUSINESS

One thing I've learned in my 77 years on earth is this: It's not how we handle the good days that determines how well we do in life. What matters most is how we handle the bad days.

There's no question that recent corporate scandals have given business a black eye. Some people have lost trust in corporations and their business leaders. You might say the last few years have been a "bad day" for business.

Perhaps.

Business does have work to do to regain the public's prior support. As an eternal optimist, I am convinced we will rise to this challenge.

I speak from personal experience. You might look at my life and conclude that I've had a few bad days of my own.

Right after World War II, I started a flying school with my lifelong friend and business partner, Jay Van Andel. We thought it would take off, but it never did as well as we had expected. We got out of that business.

On a trip Jay and I took to South America we nearly went down with our leaky sailboat, which sank off the coast of Cuba. We survived that challenge and went on to visit several South American countries. We set up some businesses importing products from that region, but those ideas didn't pan out, either.

In 1959, when the two of us started the direct-selling company Amway, we were promoting small business ownership at a time when big business was king. We met a lot of resistance over the years— including a major FTC investigation, an international customs case and a series of media challenges. Often, it seemed we were swimming against the tide. Still, we persisted.

In the 1990s, I had a couple of major heart surgeries. And seven years ago, at age 71, I had a heart transplant. Waiting several months for the perfect donor, it looked like my life's end was near. But through God's grace, I ultimately received the heart of a 39-year-old woman, and today I have a new lease on life.

No human life is problem-free. But I've always tried my best to view problems as challenges and to never lose hope. I've always believed that every challenge presents new opportunities — to learn, grow, gain strength or reach a higher goal.

So it's no surprise that I view the current mood toward business as an opportunity for us to get things back on track and show what's right about business.

Without question, the business world is different today. It is faster, more global and, in some ways, more complex than when I was a chief executive.

Despite these differences, I believe we can improve attitudes toward business, and there are some important lessons from the past that can assist us.

Specifically, I have five ideas that I believe will help business regain what has been lost in the wake of recent scandals. These echo the principles for business success articulated by Arthur Page many years ago.

HEART

First, one of the things I see missing in many corporations today is heart. We need to bring heart back into business.

Today, many CEOs and their management teams spend most of their time talking about "maximizing shareholder returns."

Is that really the only purpose of business?

It's true that companies can't continue to serve customers, employees and neighbors if they don't make a reasonable profit.

But with so much time and energy concentrated today on beating the next quarterly earnings estimate by a penny, what happens to serving customers, motivating employees and helping neighbors? They become secondary, of course. And sometimes they become an afterthought. It's no wonder that Enron and others failed. They had their eye on the wrong ball. They needed more heart.

To rebuild public trust, many companies are revisiting their vision and mission statements. They are asking: Who are we—really? What do we stand for?

Those are great questions. And they are a great place for business to start its journey to restore trust.

If honest in their introspection, many companies will find that their visions on the wall plaques in far-flung hallways don't consistently match up with their actual business behaviors.

Some companies say they care about people. But it's evident to most that they put people below profits on their list of priorities—at least those priorities that are measured by their investment in time and attention. Their actions speak volumes more than their words.

Businesses make and distribute all kinds of things. But no matter what we make or distribute, we all exist to help others. That's why we're here. If we do it wisely and well, we will serve our stakeholders and provide them with a reasonable return, too.

Because people are the core of our business, our company has a simple yet profound vision statement—helping people live better lives. For our customers, we provide nutrition and beauty products, among others, that will help them feel and look better. For those who sell our products, we offer business opportunities that satisfy a wide range of personal and professional priorities and interests. For employees, we create opportunities to make a difference. For our neighbors, we share generously to improve the quality of community life.

We believe it's essential to be more than a corporation that simply makes or markets stuff. To remain viable, we know we must first improve the well-being of people around the world.

So you could say that we're a business with tremendous heart. We're not alone, of course. There's a heartbeat in every company—stronger in some than others, but there regardless. Together, we must find new and better ways to make passion and caring for others paramount. If we do that, shareholder returns will follow.

VALUES

My second observation is that in many ways, we've strayed too far from the basics. We need to go back to the values that we've put on paper, and then live and breathe them every day.

When we started Amway, my partner and I centered the business on some basic values, such as reward, recognition, family and hope.

These were crucial to our early success. And they remain instrumental to the success our business continues to have, 44 years later.

Our core values are simple, clear and concrete. People around the world, no matter what their background may be, understand them. They relate and aspire to these ideals.

Unlike "maximize shareholder returns," our values mean something specific to everyday people.

We believe we need to inspire people, to infuse them with hope that they will have a better, more fulfilling future.

We believe people want to be financially rewarded when they sell products and when they help other people sell products. The more they achieve, the more they are rewarded.

Moreover, we believe people want to be recognized. To be told, "Good job" and thanked for their efforts, large and small. To be supported even when they might fall short of their goals or make a mistake. It amazes me how many managers and leaders overlook this fundamental point, even today.

So this is a great time for businesses to revisit values and make them a centerpiece of their work going forward.

COMMUNICATIONS

My third observation is that people today are very smart. Thanks to the Internet, they have a world of information right at their fingertips. As a result of this, along with decades of consumer education, they can spot a corporate smoke screen miles away. So they want and expect clear, straightforward, open and interactive communications. They expect companies to respect them first. So we must always be straight about who we are and what we do as businesses.

We are not the only company, of course, that values communications excellence. Fortunately, that's the rule today—rather than the high-profile exception. But allow me to share a few brief examples simply to demonstrate my point.

Our board of directors sets expectations for ethical behavior, and these expectations are integrated in our performance criteria for employees. These expectations are based on values and principles that our two founding families first articulated decades ago. They remain relevant thanks to the efforts of the second generation of family members now on the board, as well as the fresh perspective of three non-family directors.

Our values underpin several internal tools, including a Code of Conduct for the more than 3 million independent business owners

(IBOs) comprising our global sales force. Though not employees, the actions of a single IBO can affect our entire reputation—good or bad. When IBOs are not willing to abide by our code, then they no longer can be affiliated with our organization. It's that simple.

Our corporate staff—including those in communications—act as a sort of conscience for the enterprise. With our corporate reputation uppermost on their minds, they monitor people and situations. With their help, decisions are made with the company's long-term interests in mind, and always based on our core values. In fact, it's common to sit in a meeting and hear people say we won't pursue a new revenue opportunity or acquire a company because it wouldn't fit with our values.

Openness in a corporate culture starts with listening. That's why our company leaders hold regular company-wide meetings with employees, along with special sessions where only our co-CEOs—with no corporate staff present—meet with employees from all areas of the company to hear their comments, suggestions and criticisms. There's follow-up on the action items, of course.

Our corporate Intranet features a feedback site where we post straightforward answers to employees' questions on any subject. We also have a videotape series in which our chief executives discuss our core values in practical ways that are "real" for all employees.

We pose some of the most obvious questions and answers about our businesses for anyone to see on the Internet. At our Web site (www.amway.com), for example, you can find the answers to direct questions like these:

- Why do Amway meetings appear to some people like a cult?
- Is it true that Amway endorses one religion?
- Is it true that you don't have to sell, just buy the products for yourself and recruit others to do the same?

All this is part of our commitment to clear, straightforward, open and highly interactive communications. We start by listening, and we keep communicating to build and keep trust.

FAITH

The fourth change I've observed over the years is that faith seems to get checked at the door when people arrive at work. Corporations are not unique in that regard; organizations throughout society seem to go out of their way sometimes to avoid discussions about faith.

As we were growing up, our role models—teachers, parents, neighbors and clergy—helped set society's expectations. They taught us to be honest…to tell the truth…to treat others as we would like to be treated.

Basic principles like honesty, integrity and accountability can be found at the core of many different faiths. They are common human values, resident in all types of societies and cultures.

As we consider ways to restore trust in business, I'm struck that many basic concepts and principles are already deeply ingrained in us through our faith experience. Faith-based morals are right there, yet often they remain buried beneath the surface in the workplace.

So why not admit the obvious? Many of the principles that guide our business behaviors trace back to our personal religious beliefs.

Instead of acting like faith has no place in the workplace, why don't we capitalize on it? Provided we respect important differences, why shouldn't faith be acknowledged in business?

Sometimes, people are surprised to hear a former CEO of a large, global company discuss the importance of spiritual things. But I'm here to tell you that faith matters at work, too. My faith is the foundation for everything in my life; it is my greatest asset. Absent faith, the universe—including work—would seem a meaningless place to me. Nothing would have the same sense of purpose or direction.

My point is that faith-based values and principles are good. Don't check them at the office door. Don't hide them under the desk. Don't deny their existence. Encourage employees to bring them to work, and to use them in their own way and style—especially when a moral or ethical dilemma arises. Business will prosper for it.

RESPECT

Over the years, I've thought long and hard about what constitutes a good leader and what particular qualities make her or him effective. I've concluded that respect for others is the most essential trait a leader must possess. So that's my fifth and final suggestion to help business restore trust.

People know when you value and respect them—and they know when you don't. You can't hide disrespect or a lack of respect. People sense your attitude instinctively, even if they don't put it into words.

Respect is reciprocal. What goes around comes around. If you want to be respected, you must respect others. The nuts and bolts of running a business or organization are important, but they are of little consequence if you don't respect the people with whom you work—your colleagues, your employees and your customers.

Our challenge is to be regarded as honest, inspiring leaders. If people don't respect us, then we are not complete leaders, and our businesses will not live up to their potential. Moreover, business will continue to be a dirty word. None of us wants that. It doesn't have to be that way.

CONCLUSION

At age 77, I still have much to learn. And though I may tend to oversimplify some points, I'm not naïve. I'm not suggesting that these five fundamental concepts—heart, values, communications, faith, respect—are the panacea for what ails business today. It's not that easy, of course.

Six years ago, doctors ran some tests and determined I needed a new heart. The diagnosis was the easy part. Finding a heart that matched my body, and then overcoming all sorts of fears and challenges once it was implanted in my chest, was the hard part.

As I look at business trust today, I admit it's much easier to diagnose the problem than to fix it.

But since I'm 77 and essentially retired, I'll delegate the important job of restoring trust in business to today's very capable leaders. They have the ability. And thanks to some of the high-profile failures, they now have the will. I have no doubt they will succeed, and business will resume its respected place in society.

Meantime, I would like to close by sharing one of my favorite quotations from Aldous Huxley: "Experience is not what happens to you; it is what you do with what happens to you."

The events of our lives flow and change. Nothing stays the same. Business has taken a beating lately—rightly so, in some cases. That's happened to us. Now it's time to do something about it.

I believe we can restore trust in business if we show more heart. If we remember our values and make them a regular part of our daily conduct. If we listen and communicate, and we acknowledge the existence of faith in the workplace. And even if we do none of that, which I certainly hope is not the case, if we just treat others with greater respect, then there is no doubt in my mind that business is going to earn new levels of trust and support.

I believe that with all my heart.

Rich DeVos
CO-FOUNDER AND FORMER PRESIDENT
AMWAY CORPORATION

In 1949, Rich DeVos and Jay Van Andel formed the Ja-Ri Corporation and began distributing products on a direct sales basis. In 1959, DeVos founded Amway Corporation with Van Andel and served as president until 1993. In 2000, Amway became one of four subsidiaries under a new parent company called Alticor Inc.

A renowned speaker, DeVos' recorded talk, "Selling America," received the Alexander Hamilton Award for Economic Education from the Freedom Foundation. He has written three books: BELIEVE!, Compassionate Capitalism *and, most recently,* Hope From My Heart: Ten Lessons for Life.

His civic service has included: Chairman, National Speakers Bureau, United Network for Organ Sharing, Council of Trustees, Freedom Foundation; Board Member and Founding Chairman, National Organization on Disability; Board of Trustees, Gerald R. Ford Foundation; Past Finance Chairman, Republican National Committee; and Past Member, Presidential Commission on AIDS.

His awards and achievements include: Inspiration Award, International Association for Organ Donation, American Spirit Award, Republican House and Senate; National Business Hall of Fame, Junior Achievement; Horatio Alger Award; Edison Award, American Marketing Association; William Booth Award, Salvation Army; Sales & Marketing Executives International Academy of Achievement Charter Inductee; Napoleon Hill Gold Medal Award for Free Enterprise Achievement; Direct Selling Association Hall of Fame Award; Thomas Jefferson Freedom of Speech Award, Kiwanis International; and American Enterprise Executive Award, National Management Association.

A native of Grand Rapids, Michigan, DeVos attended Calvin College and served in the U.S. Air Force from 1944 to 1946. He holds eleven honorary doctorate degrees from various colleges and universities across the country. DeVos owns the Orlando Magic, the National Basketball Association franchise, of which he is chairman.

ALTICOR INC.

Alticor Inc. is a global corporation offering products, business opportunities and manufacturing and logistics services in more than 80 countries and territories worldwide. Alticor is the parent company of:
- Amway Corp.—one of the world's leading direct-selling brands;
- Quixtar Inc.—a leading e-business in North America; and
- Access Business Group LLC—a manufacturer and distributor of quality products worldwide for both Alticor and non-Alticor companies.

Headquartered in Ada, Michigan, Alticor has more than 11,000 employees worldwide. In addition, through its Amway and Quixtar business opportunities, Alticor helps more than 3.6 million people own and operate their own independent businesses.

Alticor companies focus on nutrition, wellness, beauty and home products and manufacturing and logistics services. Vitamins, food supplements and cosmetics are among the company's leading global brands. Alticor's company vision is "Helping people live better lives," and its products and business opportunities focus on making a difference in the health, happiness and personal fulfillment of people around the world.

Alticor's history dates back to 1959, when Jay Van Andel and Rich DeVos founded the direct-selling company Amway. Amway now operates in more than 80 countries and territories around the world. In 2000, Alticor was created as the parent company of Access Business Group, Amway, the Amway Grand Plaza Hotel and Quixtar. Alticor had sales of $4.9 billion in the fiscal year ending August 31, 2003.

For more information, visit: www.alticor.com.

PROVE IT WITH ACTION

"*The only way to talk about ethical leadership…is in terms of how it's exhibited in the everyday actions of the people.*"

– Ivan Seidenberg

"*How we act as individuals has a profound effect on whether the organizations we represent achieve their full potential.*"

– Rick Wagoner

"*[Our] employees do whatever is required to provide product and service whenever and wherever it is needed.*"

– Art Collins

"*Let me be clear—we did it right.*"

– Dr. E. Linn Draper

Ivan Seidenberg

CHAIRMAN AND CHIEF EXECUTIVE OFFICER
VERIZON COMMUNICATIONS, INC.

"Leadership has less to do with any single individual…than it does with the culture, norms and values of the institution itself."

– Ivan Seidenberg

ETHICS IN ACTION

Much has been made in recent months about the importance of executive leadership and integrity, particularly at the top levels of corporations, and rightly so.

The public is absolutely right to hold corporate executives to the highest standards of conduct. Employees are right to look to their leaders to exemplify ethical behavior. And shareholders are right to demand that corporate leaders make decisions in the best interests of our owners, not merely ourselves.

Making CEOs publicly accountable for the actions of the companies we head is a crucial part of rebuilding corporate credibility. For my part, I want Verizon's shareowners to see my name when they look at our financial statements and know that I personally vouch for the integrity of our results, as well as the people and systems by which they were created. But while we're holding executives' feet to the fire, we also must look well beyond the executive suite when examining the forces that shape behavior—for better or worse—in large organizations.

The buck may stop at the CEO's desk, but it doesn't necessarily start there.

The only way I know to talk about ethical leadership—the only way the phrase is meaningful in an institutional sense—is in terms of how it's exhibited in the everyday actions of the people I work with at the company where I've spent the last 30-plus years of my life. That's because, when it comes to large organizations, leadership has less to do with any single individual—even if that single individual happens to have the title CEO—than it does with the culture, norms and values of the institution itself.

At Verizon, we've had the chance to test this thesis in two ways— first, when we formed our company in 2000, and second, when our mettle was tested in the crucible of September 11.

Most people are familiar with Verizon, the largest wireless and wireline communications company in the United States and employer of almost a quarter of a million people. But until a mere four years ago, Verizon as we know it today did not exist. It was formed from the merger of Bell Atlantic, the regional phone company in the Northeast, and GTE, one of the oldest independent telephone companies in the country. Both predecessor companies had long histories and strong cultures that were a source of pride and identity for their employees and customers.

We wanted to make sure our new company—like our antecedents—would be "built to last." If you're familiar with that phrase, made popular by the James Collins book of the same name, you know that Collins defines a "built to last" company as a "premier institution...widely admired by its peers and having a long track record of making a significant impact on the world around it." He also makes the point that elite institutions are just that—institutions, whose strength derives from the organization itself rather than from any single individual. The great institutions are those that are connected to something bigger than themselves, an idea that transcends the self-interest of any individual and motivates people to work for the good of the whole, rather than just themselves.

Our goal was to use the merger process to make ourselves a "built to last" institution by blending the best of our 100-year-old histories with the best of what we aspired to become. To do that, we thought it was important to put down on paper what our new company stood for—our values, goals, purpose and commitments.

We did that in a document called "The Verizon Promise." If you read it, you'd probably say that it sounds a lot like other corporate charters, and you'd be right *(see Appendix)*. Some of the words in it are those you'd expect to see—like "integrity" and "respect." Some you might not—like "imagination" and "passion." It says that our core purpose is to bring the benefits of communications to everyone. It talks about our obligations to customers, communities, shareholders and employees. And underlying it all—bridging every aspect of our business—is the idea of service. That's what we are fundamentally about.

So from the beginning, we were a company with a shared idea of who we are, what we're in business for, and what we believe in. Our self-definition grew out of a century's worth of experience as a service company and resonated immediately with our employees. We were confident that our shared values and sense of purpose would shape our employees' actions, even when there was no precedent for what they ought to do.

On September 11, 2001, this idea of ourselves was tested in a way we never imagined possible.

The attacks of September 11 hit Verizon hard, in both our wireline and wireless operations. While all three strikes were devastating, the damage to the communications network in lower Manhattan was almost beyond comprehension. Our huge central office at 140 West St.—one of the biggest, most sophisticated communications hubs in the country—is immediately across the street from where the World Trade Center towers stood, and it was inundated by debris, soot and water from the buildings collapsing around it. In addition to once housing more than 2,200 Verizon employees, it also serves as the communications nerve center for all of lower Manhattan, from the Hudson to the East River. We also provide cellular service in the area over towers dotting the skyscrapers of Wall Street.

Altogether, 300,000 voice lines, 3.6 million data circuits and 10 cell towers were disrupted or destroyed, affecting service to 14,000 business and 20,000 residence customers—rather like the network for a city the size of Cincinnati going down, all at once.

When you operate a vital network, you have all sorts of emergency plans and processes to rely on, all of which worked superbly to make sure essential services like 911 and police and fire department communications remained up and running. But no disaster plan could have prepared us for the magnitude of what we faced that day. No emergency command center could have directed the actions of all the people who had to turn on a dime amid chaotic conditions. Those on-the-spot decisions have to be made by instinct.

For example, shortly after the attack, President George W. Bush issued a challenge that the New York Stock Exchange—whose communications network was destroyed when the Twin Towers fell—reopen in a matter of days. For Verizon, that meant installing more than three-and-a-half million voice and data lines, building new fiber-optic rings and restoring software systems—a project that would normally take weeks, if not months, to be done in just six days. Fulfilling this national imperative required our technicians to exhibit enormous initiative, skill and dedication in figuring out—on the spot—how to rebuild the communications network of lower Manhattan: pulling cable along trenches in sidewalks and out seven-story windows, hand-cleaning equipment and rerouting cables, walking up 23 floors to retrieve critical software...all in hellish conditions.

The result: Trading resumed on Monday, September 17—and the exchange went on to handle 2.3 billion shares on the day, the largest volume in its history.

For every Verizon employee on the streets of lower Manhattan, there were a hundred more behind the scenes, all of whom rose to a new level of leadership. They reached out to thousands of customers to help them get back on line. They worked with government authorities to ensure the security of critical communications links. They staffed the phones for telethons and donated thousands of dollars to relief efforts.

Verizon became a whole company of leaders, animated by the spirit of service and empowered by a commitment to a common goal. The actions by our people in the wake of the September 11 attacks illustrate to me what leadership looks like:

- First — It's based on skill, requiring people who are highly trained and proficient in their jobs.
- Second — Leaders are visible; rather than shrinking from problems, they go to the trouble and stay until it's fixed.
- Third — They are accountable for the bad news, as well as the good.
- Fourth — They communicate early, often and openly.
- And fifth — They don't need a "boss" to tell them what to do. Instead, their actions spring from within — a set of values that gives them a reason to do what they do. In our case, it was that America needed the ability to communicate. It was as simple — and as profound — as that.

Obviously, the actions of the individuals who did the work in those harrowing times reflect extraordinary personal character. But from a leadership perspective, the key lesson of September 11 is that it proves the "built to last" thesis: Great institutions produce great leaders, not the other way around. If it's not in your DNA to do the right thing in normal circumstances, you'll never do the right thing in extraordinary circumstances. If that's the case, then it means that the "system" counts — strong, values-based systems that empower individuals to act in such extraordinary ways that the whole becomes greater than the sum of its parts.

Now comes the hard part.

The job of the Verizon leadership team is to take all the history and tradition of the *last* 100 years—the rock-solid culture that allowed us to rise to the most difficult of challenges—and use it to create something lasting for the *next* 100 years. The challenges of transforming the telephone business into the broadband business will require us to re-imagine how we deliver everything from education to health care to government and financial services. If we do it right, we have the opportunity to produce not only a good return for shareowners and a good living for thousands of employees, but also something of lasting value to society.

So what's my job description? At a minimum, to do no harm. At best, to figure out how to unleash the collective leadership power of a quarter of a million people to create something permanent.

But at the end of the day, it's not about me.

I accept completely the responsibility for CEOs to be accountable for the actions of our companies and to set a tone of integrity, honesty and accountability. Verizon's employees and shareowners deserve to know where I stand on the tough issues and look to me to exemplify our values and express our point of view.

But I truly believe that the most important thing I can do for Verizon, long term, is be faithful to the principles of my institution, to guard its values and make sure they remain in sync with society's, and to reward employees' behaviors that exemplify and perpetuate them.

Great institutions—like great ideologies—transcend and survive the self-interest of any single individual, no matter where he or she sits in the corporate hierarchy.

Scandals happen when people act as if it's the other way around.

Ivan Seidenberg
CHAIRMAN AND CHIEF EXECUTIVE OFFICER
VERIZON COMMUNICATIONS, INC.

Ivan Seidenberg is chairman of the board and chief executive officer for Verizon. He began his communications career more than 38 years ago as a cable splicer's assistant. His career has encompassed numerous operations and engineering assignments, including various leadership positions at AT&T and NYNEX.

As chief executive of Bell Atlantic and previously of NYNEX, Seidenberg was instrumental in reshaping the communications industry through two of the largest mergers in its history: the merger of Bell Atlantic and NYNEX in 1997 and the Bell Atlantic merger with GTE in 2000. He also led efforts in September 1999 to form Verizon Wireless, the nation's largest cellular business composed of the wireless assets of Bell Atlantic, GTE and Vodafone Airtouch.

Seidenberg also champions diversity both within and outside the company. Under his leadership, Verizon has made great strides in increasing minority employment and initiated a partnership with the U.S. Small Business Administration to increase the company's purchasing from minority suppliers. The company was cited by Fortune *magazine in its list of "The 50 Best Companies for Minorities."*

Seidenberg's commitment to education and advocacy of connecting students and teachers to technology led to his involvement with The New York Hall of Science and Pace University, on whose boards he serves. Seidenberg also serves on the board of directors of Honeywell, the Museum of Television and Radio, Viacom Inc., the Verizon Foundation and Wyeth.

He earned a bachelor of arts degree in mathematics from City University of New York and a master's degree in business administration and marketing from Pace University. He and his wife, Phyllis, have two adult children and reside in New York City.

VERIZON COMMUNICATIONS, INC.

A *Fortune* 10 company, Verizon Communications is one of the world's leading providers of communications services, with approximately $67 billion in revenues. Verizon companies are the largest providers of wireline and wireless communications in the United States, with more than 139 million access line equivalents and 36 million Verizon Wireless customers.

Verizon is the third-largest long-distance carrier for U.S. consumers, with nearly 16 million long-distance lines. The company is also the largest directory publisher in the world, as measured by directory titles and circulation. Verizon's international presence includes wireline and wireless communications operations and investments, primarily in the Americas, Europe and Asia. Verizon in headquartered in New York City.

The mergers that have formed Verizon were several years in the making, involving companies with roots that reach back to the beginnings of the telephone business in the late 19th century.

For more information, visit: www.verizon.com.
Stock Symbol: VZ

Rick Wagoner

CHAIRMAN AND CHIEF EXECUTIVE OFFICER
GENERAL MOTORS CORPORATION

"Integrity transcends borders, language and culture. It's not something we can impose but it is something we can influence and monitor…"

– Rick Wagoner

DRIVING INTEGRITY

In recent years, in fields ranging from business to sports and from government to religion, we've been reminded time and again of the serious consequences that can result from lapses in personal integrity. In the world of business, careers have been tarnished and entire companies have been jeopardized because of poor choices.

Regardless of where we work or what we do, we cannot ignore the fact that how we act as individuals has a profound effect on whether the organizations we represent achieve their full potential. Integrity has a direct impact on both the bottom line and the long-term viability of every company.

Integrity transcends borders, language and culture. It's not something we can impose, but it is something we can influence and monitor by creating an environment that supports and requires proper business and personal conduct.

At General Motors, we certainly don't have all the answers to promoting personal integrity inside our company. But, we do enjoy a long tradition of strong corporate governance, rigorous accounting practices and accurate financial reports that I believe have helped us conduct our business in a fair, honest and open manner for many years. For this, we owe a great debt of gratitude to those who preceded us at GM. They set the tone for a high standard of integrity and conduct at GM, and I am personally committed to continuing that legacy in the years to come.

In the following essay, I will review some of the actions and programs that we at GM have undertaken which—directly or indirectly—foster, protect and promote integrity with our board of directors, employees, business partners, and customers.

A SIMPLE TEST

From time to time, I have the opportunity to speak with young people about integrity and character development. When I do, I like to tell them about a good and simple test that they can use, in any situation, to determine whether they are acting with integrity. I ask them to ask themselves a simple question: If the way they are handling a situation were reported on the front page of a prominent national newspaper tomorrow, how would their family, friends and fellow students or co-workers feel about it?

I tell them that if they'd be proud, that's terrific—their moral compass is pointing them in the right direction. If not, they better step back and reconsider what they're doing. Bottom line: How they get things done is just as important as getting them done.

A simple test, for sure—but one that I find works just as well for 50-year-olds as it does for fifth graders. At GM, we try to promote integrity by making it as straightforward and clear as this simple test. We have made integrity one of GM's core values, and we expect our employees, top to bottom, to act with integrity every day.

START AT THE TOP

At GM, we have a tradition of responsible and proactive board governance. Our board of directors was one of the first, in 1994, to formally adopt corporate-governance guidelines ensuring its independence and effectiveness.

Prior to that, GM became the first major U.S. corporation to have an African-American board member when the Reverend Leon H. Sullivan joined the GM Board in 1971. In 1977, still as a member of the GM Board, Reverend Sullivan established his landmark "Sullivan Principles," and with them a powerful tool for helping end apartheid in the Republic of South Africa. GM was the first company to adopt the Sullivan Principles 26 years ago. In 1999, GM was among the first companies to endorse the "Global Sullivan Principles," which emphasize the common goals of human rights, social justice and economic opportunity, and which now serve as the aspirational framework for our corporate responsibility initiatives.

Today, the vast majority of GM's board members—9 out of 10, presently—are independent outside directors. All of our key board committees—audit, compensation and director affairs—are composed only of outside directors. Independent auditors answer to the independent Audit Committee of the board. We do not give loans to our directors or executives, and our CEO and Chief Financial Officer have taken personal written responsibility, in our annual reports, for the company's consolidated financial statements for more than 20 years.

Of course, we realize that we cannot rest on our reputation and existing policies alone. Acting with integrity is an ongoing process, not a destination, and we have to continue promoting good corporate governance and behavior if we are to be a leader in this area.

In 2002, in response to growing public concern about the actions of Corporate America, GM took several steps to ensure just that.

- We promptly complied with the new requirements established by the Securities and Exchange Commission (SEC) for key officers to certify company financial results;

- We endorsed the new "Corporate Accountability and Listing Standards" approved by the New York Stock Exchange (NYSE);

- We adopted a new policy to expense stock options granted to employees beginning in January 2003;

- We formally supported the Sarbanes-Oxley corporate-governance legislation signed into law by President George W. Bush.

WINNING WITH INTEGRITY

At GM, we believe that our company can only realize its full potential by doing things the right way, all around the globe. To that end, we have well-established business and personnel practices, which are articulated in a set of guiding principles we call "Winning with

Integrity" *(see Appendix for summary)*. These integrity principles are shared with all new employees at orientation, and they are reviewed regularly by all of our current employees. They serve as the foundation for employee conduct everywhere we do business.

Winning with Integrity is based on GM's core values. It sets out the policies and legal obligations that help guide our business conduct around the world. In the end, of course, integrity comes down to personal responsibility, and Winning with Integrity reminds every member of the GM enterprise that they are personally accountable.

Winning with Integrity requires a commitment to personal integrity by everyone at GM: first, to exemplify our core values in their own conduct and comply with GM policies, and second, to raise concerns when they believe fellow employees are acting contrary to existing policies.

Collectively, it is the employees of GM who make up our company, and the actions of one individual can damage the reputation of all. Through Winning With Integrity, we work to foster an environment that supports and promotes proper business conduct. All GM employees know that they have both the opportunity, and the obligation, to promote integrity by demonstrating good judgment and setting strong personal examples every day.

A TRADITION OF TRANSPARENCY

At GM, we place a high value on communicating clear, consistent and accurate information about our performance. Our business processes, internal controls and reporting systems are structured to ensure that any potential issues are promptly highlighted. Our board of directors provides robust oversight—and believe me, they ask a lot of tough, probing questions!

At GM, our goal is simple: to build great cars and trucks that improve people's lives, and to do so the right way, the way that GM stakeholders expect. We understand that upholding this commitment is much more than a one-time exercise—it's a way of doing business.

To help us get there, we set annual targets for our economic, environmental and social progress, and measure our performance against those targets. We then publicly report our results in an annual Corporate Responsibility and Sustainability Report, using the standardized reporting guidelines set forth by the Global Reporting Initiative. This allows our stakeholders to evaluate our performance in a consistent and open manner. GM has been issuing this report since 1994, and was the first automaker in the world to do so.

To further underscore our commitment to transparency and open communication, we developed our "GMability" Web site in 2000. In today's Internet age, we realize that our Annual Report and our Corporate Responsibility and Sustainability Report may not reach everyone interested in our activities. GMability allows us to use the Internet to help bridge geographic and cultural boundaries.

In addition to these annual reports, GMability provides detailed information about many of our initiatives, including those in the areas of environment, safety, philanthropy and diversity. Visitors to GMability can learn about our work in advanced technology, including fuel cells; find detailed information on the GM plants in their communities; compare our fuel economy to that of our competitors; discover more about safe-driving initiatives, such as the donation of child safety seats to low-income families and at-risk children; and even contribute online to disaster relief efforts through GM Global Aid.

At GM, we want to be held accountable for our actions, and we believe our actions can be best understood when we highlight key business issues, provide key metrics to measure our performance, and communicate information that allows others to judge our progress.

TEACHING OUR OWN

Of course, there is more to integrity than simply adhering to the letter of the law. Adlai Stevenson once said, "It is often easier to fight for a principle than to live up to it." In the end, I believe the companies that succeed will be the ones that live up to the principles of integrity that they instill in their business practices.

At GM, we try to increase the odds that our employees will "live up to it" by teaching them how to act with integrity—teaching them in a formal sense, at our GM University (GMU), a virtual enterprise consisting of a number of "colleges" that represent the functional areas within our company. GMU's charter is to increase the skills and capabilities of the workforce, and create a more performance-driven culture to achieve better business results.

Two of the many courses taught at GMU are "GM Corporate Citizen Overview" and "GM Corporate Citizen Conflict of Interest." The former is designed to promote good corporate citizenship by teaching GM employees from around the globe about GM's vision, core values, cultural priorities and guidelines for employee conduct in real-life situations. The latter is designed to help GM maintain its reputation as a company that conducts business with the utmost integrity. It is based on the premise that GM is committed to taking all the appropriate precautions to avoid a conflict of interest, or even its appearance. The purpose of the course is to provide guidelines for addressing conflicts in various situations, including relationships with suppliers, activities with charities, outside board memberships, interests in other businesses, employment of relatives and outside employment.

In addition, the importance of integrity to our business practices is incorporated into the entire GMU curriculum. This is particularly true in the GMU Leadership College's "high potential program," which prepares the next generation of leaders at General Motors.

The Leadership College consists of three sessions over the course of nine months. I personally teach twice in every course targeted to GM's high potential talent, and most of my direct reports also serve as Leadership College instructors. A "leaders as teachers" philosophy has been instilled throughout GM leadership. In addition to the Leadership College, senior executives are highly encouraged to offer their expertise through teaching in a variety of courses at GMU. The topic of integrity is central in all my courses and presentations, and the same goes for the GM senior leadership team.

DEEDS, NOT WORDS

To sum up, we at GM believe that in these times of corporate turbulence, every company must do its part to help restore investor and consumer confidence in our free-enterprise system. At GM, we try to do that by running our business, day in and day out, with accountability, transparency and integrity—the way that GM tradition expects and demands.

We strive to back up our approach with tangible, measurable actions, because we believe that, in the end, a company's reputation is determined much more by what it does, than what it says. In the words of Jack Smith, our recently retired Chairman, we rely on "deeds, not words." At GM, we'll continue to behave as if our company's current and future success hinges on our every action—because, in truth, it does.

Rick Wagoner
CHAIRMAN AND CHIEF EXECUTIVE OFFICER
GENERAL MOTORS CORPORATION

Rick Wagoner was elected chairman and chief executive officer of General Motors on May 1, 2003. He had been president and chief executive officer since June 2000. He is a member of the boards of directors of Hughes Electronics Corporation and General Motors Acceptance Corporation, both GM subsidiaries.

Wagoner was elected president and chief operating officer in 1998 and had been executive vice president of GM and president of North American Operations since 1994. He served as executive vice president and chief financial officer from 1992 to 1994 and also had responsibility for worldwide purchasing from 1993 to 1994.

Wagoner was president and managing director of General Motors do Brasil (GMB) in 1991 and 1992. Prior to that, he was vice president in charge of finance for General Motors Europe based in Zurich, Switzerland, in 1989 and 1990.

Born in Wilmington, Delaware, and raised in Richmond, Virginia., Wagoner received a bachelor's degree in economics from Duke University in 1975 and a master's degree in business administration from Harvard University in 1977.

Wagoner began his GM career as an analyst in the Treasurer's Office in New York in 1977. After several promotions there, in 1981 he became treasurer of GMB in São Paulo. In 1984, he became executive director of finance for GMB. He moved to GM of Canada Limited in 1987 as vice president and finance manager. In October 1988, he became group director, strategic business planning, for the former Chevrolet-Pontiac-GM of Canada Group.

Wagoner is a member of the boards of trustees of Duke University and Detroit Country Day School and the Board of Dean's Advisors of the Harvard Business School. He is chairman of the Society of Automotive Engineers and A World in Motion Executive Committee, and is a member of The Business Council and The Business Roundtable.

DRIVING INTEGRITY

GENERAL MOTORS CORPORATION

General Motors Corp., the world's largest vehicle manufacturer, employs 341,000 people globally in its core automotive business and subsidiaries. Founded in 1908, GM has been the global automotive sales leader since 1931. GM today has manufacturing operations in 32 countries, and its vehicles are sold in more than 190 countries. GM's global headquarters is in Detroit, Michigan.

GM's automotive brands are Buick, Cadillac, Chevrolet, GMC, Holden, HUMMER, Oldsmobile, Opel, Pontiac, Saab, Saturn and Vauxhall. In some countries, the GM Group distribution network also markets vehicles manufactured by GM Daewoo, Isuzu, Subaru and Suzuki.

GM parts and accessories are sold under the GM, GM Goodwrench and ACDelco brands through GM Service and Parts Operations. GM vehicle engines and transmissions are marketed through GM Powertrain.

GM operates one of the world's leading financial services companies, GMAC Financial Services, which offers automotive and commercial financing along with an array of mortgage and insurance products. GM's OnStar is the industry leader in vehicle safety, security and information services. GM's other major businesses are Hughes Electronics Corp. (NYSE: GMH), which provides digital television entertainment and satellite-based services, and GM Electro-Motive Division, which manufactures diesel-electric locomotives and commercial diesel engines.

In 2002, GM set industry sales records in the United States, its largest market, for total trucks and sport utility vehicles. GM became the first manufacturer to sell more than 2.7 million trucks in a calendar year and the first to sell more than 1.2 million SUVs.

For more information, visit: www.gm.com.
Stock Symbol: GM

Art Collins

CHAIRMAN AND CHIEF EXECUTIVE OFFICER
MEDTRONIC, INC.

*"We were able to anticipate and incorporate
many of the leading edge practices
well before they were dictated…"*

– Art Collins

LIVING THE MISSION

We live in a time when many corporations are casting about for new principles and new directions in response to the issues of ethics and corporate governance that received heavy media and public visibility during the past several years.

Medtronic, Inc., the world's largest medical technology company, has found this unnecessary, since its Mission and operating principles, established over 40 years ago, have positioned the company to deliver consistently strong business results while maintaining good corporate citizenship.

It's been nearly half a century since Medtronic Founder Earl Bakken wrote our company's Mission. Since then, our employees have continued to advance the frontiers of medicine by focusing on one common goal: *To apply biomedical engineering to alleviate pain, restore health and extend life.* Our Mission also clearly states that we expect to fulfill our corporate purpose *by directing our growth in the areas where we display maximum strength and ability, and avoiding areas where we cannot make unique and worthy contributions; by striving without reserve for the greatest possible reliability and quality in our products; by recognizing the personal worth of employees; and by maintaining good citizenship as a company.*

The Mission works because it unifies our purpose, guides us with clarity and keeps our priorities straight. The Mission also works because we live it every day.

We recognize that to fully achieve our goals, the company must continue to grow and remain healthy. As a result, our Mission also states that we expect to earn *a fair profit on our operations*. While profit is important, it is not our primary goal. We believe that if we act responsibly and focus on meeting our customers' needs, strong financial performance will follow. This has been our experience in the past and again this year as we announced record financial results, and we expect it will continue to be the case in the future.

However, at Medtronic, the most important statistic we track is not financial in nature. It is that today, every six seconds, someone, somewhere in the world is alive or living a fuller life because of a

Medtronic product or therapy. Maura Lopez, from La Mirada, California, is one of those people. Maura is 11 years old and has diabetes. She is just one of more than five million people around the world who are insulin dependent. It's exciting and rewarding to help people like Maura who, thanks to Medtronic insulin pump therapy, now enjoy a vibrant, active life. What does she appreciate most about her insulin pump? "No more shots! And for the first time, mud pie for my birthday!"

Sometimes we touch the lives of an entire family, like the Sorrells from Little Rock, Arkansas. Their story is about hope born from tragedy. After two of her children died suddenly, Cindy Sorrells was diagnosed with Long QT syndrome, a serious heart arrhythmia condition that can be passed from one generation to another. As a result, Cindy and her children — Missy, Amber, Renee and Jeremy — have all received Medtronic cardioverter defibrillators to treat this potentially life-threatening condition. "For the first time, we have true peace of mind," Cindy told me when we first met. "Now I know my family will be safe."

For my 30,000 co-workers, Maura Lopez's and the Sorrells' story, together with millions of other stories like theirs, provide immense pride and inspiration for what we do on a daily basis.

As our record indicates, Medtronic is not a growth story for one quarter or one year. We work hard to maintain our momentum and prepare for tomorrow. In this regard, we have recently enhanced our infrastructure and expanded technical and sales support to meet rapidly growing demand for our products and to provide even better service to our customers. In order to further extend our industry-leading position, we also have invested heavily in research and development.

These investments have continued to pay off with approximately two-thirds of our current revenues generated from products introduced in the past two years. More importantly, new products are now providing more cost-effective and improved medical outcomes for millions of people around the world.

Today, Medtronic is the industry leader successfully treating some of the world's more challenging and costly medical problems, including: sudden cardiac arrest, which strikes one American every two minutes and is the leading cause of death in the United States; congestive heart failure, the progressive deterioration of the heart's pumping capability that afflicts more than 22 million people worldwide; coronary artery disease, which forces more than two million people each year to seek treatment to restore normal blood flow in the heart; diabetes, which afflicts more than 170 million people worldwide and about 20 million in the United States; and a broad array of spinal and neurological disorders that restrict mobility and result in pain for millions of people worldwide.

In addressing these pressing healthcare challenges, Medtronic's most important resources are not listed on the balance sheet or income statement. Our most precious and productive resources are the nearly 30,000 employees who individually and collectively represent the key to future medical breakthroughs and are the most important ingredient in our ongoing success. Our employees live on every continent. They speak different languages and come from different cultures. While they are diverse in many ways, they have one resolve when they go to work: to serve the people who count on them, and to live our Mission every day. Whether supporting physicians and the patients they treat on a daily basis, or responding to a crisis like the terrorist attacks on September 11, 2001, Medtronic employees do whatever is required to provide product and service whenever and wherever it is needed.

Just as Medtronic is committed to helping people live healthy and productive lives, we are dedicated to improving the communities in which we live and work. As Medtronic celebrates 25 years of formal philanthropic work, we remain steadfast to our Mission by maintaining good corporate citizenship and sharing our resources. Our employees support numerous civic and charitable efforts with significant donations of time and money. In addition, this past year corporate giving, product donations and Medtronic Foundation grants exceeded $30 million, focusing on building partnerships and empowering patients with chronic diseases, preparing future generations of scientific innovators and health professionals, and supporting numerous community outreach programs.

During the 2002 Annual Shareholders Meeting, I spoke at some length on the impact of a number of corporate scandals starting with Enron, and the steps we had taken to further enhance previously strong corporate governance and financial control and reporting systems at Medtronic. It is clear that a number of adverse events over the past several years have shaken investor confidence and have resulted in a number of mandated corporate reform measures. With the Medtronic Mission as the basis for much of what we have put in place over the years, we were able to anticipate and incorporate many of the leading edge practices well before they were dictated by the Sarbanes-Oxley Act, the New York Stock Exchange guidelines and other recent reform measures. We really believe that if we are to serve our various key constituencies well, we must, as Arthur Page pointed out many years ago, manage our business for the long term.

In addition to taking a great deal of care to conform with new reporting requirements when preparing our Annual Report and required periodic financial disclosures, we have attempted to expand communication with our shareholders and other important external constituencies. We have worked hard to write and speak clearly, with the intent of making important information understandable to all those with whom we communicate.

We also are fortunate to have a capable, highly engaged and fiercely independent board of directors. Our directors take their responsibilities very seriously and work hard to enhance and safeguard the company and our shareholders' investments. The quality of our board of directors was recently recognized when *Business Week* magazine selected Medtronic as having one of the 10 best boards in Corporate America. Let me relay a few additional facts about the Medtronic board:

- I am the only member of management on the board. This means that 90 percent are outside, independent directors. I do not serve as a standing member on any board committee, including the Nominating Committee that recommends new board members. Also, I am not affiliated in any way with any of our directors' companies or institutions.

- Routinely at each meeting of the board of directors, including committee meetings, the board meets privately in Executive

Session, without me or any member of management present. The board has access to independent experts—lawyers, accountants and compensation consultants—to turn to for counsel regarding specific Medtronic policies and activities.

- The Audit Committee of the board meets privately with the head of our internal audit group, and then privately with our independent auditors at the end of each committee meeting. Prior to issuance, the head of our Audit Committee also reviews quarterly and year-end financial statements and the associated press releases with our financial management and the independent auditors.

- The Audit Committee also reviews the performance of our external auditors each year and then votes on whether or not they should be retained. Our external auditors now have their assignments limited to audit work and selective tax assignments. As a result, they are not allowed to bid on consulting-related assignments.

- The head of our Corporate Governance Committee serves as a lead director and has private access to any member of management he wants. He also acts as a clearinghouse for board meeting agenda topics or any requests from individual board members.

While we have excellent corporate governance and strong financial control and reporting systems already in place, there is no substitute for effective corporate management and strong board members who understand their duties to safeguard the company and the interests of employees and shareholders. In that regard, I speak for myself and for Medtronic's senior executive management team and Board of Directors when I say that we make every attempt to stay current on important activities and events that impact the near and longer-term performance of the company. We have and will continue to report Medtronic's business activities and financial performance clearly and accurately. We will continue to discuss good news and bad news in terms that everyone can understand. We will stand behind what we say and do, and be accountable for the consequences. We will live our Mission with passion and integrity, and we will do our best to deliver results that all stakeholders in this great company can take pride in. No ifs, ands or buts.

Even though we all live in a more uncertain, complicated world with no small number of challenges, the opportunity to positively impact the lives and health of so many has never been greater. At Medtronic, we remain dedicated to advancing medical technology and providing better and more cost-effective medical outcomes for an increasing number of people around the world.

Let me conclude, as I have in the past, by thanking all of Medtronic's employees, customers and shareholders for their ongoing support. I remain convinced that by staying true to our Mission, Medtronic's best years are yet to come.

Art Collins
CHAIRMAN AND CHIEF EXECUTIVE OFFICER
MEDTRONIC, INC.

Art Collins assumed the role of chief executive officer of Medtronic, Inc. in April 2001 and became chairman of the board in April 2002. Collins was elected chief operating officer and member of the board of directors in 1994, and president in 1996. Previously he was corporate executive vice president and president of Medtronic International with responsibility for all Medtronic operations outside the United States.

Collins joined Medtronic in 1992 from Abbott Laboratories, where he had been corporate vice president with responsibility for Abbott's worldwide diagnostic business units since 1986. He began his 14-year career with Abbott in 1978 as manager of corporate planning and development and joined the diagnostics division a year later, where he subsequently held a number of general management positions in the United States and Europe. He was elected a corporate officer in 1989.

Before joining Abbott, Collins served as a naval officer from 1969 to 1973 and a consultant with Booz, Allen & Hamilton, Chicago, from 1974 to 1978. With Booz, Allen, he conducted major assignments in the areas of business strategy development, marketing, organization planning, financial analysis and financial systems design.

A 1969 graduate of Miami University of Ohio, Collins also holds a master of business administration degree from the Wharton School of the University of Pennsylvania where he was a member of the undergraduate faculty.

Collins serves on the board of directors of U.S. Bancorp and Cargill, Inc. He is also a member of the board of overseers of the Wharton School at the University of Pennsylvania, chairman of the industry association, AdvaMed, and serves on the boards of numerous civic organizations.

MEDTRONIC, INC.

Medtronic is the world's leading medical technology company, providing lifelong solutions for people with chronic disease. Medtronic does business in more than 120 countries and employs approximately 30,000 employees worldwide.

Medtronic Cardiac Rhythm Management develops products that restore and regulate heart rhythm, as well as improve the heart's pumping function. The business markets implantable pacemakers, defibrillators, cardiac ablation catheters, monitoring and diagnostic devices and cardiac resynchronization devices, including the first implantable device for the treatment of heart failure. In addition, the business markets automated external defibrillators (AEDs)—which are increasingly being placed in public places—and the industry's first Internet-based network to enable physicians to remotely manage patients with cardiac devices.

Medtronic Cardiac Surgery develops products used in cardiopulmonary and beating heart bypass surgery. It markets heart valve products for both replacement and repair, and develops autotransfusion equipment and disposable devices for handling and monitoring blood during major surgery.

Medtronic Vascular's products and therapies treat vascular diseases and conditions. These products include coronary, peripheral and neurovascular stents, stent graft systems for diseases and conditions throughout the aorta, and the industry's first distal protection system. The business is also moving forward with the development of a drug-eluting stent to prevent restenosis. Medtronic Vascular also markets balloon angioplasty catheters, guide catheters, guidewires, diagnostic catheters and accessories.

Medtronic Neurological and Diabetes offers therapies for movement disorders, chronic pain and diabetes, as well as diagnostics and therapeutics for urological and gastrointestinal conditions. Medtronic Spinal, ENT and SNT develops and manufactures products that treat disorders of the cranium and spine.

Medtronic is headquartered in Minneapolis, Minnesota.

For more information, visit: www.medtronic.com.
Stock Symbol: MDT

LIVING THE MISSION

BUILDING TRUST

Dr. E. Linn Draper, Jr.

CHAIRMAN, PRESIDENT AND CHIEF EXECUTIVE OFFICER
AMERICAN ELECTRIC POWER COMPANY, INC.

"Our protective systems worked well and the lights stayed on in AEP's service territory."

– Dr. E. Linn Draper, Jr.

RESPONDING TO THE WORST U.S. BLACKOUT

Months after the August 14th blackout which affected 50 million Americans and Canadians, it continues to be a prime topic for both legislators and regulators. It was the worst blackout in U.S. history.

The investigation and research to reconstruct the events of that day are continuing, and the public policy debate to determine ways to minimize the likelihood of a similar event in the future has only just begun.

Because the August 14th outage has wide-ranging implications for the future of the electric utility industry, I want to share our company's perspective on these events with you.

As you will see, we believe the actions of our employees contribute significantly to building a good business reputation. Inasmuch as AEP has $5 billion invested in its 39,000-mile transmission grid, ours is certainly a unique perspective.

From the outset, let me be clear—we did it right. The AEP System held together—a point of pride for us. Our protective systems performed as they were designed to perform, our operators performed and communicated as they should, and our load and generation remained in balance before and after the blackout. Our grid is large, robust and integrated, and can therefore withstand the power swings we experienced that day. In short, our people responded correctly and we were able to avoid serious problems caused by the blackout. In fact, Michehl Gent, the president and chief executive officer of the North American Electric Reliability Council (NERC), said on August 15 that AEP's 765,000-volt transmission system is "often heralded as the world's finest transmission system."

From an operational standpoint, the 14th was a fairly typical August day until our operators first detected transmission line problems at an interconnection point with our neighboring utility to the north, FirstEnergy. When that took place, we contacted FirstEnergy's operators. Throughout this event, we maintained extensive communications with our reliability coordinator, the PJM (Pennsylvania-New Jersey-Maryland) Interconnection, and with FirstEnergy.

Power flows on the AEP System before the event, especially into Michigan and northern Ohio, were high but not unusual, given typical summer loads. It's important to note that Michigan is often a significant importer of power. Power flows on our lines continued to increase because of increased demand outside our system. We still do not know the cause of the increased demand.

As the flows of power exceeded safe operating levels across our lines, our equipment in northern Ohio operated automatically to isolate the problem. This is exactly what the equipment is designed to do. To quote the U.S. Department of Energy's National Transmission Grid Study, released in May of last year, "Electricity flows according to the laws of physics and not in response to human controls — what happens in one part of the grid can affect users throughout the grid."

The opening of the lines prevented damage to our equipment. More importantly, it avoided cascading outages across the AEP System and probably far beyond, given the central role of AEP's transmission grid in the eastern and midwestern United States. The AEP System was not the only one to respond this way. The transmission system serving Consumers Power's load in Michigan, among others, also isolated it from the problem during the event, and their system held. I do not know why all systems failed to perform in a similar manner.

Automatic tripping of lines is not simply a matter of protecting our equipment. There are serious reliability and safety implications if the automated protection mechanisms do not activate.

First, if the equipment is damaged, it can be out of service for an extended time, further burdening other lines that are already stressed. In short, the system holds for as long as it can, but at some point equipment must "trip off" to prevent further cascading outages. In this instance, tripping off stopped the cascade to the south, enabling AEP's personnel to assist others in their restoration efforts, because we did not have to deal with restorations of our own.

Tripping off also has safety implications. If current runs as high as it was during the event, it could actually cause the lines to literally melt or to sag beyond design criteria, which can result in safety hazards to the public.

I do not wish to speculate on the root causes of this event, so I can't say it wouldn't have occurred a year ago, or it will never occur in the future. The interconnected nature of our grid, and the fact that we are now using it in ways that were not originally intended, mean that these kinds of events can occur in the future, although lessons learned can help prevent a recurrence of the same magnitude.

I take great exception to the characterization of the U. S. transmission system as "a Third World grid," as some have said. The American transmission grid is the strongest in the world, although it is being pushed to its limits.

The electrical grid in this country was designed, in large part, to move a local utility's generation to its customers—not to carry thousands of cross-country and regional transactions, as the grid is now doing. In the five-year period during which wholesale electric competition first gained momentum, the number of wholesale transactions in the United States climbed from 25,000 to 2 million—an 80-fold increase. And many stakeholders are striving for continued growth. Transmission infrastructure expansion—which is an expensive and time-consuming prospect at best—did not increase 80-fold in that time frame. In fact, very little expansion has taken place.

Clearly, there is a need to strengthen the grid through greater investments—new equipment, new power lines and new technologies—to support today's use of the grid.

Several factors will hasten grid improvement. First and foremost, we need regulatory certainty. If we need to build new transmission facilities today, we must often navigate through multiple state and federal regulators to get that done. Processes vary in every state. For permits and siting, for instance, we must get approvals from multiple state regulators, and probably multiple federal regulators, as well. We proposed a 765,000-volt line in West Virginia and Virginia in 1990. After an expenditure of more than $50 million, we received final clearance to build the line during the last week of 2002. While we respect the interests of all jurisdictions in siting decisions, we'll never get where we need to be if it takes nearly 13 years to get permission to build a power line.

And for every dollar we spend—and the National Transmission Grid Study quoted a price of $1.8 million per mile for a new 765,000-volt line—we must go back to those multiple state and federal regulators to receive full recovery. In this context, it is difficult to understand recent actions by the Federal Energy Regulatory Commission (FERC) to eliminate transmission revenues from third-party or wholesale customers. If FERC's proposal comes to pass, power will be able to move from St. Louis to New Jersey for the same fee as moving power from Pennsylvania to New Jersey. Such scenarios not only jeopardize existing investments, but they also create a disincentive for future investments since full and fair cost recovery is even more difficult.

Second, and also critically important, we must improve coordination and communication among the various entities that oversee the grid. The reality is that we don't have one single transmission grid owner and operator throughout the country, nor would it be feasible or wise to do so. It's a given that there will always be seams—or boundaries—between various grid operators.

What's required is continuous improvements in the coordination among the various grid operators to ensure coordinated planning and operations, and quick response in emergency situations. On August 14, our operators did coordinate and communicate with other operators, which helped to prevent this outage from spreading even further across the country. However, we can all strive to improve. Those who are using this event to promote their desire for a single Regional Transmission Organization (RTO) administering a spot market are not only missing the boat, but misleading some people into thinking that simply installing such an RTO would answer the reliability issues that have been raised by this event.

I fear the current controversy and seemingly endless debate over the role of RTOs are hindering our ability to make progress and create an environment conducive to investment in needed transmission assets. Although AEP has committed $50 million to RTO development, many states now are opposing an expansive role for RTOs (including a number of the 11 states where AEP's transmission and distribution lines are located), while others fully support a broad role for RTOs and more federal control over the grid and the wholesale market.

While the debate about RTOs rages on, let's not forget some key points:

- AEP is in the center of the current debate largely because of the scope and the high quality of our system, which is at the crossroads of many markets. That's one big reason why we're coveted by electricity market stakeholders in their attempts to expand RTOs.

- Policies should balance both generation and transmission. Transmission owners must receive sufficient revenues to assure adequate investment.
- Parties that benefit from competitive markets should bear the costs. Those that use the transmission system to receive those benefits should pay for it.
- While some have suggested splitting up the AEP System, the idea is unacceptable and counterproductive. The AEP System has been touted as the backbone of the Eastern Interconnection. Splitting it apart amidst efforts to increase the nation's electric reliability flies in the face of reason.

We need consensus on an appropriate use of the grid. If we focus solely on competitive markets and economics, serious implications for reliability and security arise. We need a balance, but that balance must be tipped toward reliability—the fundamental foundation of the transmission grid. Without reliability, we have no market to structure.

The benefits of competitive markets should not only flow to generation owners or electricity users, as seems to be the present policy, but also to the transmission owners. They need to receive a sufficient share of benefits to assure investment in the transmission infrastructure necessary to support competitive markets.

Additionally, we must approve NERC as the enforcement entity for mandatory reliability standards. Our grid is interconnected. We must all play by the same rules, and we must have a knowledgeable independent entity—such as NERC—empowered to enforce such standards.

We will continue to work with the U.S. Department of Energy, NERC and all of the entities that are working on investigations of the events of August 14, 2003. As part of that process, I testified before the U. S. House of Representatives' Committee on Energy and Commerce on September 4, 2003. We look forward to a complete analysis and answer to exactly what happened that day, and we hope to have a voice in determining appropriate solutions or improvements. In the meantime, we can take a measure of satisfaction in knowing our protective systems worked well and the lights stayed on in AEP's service territory.

My apologies for running on a bit on this technical subject, but I believe that greater understanding of this issue will increase shareholder and consumer faith in AEP.

Dr. E. Linn Draper, Jr.
CHAIRMAN, PRESIDENT AND CHIEF EXECUTIVE OFFICER
AMERICAN ELECTRIC POWER CO., INC.

Dr. E. Linn Draper, Jr. became chairman, president and chief executive officer of AEP in May 1993. He served as president of AEP and the Service Corporation starting in March 1992, following 13 years with Gulf States Utilities Company, where he served as chairman, president and chief executive officer. Draper is also president of Ohio Valley Electric Corporation and its subsidiary, Indiana-Kentucky Electric Corporation.

Before joining Gulf States Utilities, Draper served on the faculty and administration at the University of Texas in Austin. He holds a bachelor of arts degree and a bachelor of science degree from Rice University, and a doctorate in nuclear science and engineering from Cornell University.

In 1992, Draper was elected a member of the National Academy of Engineering. He was elected to the Cornell University Council Board in 1998, appointed to the University of Chicago Board of Governors for Argonne National Laboratory in 1999, and serves on the University of Texas Engineering Foundation Council. He is a member of the boards of directors and past chairman of the Nuclear Energy Institute, the Institute of Nuclear Power Operations, the National Coal Council and the Edison Electric Institute. He is a past president and former member of the board of directors of the American Nuclear Society.

He is chairman of the Environment, Technology & the Economy Task Force of The Business Roundtable-WDC, and chairman of the Ohio Business Roundtable. Draper is also on the board of the U.S. Chamber of Commerce and the National Association of Manufacturers. He is the chairman of the Columbus Downtown Development Council and is a member of the board of directors of Borden Chemicals and Plastics.

AMERICAN ELECTRIC POWER COMPANY, INC.

American Electric Power is one of the largest electric utilities in the United States. Approximately 5 million customers in the Midwest, Middle Atlantic and Southwest regions are linked to the company's 11-state grid.

AEP operates 39,000 miles of transmission lines and more than 180,000 miles of distribution lines. The company has more than 2,000 miles of 765,000-volt transmission lines—more than the rest of the nation's electric utilities combined. AEP is also one of the largest generators of electricity in the United States, owning and operating more than 38,000 megawatts of generating capacity.

The company has become one of the nation's largest producers of wind energy. AEP owns two wind farms in Texas with a combined generating capacity of 310 megawatts. AEP also produces electricity from coal, natural gas, nuclear and hydroelectric plants.

AEP has a tradition of environmental stewardship. The company has planted more than 62 million trees since the 1940s, some as a part of its award-winning surface-mine reclamation activities and some as a part of its carbon sequestration projects. Eleven of AEP's power plants have been designated as certified wildlife habitats by the Wildlife Habitat Council, a non-profit organization. The company sponsors summer workshops for teachers, as well as its E-LAB program, which allows teachers and students to visit and study in the forests of Bolivia or Belize.

Since 1951, AEP has been a pioneer in coal ash utilization and research. Today, fly ash produced from coal combustion is used as a partial replacement for cement in concrete and is also used in the production of paints, coatings and plastics.

Founded in 1906, AEP is headquartered in Columbus, Ohio.

For more information, visit: www.aep.com.
Stock Symbol: AEP

RESPONDING TO THE WORST U.S. BLACKOUT

BUILDING TRUST

LISTEN TO THE CUSTOMER

"When technology and the nature of customer problems change—we do, too."

– Samuel J. Palmisano

"[Our customers] simply want us to look at the world through their eyes. To meet their expectations, we also have to take a pretty hard look at ourselves."

– Louis J. Guliano

"Put the client first."

– Michael H. Jordan

"When you ask consumers what they want, it boils down to more control over their health care decisions."

– John W. Rowe, M.D.

Samuel J. Palmisano

CHAIRMAN OF THE BOARD AND CHIEF EXECUTIVE OFFICER
IBM CORPORATION

"… [I]f customers are going to look to you as the leader in computing, you have to be able to drive forward the entire computing agenda, not just a piece of it."

– Samuel J. Palmisano

ALL THE WAYS
A BUSINESS SHOULD LEAD

When I joined IBM, it was one of the most respected, innovative and successful companies in the world. That was, in large part, because of the way Tom Watson Sr., IBM's founder, had shaped it. He nurtured a unique culture, a progressive set of values and the aspiration to make a difference in the world.

IBM's position was further enhanced in the 1960s, when Tom Watson Jr. took a daring, "bet-the-company" gamble on the System/360 mainframe.

It revolutionized computing and transformed the way business was done. It also spurred a radical reinvention of IBM and propelled the company to worldwide commercial leadership for two decades.

Of course, IBM stumbled badly in the early 1990s, largely because it strayed from its values and stopped listening—to customers and to its own smart people. As a consequence, the company failed to reinvent itself for new realities. Under Lou Gerstner's leadership, the people of IBM rebuilt their company. It has come back a long way.

Today, I believe we stand our best chance in decades of returning IBM to a position of leadership—in all the ways that a business should lead. I want to describe how we define leadership for IBM, because it is the context for understanding what we accomplished in 2002 and is the framework for how we will manage IBM in the decade ahead.

SEIZING THE MOMENT

An environment like the past three years, for all its challenges, is the ideal time to make decisive moves for future growth. Because of our ability to generate strong cash flows, we have invested billions in research and development, in capital expenditures and in acquisitions. We took advantage of reasonable valuation levels and acquired several companies, including PricewaterhouseCoopers Consulting (PwCC) and six strategic software firms. We acquired Rational, a leader in software development tools. We opened the most advanced semiconductor development and manufacturing facility in the world. And we also improved our competitiveness. We revamped our PC and microelectronics businesses. Our inventory levels now stand at a 20-year low. Through progress on our integrated supply chain, we've taken more than $5 billion in costs out of the business in each of the past two years.

Through it all, the people of IBM turned in a solid performance, despite a most difficult couple of years. That performance has been reflected in our market value.

However, the meaning of this period goes beyond the blocking, tackling and individual actions I've briefly described. I believe that years from now we will see this as the time we fundamentally repositioned IBM for leadership—leadership in an industry that will be very different when it comes out of the current economic slump.

A NEW GAME FOR INFORMATION TECHNOLOGY

In some ways, the IT industry will remain familiar. It will still thrive on fundamental technology innovation—an area of unparalleled strength for our company. IBM scientists and engineers have scored eleven straight years as the world's most prolific inventors, earning nearly double the number of patents than the next closest company. Over the past decade, the U.S. Patent Office has issued IBM 22,357 patents—more than the combined number for ten of our top U.S. competitors.

But in other profound ways, the industry will be very different. How? Most people don't realize it, but the IT industry has always been two, interrelated industries. One, of course, is computing. This is more than the chips, databases, operating systems, application software and other technology elements that are in a constant state of change. This is about computing as an architecture, a model, a *system*—what all of those individual pieces, when put together, make possible. The computing model doesn't change very often, but it's changing now.

The other "industry" is the application of computing to improve or transform some aspect of business (and by "business," I mean the work of every kind of enterprise and institution). This wasn't visible for many years because these services—helping customers apply and manage the technology—were bundled with the hardware or software. But it was there all the same, and hugely important. For example, although IBM pioneered the mainframe model of computing, it would not have taken the market by storm if we had only brought customers a new machine. We had to bring them a *new idea about business*, and we had to show them how to apply mainframe systems to transform back-office functions like accounting, payroll and inventory management.

I don't think it's an overstatement to say that IBM has been unique in stepping to the forefront of both these capabilities—computing and its application to business—for most of IT's history. Today, once again, both are changing in significant and interconnected ways.

Consider what's happening in computing. Our customers have stopped thinking of their technology needs just in terms of data centers, storage systems, PCs, or even the network. Today, it's the *entire technical infrastructure* on which their businesses run, a vital infrastructure that must connect with and support relationships and transactions with other businesses, devices of all kinds and all the people using those devices.

My point is, if customers are going to look to you as the leader in computing, you have to be able to drive forward the entire computing agenda, not just a piece of it.

We see a parallel situation in how computing is being applied by customers. For the most part, businesses and institutions have automated and digitized their standalone operations and processes—the back office, the manufacturing floor, procurement, logistics, customer-facing systems. They've extracted great efficiencies by doing so. Now they want to transform processes that cut across all of those systems. Why? Because they want to build a business that can respond dynamically to whatever the world throws at it. And goodness knows, the world has been doing a lot of throwing lately.

A NEW GAME FOR BUSINESS

All of this is what we mean by "e-business on demand," which you will be hearing a lot about in the months and years to come. The promise of "on demand" is that a company or institution can provide products, services, information, health care, education, government services and so on—all "on demand" for customers, citizens, patients and students. These "sense-and-respond" or "real-time" enterprises enjoy enormous competitive advantages. They are able to convert fixed costs into variable costs. They can greatly reduce inventories. And, most compellingly, they are extremely responsive to the needs of their customers, employees and partners.

That is obviously very appealing, especially in times like these. However, consider the magnitude of the business transformation it requires. It's almost as if a business were turned on its side—moving from a collection of vertical "silos" to a seamlessly integrated, horizontal flow across value chains. That's a major, major shift—in business design and in management thinking—and pulling it off requires deep business expertise and know-how.

This may sound rather grandiose to some. And, of course, all technology companies envision ways in which their products will change business and society. Most do so with great bravado. More often than not, though, they are just plain wrong. The dot-com era was just the latest reminder that creators of databases, PCs and printers have no special qualifications to understand the future of serious business. In fact, they are probably the last people customers should look to for this kind of insight.

To be honest, when we at IBM began to understand the future course of technology and its sweeping implications for business, we looked in the mirror and saw some serious deficiencies in our own company. True, we had in recent years built up quite a bit of consulting capability. But we lacked a critical mass of business expertise to help our customers become on demand enterprises.

It was this realization that drove us to acquire PwC Consulting. We now have nearly 60,000 professionals in industries ranging from financial services to health care, with business process expertise in areas like supply chain, customer relationship management, human capital solutions and business transformation outsourcing.

We considered forming a web of alliances to gain the business insight we lacked. Others have chosen this path, and it's a perfectly respectable strategy—but not for us. IBM's brand and business model are very different from those of our competitors. Fundamental to our identity as a corporation is this fusion of business insight and technology leadership. Our learning in each realm informs what we do in the other. So we need an intimate linkage between them.

ALL THE WAYS A BUSINESS SHOULD LEAD

LEADERSHIP ON DEMAND

We have mobilized the entire IBM company and our expanding network of partners to make our e-business on demand strategy a reality. That work comes down to three main thrusts:

1. **Helping our customers become "on demand businesses."**
   Through IBM Global Services, we are applying IBM's considerable business process and industry expertise to help customers build businesses that are almost intuitive in their responsiveness to changes in demand, supply, pricing, labor, capital markets and customer needs. This requires a great deal of integration of business processes and operations, and of applications and the underlying IT systems. It means making them resilient in the face of changes and threats, from hackers to hurricanes. And it means helping them focus on what differentiates them, on their core competencies, and outsource or tightly integrate with strategic partners to supply the rest.

2. **Evolving the computing model to an On Demand Operating Environment.**
   On demand business creates new rules for IT infrastructure. Computing must be integrated and must support integration of business processes and operations, which is why our WebSphere software is growing so rapidly. Computing must be built on open technical standards and platforms, which is why IBM will continue to be a leader of the open standards movement—a leader in Linux, Web services and other emerging technical standards. Applications must be developed for this new, open model, which is why we acquired Rational; it gives software developers a compelling alternative to proprietary approaches.

In addition, an emerging technology called grid computing, built around another set of open specifications, allows the sharing and managing of separate computing resources as if they were one huge, virtual computer. This will dramatically increase utilization rates and give customers access to enormous computing capacity. Finally, IBM technologists are also pioneering ways to make IT systems "autonomic"—more self-managing and self-healing. This, too, is critical, as the increasing complexity of systems is making them unrealistically costly to manage and maintain.

3. **Establishing utility computing—computing on demand—as a viable and attractive alternative for accessing and paying for IT.** This effort has gotten a lot of attention. Yes, we intend to be a leader in utility computing services, so that customers can acquire computing and applications and pay only for what they use. IBM Global Services is already pioneering such services—server and storage capacity, as well as business processes like procurement and claims processing—for companies such as American Express, The Dow Chemical Company and Mobil Travel Guide. But we also want to equip and help customers to build their own internal utilities—software to manage and balance workloads, and server and storage systems to provide additional capacity on demand.

Clearly, the bet we're placing on e-business on demand is a big one. And part of what makes it big is that it encompasses where both computing *and* business are headed. Driving both at the same time requires a lot of work, but it's necessary, if you aspire to lead this industry.

IBM'S CENTER OF GRAVITY

Throughout IBM's history, we have reinvented ourselves over and over again. The most visible manifestation of this has been how radically our product line has changed over time—from clocks and scales to tabulating machines, to mainframes, to Selectric typewriters, to everything we do today.

How were we able to make those transitions without having a jarring identity crisis? It's because we never defined ourselves as a clock and scale company, or a mainframe company, or a typewriter maker, even when we were the undisputed leader in those markets. We simply committed ourselves to being the leader in inventing state-of-the-art technology and helping customers apply it to solve their problems. When technology and the nature of customer problems change—we do, too.

As I said earlier, the one time we forgot that and held on too long to products and ideas that were giving way to new ones, we nearly lost the whole ball game. That's a lesson we will not forget.

Today, with e-business on demand, we are again redefining the value we bring to customers. It's driving us to grow certain businesses aggressively—especially services and software—and to de-emphasize others, as we did in 2002. I have no doubt whatsoever that 15 or 20 years from now, we will be in a bunch of new and different businesses. Technology and customer problems will have marched on, hopefully with our company at the forefront. But we will still be IBM.

SAMUEL J. PALMISANO | IBM

THE PURPOSE OF A BUSINESS

As you might guess by now, we have been doing a lot of thinking about what leadership means for IBM. To lead our industry, we must be the company to which our customers look to understand the future of IT and how it can help them create business value. But there are additional aspects of leadership that are also important aspirations for our company: as an investment, as an employer, and as a member of the community.

Now, companies often say that being a great employer or a responsible citizen is as important to them as creating shareholder value or delighting customers or beating competitors. But they don't elevate them as business priorities, to be managed with the same kind of investment and discipline—and competitive passion—that they apply to managing R&D, manufacturing and sales. We do.

Why? Because over time, failure to understand change in these realms can be as damaging as failure to stay abreast of markets or technology. Maybe more so. What do investors value? What will attract and motivate the best workforce in the world? What do communities—nations and neighbors—expect of companies? As with technology and customer requirements, these are all moving targets.

We believe investors, particularly those who invest in the technology sector, reward companies that adapt, that continually create and lead the high-value spaces—because that's the only way to deliver consistent, long-term earnings growth in an industry that is constantly evolving. We believe investors reward companies that manage for the long haul, run highly efficient operations and are managed by experienced and disciplined leaders. And, at a time when industry growth projections are highly unreliable, investors reward companies that outperform their competitors—no matter the rate at which the industry is growing or contracting. This is why we have made marketshare a top priority.

I joined a company that was *the* place to work. It was progressive, fair and principled, and it invested in its people and their development. All of that stemmed from the commitment to have the best talent in the world, a commitment we reaffirm today. How you achieve that with programs and benefits depends on the times. As the composition of the workforce and their expectations changed, so did IBM, often far ahead of other companies or government mandates.

We know that employees today value flexibility and mobility, yet they want to feel part of a team, a community of colleagues. They value skill enhancement, but they want lifelong learning, not just classroom training. Most of all, while they are attracted to IBM's breadth and global presence, they don't want to get lost in a big company. They want to make a difference, have impact. All of this represents opportunities for us once again to innovate as an employer.

Finally, we need to adapt if we aspire to be a respected and engaged participant in our communities. This is more, far more, than philanthropy—although IBM takes a back seat to no one in contributions and volunteerism. It's about building relationships based on respect, trust and integrity—IBM's bedrock values *(see Appendix)*. And it's about using our remarkable scientific, managerial and analytic assets—some of the best minds on the planet—to help local, national and international communities solve problems and stimulate economic growth.

Right now, we have as many questions as answers, and more a sense of where we must go as a company than a clear path to get there. Yet we believe these are all appropriate and worthy aspirations for IBM and IBMers. They are consistent with the kind of company we want to be and have been for most of our history. This is IBM's DNA. The challenge, of course, is to bring the best of that forward without for a moment taking our eye off the customer, marketplace execution and strong results.

In the end, this goal of leadership, broadly defined, is what makes our company unique. It's why people come to work at IBM—and why millions more have wanted to be associated with it. There are certainly many places where a person can earn a very good living and build a highly gratifying career. You come to a big, complex company like ours if you want to be part of something whose impact is larger. And you come to this particular enterprise to be part of something whose impact will last, a company that explores, a company that matters.

That was the company I joined 30 years ago. Yes, the world has changed, and there's no going back. But my 316,000 colleagues welcome the challenge. We are determined to make IBM a truly great company—a great partner, investment and employer—for our generation and for our times.

This essay was adapted from Sam Palmisano's letter to shareowners in the 2002 IBM annual report.

Samuel J. Palmisano
CHAIRMAN OF THE BOARD AND CHIEF EXECUTIVE OFFICER
IBM CORPORATION

Sam Palmisano is chairman of the board and chief executive officer of the IBM Corporation. He was elected chairman in October 2002, effective January 1, 2003, and has served as chief executive officer since March 2002. Prior to his appointment, Palmisano was president and chief operating officer.

Palmisano has held a number of key leadership positions during his IBM career, including senior vice president and group executive for IBM's Enterprise Systems Group, where he led IBM's adoption of the Linux operating environment, as well as the launch of the company's unified eServer family. Prior to that, Palmisano was senior vice president and group executive for IBM Global Services, with responsibility for the worldwide operations of the largest and most diversified IT services organization in the industry.

Palmisano has served as senior vice president and group executive for IBM's Personal Systems Group; led IBM's strategic outsourcing business; and was president of the Integrated Systems Solutions Corp. (ISSC), an IBM wholly owned subsidiary, and now part of IBM Global Services. Before joining ISSC, Palmisano was IBM senior managing director of operations for IBM Japan. He joined IBM in 1973 in Baltimore, Maryland.

INTERNATIONAL BUSINESS MACHINES CORPORATION (IBM)

IBM is the world's largest information technology company, the world's largest business and technology services provider, and the global leader in IT financing, with revenues of more than $89 billion in 2003. Its 316,000 employees serve clients in more than 160 countries worldwide.

During IBM's 92-year history, the company has provided leadership and innovation in both the advancement of information technology and its applications to businesses and institutions worldwide. Today, IBM continues to lead in the invention, development and manufacture of the industry's most advanced information technologies, including computer systems, software, storage systems and microelectronics. IBM translates these advanced technologies into value for clients through its professional solutions, services and consulting businesses worldwide.

IBM is committed to corporate citizenship and counts education as the top priority in its philanthropic efforts. Through "Reinventing Education" and other strategic efforts, IBM is working to solve education's toughest problems with solutions that draw on advanced information technology and the best minds the company can apply. In addition, IBM recently launched the "On Demand Community," a unique initiative to encourage and sustain corporate philanthropy through employee volunteerism.

IBM has received many recent industry awards and honors, including ranking in *Business Week* as the world's third most valuable brand (2002), ranking No. 1 in *Fortune* magazine's annual list of the Top Ten Most Admired Companies-Computer Industry" (2002), and topping *Forbes'* rankings of the most powerful technology industry companies on their "Computers and Electronics" list (2002). IBM's global headquarters is in Armonk, New York.

For more information, visit: www.ibm.com.
Stock Symbol: IBM

ALL THE WAYS A BUSINESS SHOULD LEAD

BUILDING TRUST

Louis J. Giuliano

CHAIRMAN, PRESIDENT AND CHIEF EXECUTIVE OFFICER
ITT INDUSTRIES, INC.

*"Our customers have quite reasonable expectations.
They want products and services on which they can rely.
They want them delivered on time. They want us to provide good value."*

– Louis J. Giuliano

SERVE CUSTOMERS BETTER, GROW FASTER

At ITT Industries, we spend a great deal of time focusing on creating value. Value has many dimensions—to customers, to investors and to employees. But the real value of ITT Industries is embodied in our people. In a recent annual report, we tried to capture that value by showing the faces of more than 150 of the men and women who serve our customers and our shareholders around the world each day. In addition to their own achievements, they represented the creativity and commitment of 36,000 co-workers who, together, make ITT Industries so strong.

In the annual report, we prominently featured a few of their stories—stories of creativity, heroism, imagination, and dogged determination to find a better way to serve their customers and to pursue a higher purpose. For example, we told the story of how a few of our people, and some of our equipment, played a pivotal role in saving the lives of nine miners in Quecreek, Pennsylvania. The story of the rescue of these miners has been told many times, but what isn't as well known is that at a critical point in the rescue attempt, one of our vertical turbine pumps was used to reduce the water level in the mine shaft in which the nine men were trapped. It took heroic efforts on the part of several ITT Industries employees to manufacture that custom pump in record time and get it moved from Texas to Pennsylvania in time to help rescue the miners. Our stories aren't always this dramatic, but they share some common themes—a desire to make a difference, a passion for engineering, and an understanding that the products and services we provide serve critical needs for our customers.

A FOCUS ON LEADERSHIP

Our stated vision is to become a premier multi-industry company, premier in every sense of the word, creating value for all of our stakeholders—employees, customers, shareholders and communities. We are making progress towards this goal by focusing on key strategies. It begins with our commitment to developing leadership talent throughout the organization. We are continuously improving the quality and efficiency of our products and services, as perceived by our customers. By focusing on leadership and operational excellence, we can provide the steady growth in value creation our shareholders rightfully expect.

In my view, the starting point for the deployment of our strategies is leadership development. The leadership skills of all of our people are the driving force behind our strong financial and operating results, and the reason our customers and investors have such confidence in our company. We recognize that we have effective leaders at every level in the organization—not just at headquarters or in the executive ranks. I believe that one of the most critical responsibilities of all of us who lead ITT Industries is to create a caring environment for our employees. Our company prides itself on the engineering talent we have throughout the organization. While engineers may be quite comfortable with the precision of math and physics, they aren't always so comfortable with what is needed to create an environment in which each employee can reach his or her maximum potential. We all have to work at it. I have learned in my career that when employees know they are respected, when their contributions are recognized, they are capable of incredible accomplishments.

I'm energized by seeing employees who are excited about what they are doing. It's contagious. What most employees want more than anything is to feel that their contributions to the organization are making a difference. It's our job to create the environment in which they can.

SEEING THE WORLD THOUGH OUR CUSTOMERS' EYES

Our customers have quite reasonable expectations. They want products and services on which they can rely. They want them delivered on time. They want us to provide good value. They want to know that they can depend on us, both at the time of the sale and long afterward. They want us to conduct our business dealings with integrity. They simply want us to look at the world through their eyes.

To meet their expectations, we also have to take a pretty hard look at ourselves. We have to continuously challenge the status quo, finding new ways to get better.

The linchpin of our continuous improvement efforts is what we call Value-Based Six Sigma (VBSS), now an integral part of the ITT Industries' culture. We are striving to make VBSS a way of thinking and managing. As I like to remind our employees, VBSS is one of our most effective growth strategies. By reducing our time to market, by enhancing the quality of our products and services, and by delivering these products on time, we will serve our customers better and grow faster as a result.

Internally, our growth is fueled by a steady stream of new, differentiated products and services. Over the years ITT engineers have played a critical role in the development of technical innovations that today are commonplace, among them television, fiber optics, global positioning satellites, submersible pumps and night vision.

In 2002, we launched a new effort aimed at making sure our solutions solve real customer problems. With Value-Based Product Development, we are training our business development, marketing and engineering teams to better capture the voice of the customer so that we can develop products that meet both the customer's spoken and unspoken needs. This initiative can have a major impact on our future growth by enhancing our ability to listen to our customers and respond to their needs with well-designed solutions.

Looking at the world through our customers' eyes has helped us develop new products that meet critical needs, such as our revolutionary N-pump, a wastewater treatment pump that dramatically reduces clogging, thus addressing the costly problem of down time. We have also developed energy-efficient water treatment approaches that address the most costly aspect of water treatment: energy consumption. As the major supplier of Night Vision to the armed forces, we are currently working on the next generation of these devices, featuring innovative features such as panoramic displays. Our marine products group has developed a new global shipboard compass that automatically re-calibrates settings based on the geographic location of the vessel.

Our employees enjoy these challenges. It's gratifying to solve problems and find new ways to add value. Our competitive advantage depends on our willingness to embrace change and continually improve. Again, it is not easy, but it is rewarding.

FINANCIAL PERFORMANCE IS ONLY PART OF THE STORY

It is increasingly clear that investors are seeking companies in which to place not only their dollars, but their trust. In the past few years, the confidence of the investing public has been undermined by a seemingly endless stream of accounting scandals, insider trading and a disturbing lack of oversight by those responsible for corporate governance. The Principles articulated by Arthur W. Page resonate more clearly now than ever. Each deals with an element important to corporate success. At ITT Industries, our commitment to ethical behavior is captured on the cover page of our Code of Conduct: "Do the right thing—always." This phrase provides a foundation for the values with which we do business.

Our Code of Conduct *(see Appendix)* has served as the focal point for our statement of business principles for many years. It is published in multiple languages, updated on a regular basis and distributed to our employees around the world to provide a clear and unequivocal affirmation of our commitment to the highest ethical standards.

When I speak to groups of ITT Industries employees, I try to make it clear that we are willing to make the tough choices necessary to preserve the spirit and intent of our Code of Conduct. It's as simple as this: If we have to walk away from business to avoid violating our Code of Conduct, then that is what we must do. In the long run, we will overcome any short-term effects of losing a contract by avoiding the inevitable liabilities of operating in the gray areas.

It takes continuous communication with our employees to maintain the viability and relevance of any statement of business ethics and principles. It also requires that we take a close look at what we are rewarding and recognizing in the organization. A Code of Conduct document, no matter how well written, can't overcome reward systems that look the other way, or that are unbalanced or inconsistent with the company's values and ideals.

SERVING A HIGHER PURPOSE

It is gratifying to know that many of our products serve critical purposes that truly affect the lives of those who use them. Our water technology equipment helps deliver fresh water to a thirsty world, and then cleans that water so that we can use it again. Our Night Vision products help protect military and law enforcement personnel, and these devices often make the life-saving difference in successful search and rescue missions. We make highly-engineered valves and other devices used in producing vaccines and other bio-pharmaceutical products.

As the world's largest producer of pumps and water technology, we feel a special responsibility to share our knowledge and expertise in meaningful ways in the communities in which we live and work. For example, for several years we have been the global sponsor of the

Stockholm Junior Water Prize. This award is presented annually by the Crown Princess of Sweden, Victoria, to a high school student, or team of students, for achievement in the field of water resource management. Students from 28 countries competed for the prize in 2003, and hundreds more competed at the national level for the privilege of representing their countries in Stockholm. In addition to global sponsorship, ITT Industries serves as the local sponsor in four countries, including China.

This competition has helped raise the awareness of the world's water crisis among high school students, the leaders of tomorrow. Despite the many global advances we have made, it is still a reality that more than 1.2 billion people, one-fourth of the developing world, do not have access to reliable sources of clean water. Though hard to believe, it is a sad fact that more than 2 million children die each year because of preventable water-borne disease.

We continue to look for new ways to help. For example, in Malawi, an ITT Industries pump brings fresh water to the Malawi Children's Village, home to children orphaned by the AIDS epidemic. In addition to meeting immediate needs for water, this pump has also enabled the village to become an important source of seeds for local farmers. A relatively simple pump has brought hope to an area ravaged by poverty, hunger and disease.

We have also donated ITT Industries Night Vision devices to a number of local law enforcement agencies and search-and-rescue teams to assist in their local community efforts. We are constantly looking for additional ways to share our technology, our expertise and our people in solving similar problems around the world.

EMBRACING THE FUTURE

My confidence in ITT Industries' future is based on my personal belief that we have the right people for the road ahead. Our company is filled with leaders, innovators, problem-solvers and solution-providers. They are committed to solving our customers' problems and creating a work environment in which each of our employees can make a meaningful and appreciated contribution. I am grateful to our employees for their ongoing commitment. They take pride in knowing that the jobs they are doing truly matter to our customers and to the world at large. I take pride in serving with them in this mission.

Louis J. Giuliano
CHAIRMAN, PRESIDENT AND CHIEF EXECUTIVE OFFICER
ITT INDUSTRIES, INC.

Louis J. Giuliano was named chairman, president and chief executive officer of ITT Industries, Inc. in March, 2001. In this role, he is responsible for setting the strategic and operating direction for this Fortune 500 Company. Immediately prior to being named to his current position, Giuliano was president and chief operating officer of the corporation, responsible for the ongoing operations at the company. He has played a key role in improving the company's operating performance, leading to stronger margins and higher cash flow. Most recently he has led the company's Value-Based Six Sigma introduction, a program designed to streamline processes and increase operating effectiveness throughout the company.

Prior to being named president and chief operating officer of ITT Industries in 1998, Giuliano was president and chief executive of ITT Industries' Defense and Electronics businesses and senior vice president of ITT Industries. During that time, the businesses entered new, rapidly growing markets, and achieved consistent sales and income growth.

Giuliano joined ITT in July 1988 as vice president of ITT Corporation and vice president -Defense Operations at ITT Defense after a 19-year career at Allied-Signal, where he served in a number of roles, ultimately becoming president of the Avionics Systems Group, responsible for seven operating units nationwide.

Giuliano is a graduate of Syracuse University with a bachelor of arts degree in chemistry, and a master of business administration in marketing. In February 2003 he was elected to the board of directors of Engelhard Corporation. He also serves as honorary chairman of the Westchester County Red Cross Armed Forces Emergency Services.

ITT INDUSTRIES, INC.

ITT Industries, Inc. is a global engineering and manufacturing company with leading positions in the markets it serves. It is the world's premier supplier of pumps, systems and services to move and control water and other fluids. The company is a major supplier of sophisticated military defense systems, and provides advanced technical and operational services to a broad range of government agencies. ITT Industries also produces connectors, switches, keypads and cabling used in telecommunications, computing, aerospace and industrial applications, as well as network services. Further, ITT Industries makes industrial components for a number of other markets, including transportation, construction and aerospace.

Since becoming an independent company in 1995, ITT Industries has taken steps to strengthen its key businesses with significant potential for profitability and growth through a series of acquisitions (Goulds Pumps, Kaman Sciences, Stanford Telecom and C&K Components, among others) and divestitures.

ITT Industries is dedicated to being a good neighbor and corporate citizen and supports many worthy causes. The company has endorsed the principles of the Coalition for Environmentally Responsible Economies (CERES). ITT Industries is also a founding co-chair of the Engineering Alliance, which began in 1999 for the purpose of improving public awareness, understanding, and recognition of the engineering profession, including encouraging the study of engineering in U.S. colleges and universities.

Headquartered in White Plains, New York, the company generated $5.6 billion in 2003 sales.

For more information, visit: www.itt.com.
Stock Symbol: ITT

SERVE CUSTOMERS BETTER, GROW FASTER

BUILDING TRUST

Michael H. Jordan

CHAIRMAN AND CHIEF EXECUTIVE OFFICER
EDS CORPORATION

*"We want to be our clients' most trusted ally.
We are in business to serve our clients.
We have no success without client success."*

– Michael H. Jordan

PUTTING THE CLIENT FIRST

I came out of retirement to become chairman and CEO of EDS. Before EDS, I spent more than 30 years with companies such as PepsiCo, Frito-Lay and CBS Corporation.

EDS is a company with talented people and clients representing companies and governments around the world. It's a company that invented the outsourcing services industry more than 40 years ago and is now well-positioned to reinvent it. Our people, given the right leadership and direction for the times, are the ones who will make it happen.

Countless studies have been conducted on leadership over the years. Results typically reflect behavioral characteristics such as "you have to be aggressive" or "you have to present well." My point of view is that the only characteristic you need is honesty. Everything that's important springs from honesty.

At EDS, we understand the importance of being open and honest with ourselves, our clients and our shareholders. We are taking a candid view of our business and of our future. Integrity, character and common sense guided EDS to the forefront of the industry it founded. These same characteristics are leading us through our transformation.

As the new chairman and CEO, I want to share with you my experience to date, still in the early stages of our transformational journey. Let me start with a brief history of EDS. EDS began in 1962 with one man, one $1,000 check and one extraordinary vision. By the end of the 1960s it had grown to approximately 500 people with revenues of more than $16 million. Today, EDS has more than 130,000 employees. We're a $21.5 billion-plus company, with operations in 60 countries. The growth we have achieved since our founding would not have been possible without our strong commitment to integrity.

EDS was born from a core set of values centered on our people, our clients and our business. These values were an integral part of the company's early success, and they remain our moral compass today. The key is keeping them real, translating them into terms that are meaningful, and providing an environment in which people accept the company's values as their own and incorporate them into everyday thoughts and actions.

OUR PEOPLE

EDS is a services company. Our people are our lifeblood. Great service doesn't happen without them. We understand that when you treat people with respect and dignity, you get results.

We believe leaders model the behavior they want. They personally demonstrate how they want business issues and people to be addressed. You can shout out the words, but until you live by them, no one believes you. When I arrived at EDS, I received an outpouring of suggestions and comments—50 e-mails a day. Our people had lived through a difficult 12–18 months. They wanted me to know how they felt. They wanted to share their deeply held ideas to make their company better. It's a testament to their indomitable spirit. Over time, benefits had changed and compensation and severance programs had been reduced. We had issues to address.

We've put in place a number of significant human-resources changes. We started with an improved U.S. severance plan effective on the first day that I came onboard. We upped the funding of base salary budgets to provide salary increases to more employees. We increased project and performance bonus budgets. We also improved personal leave options, giving employees the much-needed flexibility to balance work with their private lives. Now, we're modifying incentive plans to better align them with expected business and individual performance. More changes are in the works.

It all makes a difference. When our employees feel respected and valued, they convey that confidence to our clients through outstanding service and pride in their work.

OUR CLIENTS

EDS founder Ross Perot said, "An outstanding leader always puts others first, puts his company first and puts the customer absolutely first in line."

One of the things I admire about EDS is its service culture and work ethic. We deliver for our clients. We out-execute our competitors time and again. By way of example, in my early meetings I met with a client who was in bankruptcy. The chief executive wanted to renegotiate our contract but couldn't get our attention. So, he stopped paying us for two months. He got our attention all right, but he noted the service his company received never wavered. The EDS team continued to deliver 100-plus percent. The lasting impression made on that client strikes at the heart of our philosophy: Put the client first.

When I first came here, clients saw the people of EDS as both committed and dedicated. That hasn't changed. Clients, however, also thought we got in our own way at times. They told us: EDS had too many client touchpoints and an overly complicated organizational structure. We heard them loud and clear, and we moved to change that dynamic.

Our goal is to ensure our clients get what they need from us when they want it—easily. We want to be our clients' most trusted ally. We are in business to serve our clients. We have no success without client success. Understanding that special relationship—and being able to deliver on it globally—is what sets us apart in the marketplace. To do that we must, as Arthur Page suggested long ago, listen to what they say.

Just as we aim to make our clients' businesses more competitive, we, too, must become more competitive. Our transformation is designed to do just that. One of the most challenging aspects is overhauling our operating model. The new model makes it easy to do business with—and in—EDS.

We are driving hard to increase sales, reduce costs, invest in our future and focus on sectors where we can win business.

OUR BUSINESS

Many of you have asked: "With increased criticism and skepticism of corporations across America, what is EDS doing to increase its corporate responsibility and accountability?"

Corporate responsibility and accountability is an area the EDS leadership team is particularly in tune with, and we are committed to the measures we are incorporating to address the issues confronting Corporate America today. We are attending to corporate governance, executive compensation and succession planning—top-of-mind issues for employees, clients and investors.

The EDS board has been focused on corporate governance for years. EDS had committees composed entirely of outside directors with written charters—long before Sarbanes-Oxley and the New York Stock Exchange (NYSE) rule proposals made them mandatory. These included a committee focusing on governance issues, an audit committee with a financial expert as chairman, and a committee required to review and approve the compensation of all senior officers. There also were such measures as an annual CEO evaluation, regular board evaluations, an annual review of the independence of directors and board oversight of charitable contributions. These governance practices were described for our shareholders in our public filings and communications every year. As the new rules under Sarbanes-Oxley and NYSE governance standards were added, EDS moved to comply before it was required. The board adopted written governance guidelines, incorporating many of its practices that go beyond what the rules require. Together with the amended charters of its committees, EDS posted these guidelines on our Web site (www.eds.com) for our shareholders. EDS posted reports on stock trades by EDS executives on the site before mandated as well.

Our transformation also provides an opportunity for us to size compensation in terms of new company direction. The EDS board initiated a review of all compensation and benefits programs. Executive pay is based on realistic, market-based pay packages, starting with me. Our incentive design for 2004 will continue to evolve to emphasize collaboration and accountability. The board is heavily involved in shaping our compensation and benefits strategy, with robust discussions around how our policies align with EDS' business direction and how to identify the right programs for success.

We've engaged our board members in a continuing education program to ensure they remain highly knowledgeable about our business and the rapid changes characteristic of our industry. The primary focus of the program is to provide our directors with improved information regarding our client-facing activities, competitive positioning and business priorities. As a result, they will be able to more effectively guide our strategy and goals as they continue to evolve.

In line with our transformation, we decided we needed to add some fresh perspectives to EDS' executive talent and to build a deep bench of talent. A thorough selection method and a development program linked to company strategy help us plan beyond the CXO level. Upgrading our succession planning process is a priority because we recognize having the right people with the right skills in key positions is a source of competitive advantage. It is an essential component of an effective transformation. We are developing a more focused approach aligned to our strategic transformation. In fact, the first phase is well under way.

Good succession planning not only leads to promotion from within, but also to some buy decisions. We intend to use succession planning as an integral part of instituting quick change—bringing people in from the outside can be an effective, strategic approach. At EDS, we seek a blend of perspectives in our organization. As a services organization, it is extremely important to invest in our people's development—it's instrumental to EDS' success. Whatever we do in terms of people care, developing our people is still the most important objective in our minds.

At EDS, running our business is dependent upon how we conduct ourselves. EDS has a long-established Code of Business Conduct *(see Appendix)*. New employees, as well as existing employees, must certify annually that they have read and understood the Code, which has been translated into twelve languages for our global community. With the increased focus on corporate responsibility, that Code also has been posted on our Web site for our shareholders and others to see. We have enhanced our Code by strengthening our existing processes for receiving, investigating and reporting to our leadership and board any allegations of impropriety. Finally, by engaging the board in our annual review of the Code, we ensure the highest level of oversight. Beyond a piece of paper that details what ethical behavior entails, what it really comes down to is the way the leader behaves with his/her people and the signals he/she sends about acceptable behavior. Personal role modeling is essential—and I am a believer that CEO behavior sets the tone. At EDS, we simply don't tolerate game-playing.

At EDS:

- We want to get the job done and get it done well.
- We care about people.
- We stick together and support each other.
- We set and keep high standards of business and personal ethics.
- And above all, we deliver on our word. We do what we say we will do.

Solid business practices and sound business values—in equal measure—are essential to any organization's success. As such, corporate ethics are an indispensable pillar in rebuilding Corporate America. It requires that the chairman and CEO, board of directors, and senior executives accept the responsibility and the accountability of being role models for all to follow.

Michael H. Jordan
EDS

Michael H. Jordan, chairman of the board and CEO, joined EDS in March 2003.

Jordan is the retired chairman and chief executive officer of CBS Corporation (formerly Westinghouse Electric Corporation). Before joining Westinghouse, he was a partner with Clayton, Dubilier and Rice. During 18 years with PepsiCo, Inc., he served in numerous senior executive positions, including CFO of PepsiCo, Inc. and president and CEO of PepsiCo WorldWide Foods, which includes Frito-Lay. From 1964 to 1974, he was a consultant and principal with McKinsey & Company.

Jordan is an angel investor as well as a member of several private equity firms. He is also a partner of Beta Capital Group, LLC of Dallas, Texas. He currently serves as chairman of eOriginal Inc., an electronic commerce company. Previously, he was a general partner of Global Asset Capital, LLC, a venture capital firm. From 1999 to 2001, he was chairman of Luminant Worldwide Corporation.

In addition, Jordan is chairman of the National Foreign Trade Council, trustee of The Brookings Institution, member and former chairman of the U.S.-Japan Business Council, chairman of the United Negro College Fund, and a member of The Business Council. He also serves on the boards of Aetna Inc., WPP Group plc and several privately held companies.

Jordan received his B.S. in chemical engineering from Yale University and a master of science degree from Princeton University. He subsequently served a four-year tour of duty with the U.S. Navy. Jordan is married to Hilary Cecil of New York City.

MICHAEL H. JORDAN | EDS

ELECTRONIC DATA SYSTEMS CORPORATION
EDS

Founded in 1962, EDS invented the outsourcing services industry more than 40 years ago and continues to reinvent it every day. As the world's most experienced outsourcing services company, EDS delivers superior returns to 35,000 clients through its cost-effective, high-value services model. EDS works hard to be its clients' most trusted ally, developing business solutions for companies and governments in 60 countries.

EDS' core business is outsourcing services. Its portfolio of open solutions spans infrastructure outsourcing, business process outsourcing, applications outsourcing, and consulting. EDS' two complementary subsidiary businesses are A.T. Kearney, one of the world's leading high-value management consultancies, and UGS PLM Solutions, a leader in product data management, collaboration and product design software.

EDS' deep industry knowledge—including health care, manufacturing and financial services—enables it to help clients solve issues specific to their businesses. The company's unmatched global network provides the capacity and capability to serve our clients well.

Through the company's open technology platform and consortium approach, clients receive best-of-thought EDS solutions combined with best-of-breed technologies from like-minded hardware and software providers.

With 2002 revenue of $21.5 billion and $24.4 billion in total contract signings, EDS is ranked 80th on the *Fortune* 500. EDS is headquartered in Plano, Texas, and employs more than 130,000 people.

For more information, visit: www.eds.com.
Stock Symbol: EDS

BUILDING TRUST

John W. Rowe, M.D.

CHAIRMAN AND CHIEF EXECUTIVE OFFICER
AETNA INC.

"Very simply, we must listen carefully to determine what are their needs, and how we can best meet them."

– John W. Rowe, M.D.

THE AETNA WAY

How does a company deal with the conflicting demands of key constituencies in light of the reality that, as Arthur W. Page said a half-century ago, "All business in a democratic country begins with public permission and exists by public approval?" At Aetna, we believe it starts with a binding philosophy of who we are and how we operate that is understood by all constituencies.

When Aetna sold its financial services and international businesses and spun off its health care, disability, group life and other related employee benefits businesses as the new Aetna in 2000, the company brought in a new senior management team and sought to create a dramatically different approach to health care insurance in America. This dictated a new strategy, a new operating model and, perhaps most important of all, a profound change in attitude toward our constituencies.

In the preceding years, despite good intentions, the company had stumbled while seeking to become the largest player in the health care financing industry. By making market share the primary goal, the company had lost its focus on the needs of its key constituencies.

THE AETNA WAY

Our new leadership team saw an opportunity and an urgent need to redefine the mission, values, goals and operating principles of this 150-year-old company. The result was The Aetna Way, which we now reference daily as a guide to every decision we make *(see Appendix)*. In many ways, we were returning to Aetna's roots, but with a new focus and dedication that has energized the company and fueled a dramatic turnaround in constituent satisfaction and financial performance.

The Aetna Way defines a new culture based on a set of enduring values, with the people who use our services at the center of everything we do. It requires us to examine our actions from the perspective of each constituency, ensuring that we:

- Act with integrity;
- Engage employees;
- Deliver quality service and value;
- Demonstrate excellence and accountability.

All good words. But what do they really mean to our key constituencies as we go through the thousands of decisions—big and small—that we make every day as we conduct our business?

To find the answer, let's take a look at our relations with three constituencies that are important to the new Aetna—employers, consumers and physicians. While they often have similar interests when it comes to health care, their interests tend to diverge when it comes to financial issues. This creates some interesting dynamics.

EARNING PUBLIC APPROVAL

First, a bit of background, just to set the stage:

The last time medical cost inflation soared into double-digit levels in the late 1980s and early 1990s, employers embraced a new form of health coverage for their employees called "managed care." Driven by the desire of employers to slow debilitating increases in their health benefits costs, HMOs placed a variety of restrictions on access to health care.

By the mid-1990s, however, physicians and members chafing against those restrictions spawned a rising discontent that led to lawsuits, increased government regulation and the threat of legislation to reign in the perceived abuses of managed care.

The health insurance industry has responded by offering open access plans with fewer restrictions. At the same time, consumers are seeking—and physicians are providing—access to new pharmaceuticals and other new medical technologies. These trends (and a host of other factors) have led to a rekindling of double-digit medical cost inflation. Clearly, all parties want the best today's medicine can offer. But when it comes to financing access to these wonders, at a time when economic growth is less robust and jobs are not as easy to come by, the interests of our key constituencies begin to diverge.

As we think about these problems, The Aetna Way requires us to approach solutions from the perspective of each constituency. Since the issues are largely financial, let's start with the party that still pays most of the bills.

THE EMPLOYER

In the U.S. health care system, most people get access to health care through a benefits plan provided by their employer. Until recently, the employer's share of the cost of those benefits was increasing. Between 1993 and 2002, the average employee buying family coverage saw health care premiums rise 35 percent; during the same period, his or her employer's contribution rose 101 percent.

Today, those trends are being reversed. Many employers say they have little choice but to shift a rapidly increasing share of the cost of health benefits to their employees. With help from health insurers, employers are finding any number of creative ways to do this, including charging higher premiums; increasing copays or eliminating them in favor of coinsurance, where the employee share is a percentage of the cost, not a fixed amount; increasing deductibles; reducing benefits; or eliminating coverage altogether.

Today, employers have two concerns: How can they avoid some of the increasing costs, and how can they ensure they're getting full value for the money they do pay.

THE CONSUMER

Most consumers clearly want fewer restrictions on access to care, and for the most part, they're getting that with more open access plans.

But taking a consumer view leads quickly to an alarming realization: Consumers spend billions of dollars on health care and have virtually no control over the way those dollars are spent. When you ask consumers what they want, it boils down to more control over their health care decisions. As employers shift a bigger share of the cost of health care to employees, and they have more of their own dollars at risk, this becomes even truer.

Consumers also find the health care system confusing and intimidating. Reliable information about what they're entitled to and the quality of care they are likely to receive can be hard to obtain.

THE PHYSICIAN

If there were a constituency even more dissatisfied with the nation's health care system than consumers during the past decade, it would be the nation's physicians. They saw managed care as a threat to their ability to serve their patients well and worried that insurers' claims-processing practices denied them their due. The result was a spate of class-action lawsuits against insurers by state medical societies.

At the same time, ironically enough, many physicians are beset by medical malpractice lawsuits that have driven their malpractice insurance premiums to nearly intolerable levels.

Physicians want to be able to treat their patients effectively and to be fairly compensated for their efforts.

TWO SOLUTIONS

As we thought about the needs of our constituencies from their perspectives, we began to see some common threads that have led to some interesting new approaches to health care that go well beyond managed care. Two of these innovations are consumer-directed health plans and cooperative care management.

CONSUMER-DIRECTED HEALTH PLANS

By listening to both employers and consumers, and thinking about issues from their perspectives, we've developed one of the leading products in a new model called "consumer-directed health plans." The goal is to give consumers more control over how they use their health care dollars and make them better purchasers of health care services.

Our new plans cover preventive care in full to ensure people won't forego the routine tests and checkups that can keep them healthy. These plans also cover the major expenses associated with serious illnesses. In between, members receive an employer-funded health account that covers part of their deductible expenses and that can be rolled over to the following year if it is not used in full. Once the employer-funded account is expended, the member is responsible for payments until an out-of-pocket maximum is reached.

Critics have suggested that consumer-directed health plans are merely a means to shift costs from employer to employee. In reality, however, an employer may adjust the cost-sharing equation of any health plan by changing the premium subsidy, deductible and coinsurance levels. The difference with consumer-directed plans is that they give members greater control over how they spend their health care dollars.

For a consumer-directed health plan to work, however, members must receive both incentives and tools to help them manage the middle ground where more consumer involvement can result in more cost-effective decisions. Providing consumers with incentives to be more conscious of their health care spending as they are aided in making more informed decisions will lead to a more efficient system with better outcomes for patients.

A recent study of the experience of a *Fortune* 500 employer that moved all its employees into a consumer-directed health plan showed that members in such a plan are likely to select cost-effective approaches and reduce utilization in some discretionary health services, while maintaining overall benefit and preventive health care levels. In simple terms, the overall costs of medical plans will be reduced without negatively affecting the member's health.

This approach seems to meet the needs of all constituencies. Employers can offer preventive care benefits and good protection against serious health-related expenses while providing a meaningful cost-sharing balance for more routine medical care. And they know that consumers will take on some of the responsibility for managing costs.

Consumers see their costs going up under any scenario. With a consumer-directed plan, they get more ability to make the choices that are right for them, and better tools to help them make those decisions effectively.

Physicians also benefit. Consumer-directed care and the tools that surround it offer unprecedented transparency to such elements as treatment options, medicines, costs and risks. This means that physicians and patients can discuss medical issues on a new level. They can have an active, informed dialogue about medical options and cost-value trade-offs, and work together to make the right decision for the circumstances. These discussions will build a much stronger physician-patient relationship.

COOPERATIVE CARE MANAGEMENT

The second area where listening to constituents has suggested an innovative approach is in case- and disease-management programs designed to help patients get the care they need.

As a health insurer, Aetna has access to a significant amount of health care data on our members that physicians often don't see. By connecting the dots between disparate pieces of information, we can be very helpful to patients and their physicians.

Our disease-management programs, for example, identify patients with chronic conditions and assign nurse case managers to encourage them to take their medicines, get their checkups and follow their doctors' orders. Our MedQuery program alerts physicians to drug interactions or gaps in treatment that may have escaped them because they were unaware of the actions of a second physician, for example.

These programs would be impossible if we were in an adversarial position with physicians. When we thought about the issues raised by physicians in their class-action lawsuits from their perspective, it was easy to see how they needed more clarity around our policies and practices. We felt that all of our actions were reasonable, yet we had to admit that from the outside, the complexity of the system made it confusing at best.

Accordingly, we set out to become the first major insurer to reach an agreement with physicians that not only would end the legal skirmishes, but also, more importantly, would launch a new era of cooperation between Aetna and physicians.

The agreement includes industry-leading improvements to physician-related business practices that set new levels of transparency in paying claims, including a National Advisory Committee of Practicing Physicians to provide advice to Aetna on issues of importance to physicians. It also establishes an independent foundation dedicated to improving the quality of health care in America.

The agreement will streamline communication between physicians and Aetna, reduce administrative complexity in the claims-payment system and help improve the quality of the health care system.

These changes are expected to result in increased predictability and speed of claims payment, creating significant value for physicians by reducing time-consuming and costly administrative burdens and giving them and their office staffs more time to focus on their central mission—providing health care to patients.

Streamlining business processes will create great value for physicians in terms of reduced overhead and greater focus on patient care, as well as reduce Aetna's administrative costs. It also means better value for consumers and employers as they benefit from our cooperation with physicians on care management programs.

GUIDING PRINCIPLES

As we follow The Aetna Way and seek innovative solutions to the problems facing America's health care system, several guiding principles governing Aetna's relations with external constituencies have emerged.

First, listen. We believe it's important to think about our policies and actions from the perspective of the external constituencies. Very simply, we must listen carefully to determine what are their needs and how can we best meet them.

Second, look for common ground. Inevitably, different groups will have different interests, which sometimes conflict. But often, with a little effort, a search for common ground can yield innovative solutions.

Third, be transparent. It's easy to suspect the worst when you can't see how decisions are being made. Being open about processes and inviting advice can eliminate suspicion and build trust.

Finally, be willing to change. No person or institution is perfect; we all make mistakes. The measure of a company worthy of the public's trust is its willingness and ability to take good advice and amend its practices when the interests of its constituencies warrant a new approach.

Aetna operates in a highly regulated sector of the economy— one that often has been controversial and criticized. We understand perhaps better than most the validity of Arthur W. Page's observation that business begins with public permission.

Furthermore, our shareholders fully appreciate that the better we do in understanding and meeting the needs of our disparate constituencies, the more they will enjoy the fruits of our success.

In 2003, we celebrated Aetna's 150th anniversary, so we have a long history of success in dealing with the needs of our customers, business partners, employees and shareholders. Today, by listening, finding common ground, being transparent and being willing to change, Aetna is seeking innovative solutions to our constituents' problems. Guided by The Aetna Way, we've begun to rebuild the pride that we feel in helping people achieve health and financial security.

John W. Rowe, M.D.
CHAIRMAN AND CHIEF EXECUTIVE OFFICER
AETNA INC.

John W. Rowe, M.D., is chairman and CEO of Aetna Inc., one of the nation's leading health care and related benefits organizations. Prior to joining Aetna, Rowe served as president and chief executive officer of Mount Sinai NYU Health (1998–2000), one of the nation's largest academic health care organizations. Before the Mount Sinai NYU Health merger, Rowe was president of The Mount Sinai Hospital and the Mount Sinai School of Medicine in New York City (1988–1998).

Before joining Mount Sinai, Rowe was a professor of medicine and the founding director of the Division on Aging at Harvard Medical School, and chief of gerontology at Boston's Beth Israel Hospital. He has authored over 200 scientific publications, mostly in the physiology of the aging process, and a leading textbook of geriatric medicine.

Rowe has received many honors and awards for his research and health policy efforts regarding care of the elderly. He was director of the MacArthur Foundation Research Network on Successful Aging and is co-author, with Robert Kahn, Ph.D., of Successful Aging *(Pantheon, 1998). Rowe is a member of the Institute of Medicine of the National Academy of Sciences and the Medicare Payment Advisory Commission (MedPAC), and is chairman of the board of trustees at the University of Connecticut.*

JOHN W. ROWE, M.D. | AETNA

AETNA INC.

Founded in 1853, Aetna is one of the nation's leaders in health care, dental, pharmacy, group life, disability, and long-term care insurance and employee benefits. The company is dedicated to helping people achieve health and financial security by providing easier access to safe, high-quality health care and protecting their finances against health-related risks.

Aetna provides benefits through employers in all 50 states, with products and services targeted specifically to small, midsized, and large multisite national employers, serving more *Fortune* 1000 companies than any of its competitors. The company also serves individuals and Medicare beneficiaries in certain markets.

In addition to its wide range of insurance and employee benefits products, Aetna offers a wide array of programs, services and information that help check the rate of increase in employee benefits costs, while striving to improve the quality of health care and increase employee productivity. These include case management, disease management and patient safety programs; integrated medical, pharmaceutical, dental, behavioral health and disability information; and quality-based specialist networks.

As one of the first national health care companies to offer a consumer-directed health plan, Aetna continues to be a leader in this area with its growing Aetna HealthFund® family of products. With more choices and control over their health plan than ever before, Aetna HealthFund members have access to convenient tools and easy-to-understand information that can help them make smart, effective decisions about their health and financial well-being. Aetna is headquartered in Hartford, Connecticut.

For more information, visit: www.aetna.com.
Stock Symbol: AET

THE AETNA WAY

BUILDING TRUST

MANAGE FOR TOMORROW

"Keeping all stakeholders in balance is key to maintaining public trust."
– Klaus Kleinfeld

"[T]o think and plan long-term is particularly critical to Pfizer's business of discovering and developing important medicines."
– Hank McKinnell

"Meeting commitments to others is essential to long-term financial performance."
– John W. Rowe

"…Trust and innovation…if you want to manage your business for tomorrow…you can't have one without the other."
– Dr. Henning Kagermann

Klaus Kleinfeld

PRESIDENT AND CHIEF EXECUTIVE OFFICER
SIEMENS CORPORATION

"By taking the long view…we've been able to offer…innovative products, systems, and solutions as [a] competitive advantage."

– Klaus Kleinfeld

RESTORING PUBLIC TRUST

I remember well attending the meeting with President George W. Bush in a small room at the White House, when he challenged our group of assembled CEOs to restore the trust of the American people in business. I was struck by the sincerity of his call to action. As one of the few leaders of a European company present that day, I was also struck, probably more than my American peers, by how important that challenge is—not just for American business, but also for companies around the world.

American corporate systems and structures have become global models. The erosion of confidence in corporate governance in the United States has put at risk the reputation of business on an international scale. This has happened at a time when the globalization of business is just beginning to bear fruit for humankind—enhancing the flow of capital and innovative technologies to developing economies, and ultimately raising the standards of living in the most remote areas of the world. So the stakes are high, and the response to President Bush's challenge is urgent.

As a Siemens executive, it is natural that I would emphasize the global implications of corporate governance. With operations in 190 countries, Siemens is the most global of all industrial companies. But of all those countries, the United States holds a special place. It is our largest market, home to 70,000 employees and the base of 11 of our worldwide businesses.

And as a member of a family that fled East Germany, I have seen firsthand the consequences of letting business standards deteriorate. Few countries had an industrial base that was as inefficient, obsolete, and corrupt in a very obscure way as East Germany's. In an economy where the state controlled business enterprises, the concept of corporate governance did not exist. And in a totalitarian society, terms like "public confidence" and "public trust" had little meaning or relevance. One knows best the value of something when one has seen the consequences of its loss.

At Siemens, we look at the public as a diverse array of constituencies. Certainly this includes shareholders, the company's owners. Our customers, without whom there would be no reason for the company. Our 425,000 employees and managers, who work to satisfy our customers and create profits for our owners. The communities where we work, the media, government officials, regulators, financial institutions, suppliers, partners, retirees, unions, and a host of other publics. Because they all have a stake in Siemens, we call them our stakeholders. It is my belief that keeping all stakeholders in balance is key to maintaining public trust. Certainly, this is consistent with the principles Arthur Page articulated so many years ago.

When one group is favored over another, troubles eventually arise. For example, while a company's executives are important, particularly in times of competition for top talent, some of the worst corporate scandals were caused by emphasizing rewards for a select group of executives. This was done without considering the interests of shareholders and other employees. Perhaps the most frequent cause of imbalance among stakeholder priorities has been the exclusive focus on investors and the financial community to the neglect of other stakeholders.

With the stock price as the most visible scorecard for corporate management, it is not surprising that a generation of executives focused on the mantra of the 1990s—maximizing shareholder value. In the interest of satisfying investors seeking short-term gains from stock price rises, some companies focused solely on financial strategies rather than investing in R&D to improve the products and services they offered their customers. Others neglected their commitment to employees, borrowing from pension funds to finance the growth that they felt Wall Street demanded.

At Siemens, the investor is a very important public, but not at the expense of other stakeholders. We challenge the argument that shareholder interests are incompatible with those of the other publics. We also resist the instant-gratification temptation so prevalent during the boom of the 1990s. In fact, many financial analysts were critical of Siemens for refusing to take advantage of the higher "New Economy" multiples by selling off industrial businesses and expanding our IT and telecommunications portfolio. That would not have served our industrial customers and strategic partners well. Given the recent crash of the technology market, it also proved to be the wrong move for our investors.

Maintaining a balanced portfolio—like balancing stakeholder interests—has contributed to Siemens' steady growth and financial stability for more than 150 years, during good times and bad. In 1884, company founder Werner von Siemens wrote to his brother: "I am not going to sell the future for a quick profit!"

Taking the long view makes it easier to satisfy all stakeholders' needs and expectations. Take, for example, our business customers. They want top-quality products and services that enable them to satisfy their own customers, and to do it better than their competitors. Innovation can be a great competitive edge, but in a tough economy many of our customers do not have the funds to invest in R&D. By taking the long view, and maintaining our traditionally high levels of research funding even when profit margins are depressed by the economy, we've been able to offer Siemens' innovative products, systems, and solutions as their competitive advantages.

Treating a customer as a stakeholder is the best way to create truly productive partnerships. It means that our customers have a stake in our development efforts on their behalf. And it means that we must understand fully each customer's needs, what creates value for him or her. For a company with a strong engineering heritage such as Siemens, this is always a great challenge. We strive constantly to overcome the temptation to let technology, rather than our customers and our market, drive the development of our products. Done right, it is an unbelievably constructive dialogue with very often outstanding results that strengthen the offerings of our customers. It also makes the world a better place: with more efficient energy production, distribution, and consumption; with easier worldwide communication; better medical diagnosis; and more effective treatments, to name just a few areas.

However, technology is not the only answer to innovation. For example, we've listened to our customers and created a solution to their needs—and made them stronger Siemens stakeholders—through a creative financing approach called "performance contracting." With capital investment budgets reduced drastically, customers often are unable to take advantage of technological improvements that could reduce their operating costs dramatically. So we are now offering contracts where we will install new technologies and our customers will only pay us as they realize the savings.

The U.S. Postal Service, known for not having sufficient funding to handle all of its modernization needs, recently awarded Siemens a performance contract to develop and install an automated mail-forwarding system. With 17 percent of the U.S. population moving each year, the postal service annually handles 40 million address changes, forwards 2 billion pieces of mail, and returns to senders another 1.3 billion pieces. By automating the current expensive and labor-intensive process, Siemens will provide the U.S. Postal Service significant savings. From those savings, Siemens will be paid for the sophisticated automatic-recognition and image-management technology we are developing for the postal service in our plants in Texas and Germany.

Besides providing the machines that handle more than 90 percent of America's letter mail, Siemens contributes to a broad spectrum of America's public services and infrastructure. Our power equipment generates one third of the country's energy; we provide the commuter trains to 11 major U.S. cities and security systems to all 438 major airports; we handle more than 150 million medical transactions every day and provide diagnostic equipment to hospitals in virtually every U.S. community; and we are responsible for building safety, security, and energy management in more than 20,000 facilities across the country.

A company in the infrastructure business knows well the importance of corporate citizenship, particularly in serving the community and treating local government officials as important stakeholders. Our employees are active in their communities, our managers serve on local foundation boards, and our executives seek out national leadership roles. Siemens is also proud to sponsor the Siemens Westinghouse

Science Scholarships, the prestigious awards for bright students from America's high schools, and the newly created Innovation Award competition as part of the National History Day program.

For busy leaders, it is tempting to support these good will efforts with encouragement and endorsements rather than personal participation. But I've always been guided by the words of the outspoken German novelist and poet, Erich Kästner, who said, "There is nothing good, unless you do it." Also I firmly believe in what Sir Karl Popper calls "piecemeal work"—the world only changes if you start in your own direct environment.

So I try to set the standard for our executives. I make sure to be present to honor the winners of the science scholarships and innovation awards. Reinforcing my interest and experience in our medical business, I serve on the board of the Centers for Disease Control Foundation. To cover both our national and local corporate citizenship obligations, I serve on the national board of the U.S. Chamber of Commerce and lead the Cybersecurity Task Force of The Business Roundtable, while also leading an investment development task force for New York Mayor Michael Bloomberg in Siemens Corporation's hometown. Reaching out to community stakeholders through high-quality national and local philanthropic programs is time consuming and expensive. There are some who say such use of the company's funds is incompatible with maximizing shareholder value; that it is a misuse of the investor's money. On the contrary, I believe that corporate social responsibility is a necessary condition for a company to be financially successful over the long term.

The Siemens culture fosters a leadership philosophy that we call "sustainable management." Based on a view that a company exists in balance with the society and environment in which it does business, our culture recognizes that all Siemens stakeholders are important to the company. Sustainable management drives Siemens to continue to be one of the world's leading investors in R&D, encourages us to adopt the toughest standards of corporate governance, and motivates us to participate in the communities where we do business. That focus on those longer-term, high-value principles such as innovation, governance, and social responsibility has produced significant returns for our shareholders, while companies that tried to take shortcuts have suffered in the stock market as well as the market of public opinion.

In many ways, the most important stakeholders for a corporation are its managers and employees. They certainly have a great stake in the company—their jobs, their livelihood, the quality of life of their families, and the pensions that provide them security and comfort in their old age. Managers and employees also provide the greatest leverage with other stakeholders. They are on the front lines with customers on a daily basis, they are the face of the company in the community, and their labors keep the company operating and providing products and services for the company's markets.

At Siemens, we give our leaders the tools and the encouragement to communicate actively with their employees, always seeking to create two-way dialogue. We provide, for example, an online information and learning exchange, called "The Leader's Forum," where the top 600 leaders share best practices, obtain career-development information for their employees, and download materials they can use to explain business news to those they supervise. Twice a month, the leaders meet online for a 90-minute chat with an author, business leader, or expert on timely topics such as selling, customer service, economic issues, and leadership strategies.

The CEO's role with the employees can be tricky. It is always a challenge to reach out to employees without bypassing the chain of command. In a company of 70,000 employees, it is also impractical for a CEO to reach all internal stakeholders in any sustained, meaningful way. So we have established a simple approach of a monthly e-mail letter personally addressed to each employee where I relate in a very personal way my observations about important happenings during the month. Each letter contains a link to a spot on our intranet, called the "President's Corner," where employees can go to learn more about the topics I write about. Each month, more than 5,000 employees take that opportunity and go to the President's Corner.

We are always looking for feedback, and I receive about 60 notes commenting on points in the letter. I answer each one personally. I also seek out employee comments through an approach we call "Listening Tours." Whenever I am visiting one of our 600 sites in the United States, I schedule 90 minutes for a meeting with 15 employees representing a cross-section of the local employee population. It's a time for listening to what's on the minds of employees, for answering questions, and for getting a feel for the local management culture. We also like to use town hall meetings for larger groups of employees, encouraging frank Q&A interchanges.

In a few isolated cases I've sensed a reluctance among employees to speak up, indicating a lack of openness or intimidation that we addressed quickly with the local managers. In most cases, the experience is encouraging, with plenty of constructive comments, and I leave with the feeling that our employees are living by the company's values and represent a good, high-performance culture. I am pleased also to see that my personal involvement in these frank, two-way interchanges have emboldened our managers to be more proactive in communicating with those they lead.

Ultimately, we will only meet the challenge of restoring public trust by setting high values and making sure that our executives, managers, and employees communicate them and live by them. Those values emphasize the company's commitments to all its publics, all those who have a stake in what the company does. Keeping those stakeholder interests in balance isn't easy, but it is essential to the long-term success of our companies.

Klaus Kleinfeld
PRESIDENT AND CHIEF EXECUTIVE OFFICER
SIEMENS CORPORATION

Klaus Kleinfeld became president and chief executive officer of Siemens Corporation on January 1, 2002, after serving one year as the chief operating officer of the New York-based company. He was named to the Siemens AG managing board on December 1, 2002.

He was executive vice president and a member of the executive board of the Siemens AG medical engineering group prior to his U.S. appointment. Before that Kleinfeld led Siemens' $1 billion worldwide angiography, fluoroscopy and X-Ray systems business. Prior to his medical assignments, Kleinfeld established and led the Siemens Management Consulting Group (SMC).

Kleinfeld began his career with Siemens in 1987 in the corporate sales and marketing group, moving a year later to Siemens corporate planning and strategy. Prior to joining Siemens, he was a strategic product manager at the CIBA-GEIGY pharmaceuticals division in Basel, Switzerland.

Kleinfeld is a member of the board of directors of the Centers for Disease Control Foundation, the U.S. Chamber of Commerce and the Metropolitan Opera. He is also a member of The Business Roundtable and serves on the boards of the American Institute for Contemporary German Studies, The Turner Corporation and the Partnership for New York City. He was instrumental in establishing the "Siemens Kinderfond" foundation and the Siemens Caring Hands Foundation.

Kleinfeld earned a master's degree in business administration/economics from the University of Goettingen (Germany) in 1982, followed by a Ph.D. in strategic management from the University of Wuerzburg (Germany). He resides with his wife and family in Connecticut.

SIEMENS USA

Siemens USA provides a broad range of products, systems and services to America's top enterprises. With 70,000 employees at 685 locations in all 50 states, Siemens USA is composed of a diverse set of business units that includes power, automation and controls, information and communications, healthcare, transportation and lighting

With $20 billion in revenues, the United States is Siemens AG's largest market. Every business day, Siemens USA:

- Treats more than 30,000 cancer patients with radiation therapy systems.
- Processes more than 150 million healthcare information transactions.
- Produces the generators that provide one-third of the nation's electricity.
- Provides consulting and managed IT outsourcing services for half of the Fortune 100.
- Handles 90 percent of the U.S. mail with its postal automation systems.
- Supplies one-third of the light rail vehicles in North America.
- Provides baggage handling systems for more than 100 major U.S. airports.
- Produces 200,000 automotive electronic components for 40 percent of U.S.-built cars.
- Manufactures 3.3 million energy-saving lamps.

As an active corporate citizen, the company dedicated about $13 million in fiscal 2002 to community programs and non-profit organizations, as well as an additional $3 million to American education through scholarships and research grants to more than 100 universities. Employees participate in Siemens Caring Hands programs in communities across the nation, volunteering to clean-up parks, walk for charities and revitalize city centers. Siemens USA is headquartered in New York City.

For more information, visit: www.siemens.com.
Stock Symbol: SI

BUILDING TRUST

Hank McKinnell

CHAIRMAN AND CHIEF EXECUTIVE OFFICER
PFIZER, INC.

"Shareholder interests are best served when management leads employees to think and act generation-to-generation, as well as quarter-to-quarter."

– Hank McKinnell

INTEGRITY: KEY TO SUCCESS

Pfizer is now the world's largest and most valuable pharmaceutical company. We have been in business since 1849 and remain headquartered in New York City, the city of our founding. We are proud of the fact that we have not missed a dividend since the Hoover Administration, and we are one of America's best performing and most widely held companies. As only the twelfth chief executive in Pfizer's 155-year history, I am keenly aware of the responsibilities we have to all our stakeholders, starting with our patients. Pfizer is one of the crown jewels in American business, and the bedrock of our century-and-a-half of success lies in our integrity.

Pfizer is unique in that not only is our stock both widely held by individuals, but is also a favored investment by institutions. We, and companies like us in American business, owe a debt of gratitude for the current quest to reform the excesses of corporate governance. I know it was not easy to keep the pressure for such reform going at full bore during the 1990s, when companies routinely announced that they had "new business models" that no one else could understand. As Pfizer's Chairman and Chief Executive, and in my new role leading The Business Roundtable, I am passionate about fairness for all stakeholders. I am also anxious to restore public confidence in American corporate leadership.

Pfizer has been a strong voice for better corporate governance, long before it became a fashionable issue. We believe in transparency and fairness for all investors. We've lived and thrived on the maxim that an independent, inquisitive, hardworking and highly intelligent board of directors is ultimately the best guarantor of that transparency and fairness. Over the long term, such a board makes managing a major company such as Pfizer easier.

We insist on making it easy for our board to get the information they need and to ask the hard questions that challenge and sharpen management's thinking. Some chief executives shy away from the hard issues of governance. I do not. I believe that a company overseen by an active, committed and strongly independent board of directors is much easier to manage than a company where the board is passive or remote. It takes thorough analysis and a strong case to get buy-in for management's strategies from our board. But once plans pass muster, the board is highly supportive of our actions. This approach to oversight made it possible for us to pursue and win Warner-Lambert in 2000. This was an unprecedented move in our industry, and represented a departure from our longtime strategy. Following the most stringent analysis and severe questioning that you could envision, we earned the board's complete and unstinting support. That made it possible to go forward with a bid for Warner-Lambert and, ultimately, to win the company, a move that propelled us to the lead in our industry.

Pfizer's board is routinely given accolades for its strength and independence. The board has won the Spencer Stuart/Wharton School Board Excellence Award, perhaps the most prestigious honor a board of directors can garner. We at Pfizer are all justifiably proud of that, but more to the point of good corporate governance, such a board and the dynamics it engenders allows us in management to think and plan long-term. In that respect we agree with Arthur Page, who said that for a business to succeed, it must manage for tomorrow.

This license to think and plan long-term is particularly critical in Pfizer's business of discovering and developing important medicines. The road to a new medicine is never easy. It may take up to 15 years and require an investment in excess of $800 million. We test some 5,000 compounds to find one that ultimately becomes, after years of rigorous study and testing, a prescribed medicine. Even then, only three of every 10 medicines we put into the hands of patients will pay back its investment. Those that do go to market must pay for the hundreds that never make it to the starting gate. The risks involved with drug discovery and development place even more focus on our corporate governance and our ability, as managers, to be responsive to the needs of all stakeholders.

Our insistence on good corporate governance adds to our competitive advantage. This is especially evident now, when many businesses are finding themselves at a crossroads, experiencing a crisis of confidence, the likes of which have not been seen in decades.

I have three points to underscore in discussing corporate governance. First and foremost, I remain extremely angry with the so-called "corporate leaders" who abused their powers. We have seen managers put greed, ego and personal gain ahead of their obligations to those with stakes in their companies. These people have also inflicted immense pain on those who believed in them, particularly their employees.

When people (especially employees) believe in a company, they are disposed to invest heavily in it. This crisis in corporate governance weighs most heavily on the people whom I, as CEO, want most on my side—committed and passionate employees.

I am also angry because those who abused the public trust affected my ability to lead Pfizer, a company where I have worked for more than 32 years, and a company I have believed in from Day One.

Those who abused America's trust poisoned the well for me and for the vast majority of my counterparts in other companies—leaders who want to do the right thing for all stakeholders. The corporate criminals among us, few as they might be, have made it difficult for honest executives to credibly speak about core values such as quality, integrity and teamwork.

No matter what the color of one's collar, criminal wrongdoing is criminal wrongdoing. Stealing is stealing, whether it happens on the street or in corporate suites. I am glad the time has come for a full and fair accounting of what happened in the Enrons and Tycos of the world. Let justice be done—the faster, the better.

INTEGRITY: KEY TO SUCCESS

Angry as I am, and angry as I know the American public is, let's take some heart in the willingness of so many corporate leaders to stand up for accuracy and fairness in their public financial statements and disclosures.

We are now at Sarbanes-Oxley, year two. While Sarbanes-Oxley is a long, complex and sometimes confusing act of law, passed in haste, America's corporate leaders have stood up to follow its spirit and intent. Thanks to Sarbanes-Oxley and other reforms, the leaders of more than 1,000 American-traded companies attested to the accuracy and integrity of their financial statements and financial disclosures. I challenge the corporate leaders of any other nation to do the same.

The performance of American business in this post-Sarbanes-Oxley era confirms what President George W. Bush said to me during the Waco summit in 2002. When asked about his confidence in American management, the President said, "Ninety-nine percent of Americans are honest and hardworking. The same is true of their CEOs."

We may run different kinds of businesses, and take different approaches to the businesses we lead. But I believe, as the President does, that 99 percent of CEOs know the difference between right and wrong, and that they set the right tone, right from the top.

This leads me to my second point. While good corporate governance takes place in a framework of laws and regulations, simply changing that framework does not ensure a higher standard of governance.

With Sarbanes-Oxley, we have seen an historic re-adjustment of the framework of laws and regulations. More changes are undoubtedly on the way, even though I personally believe America would benefit from calling a "time out" on additional major changes until the performance of Sarbanes-Oxley can be thoughtfully evaluated.

The reality is that companies that always took good corporate governance seriously were more than willing to work hard to comply with new laws and regulations, no matter how confusing or overlapping they may have been.

In fact, at Pfizer, we used Sarbanes-Oxley as yet another opening to make certain that our board was ready to ask the most difficult questions and get unstinting answers from management.

In the wake of Enron, for example, we in management went to our Audit Committee with a list of questions—along with our answers.

We said, "We know that, as independent directors, you might want to consider asking these questions of us. We want you to have the answers, even before you ask the questions."

We did the same after Sarbanes-Oxley was passed. We had no real difficulties complying with the spirit and intent of this law, but we did go through every provision, to make certain that any question by our directors could be fully answered.

I think what really makes a difference in good corporate governance isn't so much the rules and regulations, but rather, attitude of management and board members. As a company leader, you have to seek excellence in corporate oversight in order to achieve it.

As the chairman of a publicly held company, and as an independent board member of other major companies, I have found that the most significant variable in board performance is the commitment of board members to excellence in performing their work.

We at Pfizer tell our board members, upfront, to expect to spend a minimum of 200 hours per board member on the very important work of independent oversight. As a company, we invest heavily in director education, and give the board plenty of opportunity to consult without management present.

Yet, what truly distinguishes Pfizer's board and other excellent boards is an overarching commitment to good corporate governance. It's mindset over mandate. Actions speak louder than credos, and even louder than rules and regulations. Companies that truly want to govern themselves well usually do so no matter what the regulatory environment. They also understand that corporate governance doesn't start and stop with the interests of investors. Good corporate governance shapes how a company deals with all of its key stakeholders.

This brings me to my third point. It is time to revisit the concept that corporations exist primarily to maximize shareholder value.

The modern corporation does exist to serve shareholders. But blindly ascribing our existence only to investors will, over time, alienate the other stakeholders, upon whom we must rely for value creation.

Ultimately, shareholder interests are best served when management leads employees to think and act generation-to-generation, as well as quarter-to-quarter. Shareholders are also best served when customers, employees, communities, and regulatory bodies see that they too, have a real stake in the company's long-term success.

With this in mind, in 2001, Pfizer adopted a new mission: To become the most valued company to patients, customers, colleagues, investors, business partners and the communities where we work and live.

We could have put shareholders above all and simply said, "We want to be the world's most valuable company!" We didn't, and for a reason. We believe that if we work towards this "most valued" ideal, we will be a company built to last. This is the best way to produce sustainable value for shareholders.

All of us, whether we be corporate leaders, directors, or investors, can be justifiably angry with those who abused corporate power. Ultimately, we must get past the anger at wrongdoers, anxiety over new regulations and arrogance over our roles in spinning the flywheel of business.

We need to begin to repair the damage done by a relative few. That means changes in the mindsets of corporate leadership, with all of us working to restore confidence in the integrity of American business.

It's time to show, without question, that American business can make money the old-fashioned way, the way Pfizer and so many companies have done it for decades—by earning it with valued products and services, created by competent, ethical people, and sustained by investors who know that just about everything worth doing takes time, passion and commitment.

Thank you for your faith in us. We will continue to earn it, every day.

Hank McKinnell
CHAIRMAN AND CHIEF EXECUTIVE OFFICER
PFIZER, INC.

Hank McKinnell is chairman and CEO of Pfizer, Inc. Born in western Canada, McKinnell earned his bachelor's degree in business from the University of British Columbia and earned both his master's and doctorate in business from Stanford University Graduate School of Business. He joined Pfizer Japan in 1971. He was then asked to become a regional manager for Pfizer in Iran/Afghanistan, starting a string of promotions that brought him to the leadership of Pfizer Asia in the early 1980s.

Moving to Pfizer headquarters in New York City, he led the company's strategic planning group and then its medical technologies operation. He then served as chief financial officer before being named as head of Pfizer's largest operation, prescription pharmaceuticals, in the early 1990s.

In 1999, McKinnell became president and chief operating officer of Pfizer, Inc. He helped lead the acquisition and integration of Warner-Lambert in 2000. In 2001, he was elected chairman of the board and CEO.

After becoming Pfizer's CEO, he acquired Pharmacia and cemented Pfizer's position as the world's largest pharmaceutical company. He established Pfizer as an innovator in opening access to healthcare to people with limited incomes, launching programs such as the Pfizer Global Health Fellows and the Pfizer for Living Share Card.

McKinnell serves on the boards of ExxonMobil, Moody's, and John Wiley & Sons. He is the only pharmaceutical company executive to serve on the Presidential Advisory Council on HIV/AIDS. He chairs The Business Roundtable and is a fellow of the New York Academy of Medicine. McKinnell serves on the board of trustees for both the New York City Public Library and the New York City Police Foundation. He is the 2003 winner of the Cleveland Dodge Medal from Columbia University and the 2003 recipient of the United Nations Association's Global Leadership Award.

PFIZER, INC.

Founded in 1849 in Brooklyn, New York, Pfizer, Inc. is the world's largest research-based pharmaceutical company. More than 120,000 colleagues, operating in some 150 nations, bring Pfizer products to people and their prized animals, all in pursuit of longer, happier, healthier lives.

Pfizer is the number one medicines company in every region of the world. Its product portfolio includes 14 number one products, serving patients suffering from some of the world's most devastating diseases. Pfizer's key prescription medicines include Lipitor, the world's largest selling medication for lipid lowering, and Viagra for male erectile dysfunction.

Pfizer Global Research and Development is the world's largest privately funded biomedical research group. Pfizer has more than 200 medicines in development, and more than 400 more projects in earlier discovery stages.

Pfizer Global Manufacturing encompasses 93 manufacturing facilities and 54 logistics centers in more than 40 nations. It builds on a heritage that includes the broad-scale production of penicillin and the commercialization of the Sabin polio vaccine.

Pfizer Consumer Healthcare provides a range of products including Listerine for oral care, Nicorette/Nicotrol for smoking cessation, Neosporin ointment, and Benadryl allergy medications.

Pfizer Animal Health is the world's leading discoverer and marketer of products to prevent and treat diseases in livestock and companion animals.

The company donates more than $2 million, in cash and products, per day to help people worldwide. Pfizer has been instrumental in some of the world's most effective public/private partnerships for healthcare access, including the International Trachoma Initiative, the Florida: A Healthy State Initiative, the Diflucan Initiative, and Sharing the Care. Pfizer is headquartered in New York City.

For more information, visit: www.pfizer.com.
Stock Symbol: PFE

INTEGRITY: KEY TO SUCCESS

BUILDING TRUST

John W. Rowe

CHAIRMAN AND CHIEF EXECUTIVE OFFICER
EXELON CORPORATION

"Operating in today's markets requires peripheral vision and fast feet. We are seeking to build a company that consistently adds value—year after year."

– John W. Rowe

REALITY AND INTEGRITY

I have made my way in this world for the past 20 years as the CEO of utility companies—Central Maine Power, New England Electric System, Commonwealth Edison and now its parent company, Exelon. In all of these situations, my shareholders' returns have been dependent upon my ability to separate what is real from what is fancied, and upon my ability to combine aggressive financial goals with a keen sense of integrity and community responsibility.

Realism and integrity are part of the legacy I wish to leave to this company. Exelon will report its earnings honestly.

We will try to identify risks as well as opportunities. We will deliver news to our shareholders—good or bad—in a timely and forthright fashion. For example, Exelon is making it through the current turmoil in the stock market and the energy industry with highly competitive returns for its investors and gratifying public recognition. *BusinessWeek* has rated Exelon best among the utility companies for the past two years, and *Forbes* deemed us the "Best of Breed."

We have prospered because we are a real company with real customers, real generation, real transmission and distribution systems, and a power team that trades real power. We have:

- 5.1 million retail electric customers—3.6 million in Northern Illinois and 1.5 million in Southeastern Pennsylvania—the largest electric customer base in North America.
- 43,000 megawatts of generation—either owned or under contract. This includes 16,000 megawatts of nuclear capacity, as well as 2,500 megawatts of gas-fired capacity under construction.
- Over 6,000 circuit miles of transmission systems and 94,000 circuit miles of distribution systems. We have invested $3 billion improving these systems over the past three years.
- $1,440 million in reported net income in 2002—the highest among U.S. electric companies.

We have turned our principles into a succinct corporate vision that really does drive our actions: "Exelon strives to build exceptional value—by becoming the best and most consistently profitable electricity and gas company in the United States."

We are driven to:

1. Live up to our commitments.
The past two years have shown what happens to companies that forget their commitments, companies that become obsessed with spin rather than substance. At Exelon, we know that meeting commitments to others is essential to long-term financial performance. In this, as in other things, when planning for the future, actions speak louder than words.

Keep the lights on. It all starts here. Our business requires reliable service to customers at prices that are competitive and reasonably predictable. Over the past three years, our Delivery Group has improved its reliability (65 percent Outage Duration and 51 percent Outage Frequency improvement since 1999) at prices that reflect the discounts required by Illinois and Pennsylvania lawmakers.

Perform safely—especially in nuclear operations. Safety is an imperative for every electric utility. As owner of the largest nuclear fleet in the United States and the third largest in the world, Exelon must have a constant and special commitment to operating safely. The shell of the second unit at Three Mile Island (where Exelon owns the first unit in a joint partnership with British Energy) is a constant reminder of this special obligation. The responsibility for operating safely is shared among all U.S. nuclear generators, and we are dependent on each other to uphold it.

Constantly improve our environmental performance. All forms of producing electricity impose environmental costs. Our nuclear, hydro, and gas generation help limit our impacts. We have supported legislation to deal with the climate change issue and have designated a strategy team to identify new ways of reducing our own impacts.

Act honorably and treat everyone with respect, decency and integrity. Competition and new forms of regulation have changed the ground rules for utilities. In this changing world, it is more important than ever to conduct our business with ethical standards and to focus on simple integrity and decency in our dealings with employees, customers and our investors. Our voluntary separation programs have been one example of meeting this commitment.

Continue building a high-performance culture that reflects the diversity of our communities. Our operations are based upon two of the most diverse cities in the United States — Philadelphia and Chicago. We are building a diverse management team and workforce. We have come a long way, but we have more to do and we need to move faster.

Report our results, opportunities and problems honestly and reliably. In the past few years, several large companies have violated securities laws, generally accepted accounting principles and fundamental good faith. We are trying in our quarterly earnings releases, in our Securities and Exchange Commission (SEC) filings, and in our annual report to our shareholders to set a high standard of reporting.

2. Perform at world-class levels.
Relentlessly pursue top quartile performance levels in productivity, quality, safety and customer satisfaction. We know that superior operations are the best way to add value in a low-growth industry. For the full year 2002, Exelon implemented a cost management initiative, which achieved $340 million of sustainable savings relative to Exelon's original 2002 financial plan. In 2003, we are also developing a more fundamental and durable productivity improvement program called The Exelon

Way, with a goal to save another $600 million annually by 2006. And we need to work harder to improve our customers' satisfaction.

Adopt a common business model, core operating processes and best practices across the enterprise. We are consolidating and centralizing functions where it makes sense, such as in our energy delivery company. In addition, we are standardizing and simplifying our operating procedures across the company, as well as adopting the best practices necessary to reach our top quartile performance objective.

Ensure effective integration across businesses and optimize the whole. The California energy crisis of 2001 and the merchant generation failures of 2002 underscore the importance of integrating generation, delivery and customer service. This is good for Exelon. However, successful integration requires constant sensitivity to regulatory requirements and constant diligence in keeping our businesses working together. The way our Generation, Power Team, and Energy Delivery groups worked together on revising our power purchase agreements reflect this kind of work.

Promote and implement policies that build effective markets. Exelon's ultimate value depends upon efficient markets that function under fair rules. To that end, we have endeavored to build effective regional transmission organizations (RTOs) and have supported the Federal Energy Regulatory Commission (FERC) efforts to introduce a standard market design. This work was essential to FERC's approval for ComEd to join the independent system operator. Within the Pennsylvania, New Jersey and Maryland region, PJM determines each day what the region's electricity needs are, then calls on the optimal generating stations to supply that energy in the most economic manner.

Adapt rapidly to changing markets, politics, economics and technology to meet our customers' needs. Exelon operates in a number of different regions in the United States. We have formed cross-functional Regional Market Success Teams to understand and manage the changing market rules, politics, and economics of each region. Operating in today's markets requires peripheral vision and fast feet—our Regional Market Success Teams meet these needs.

3. Build value through disciplined financial management.
The electricity business enjoys modest and durable growth—but not rapid growth. The performance commitments described in our vision statement are intended to give us some additional earnings growth over the next few years. We must continue to analyze and pursue investment opportunities regularly, but we must focus more on improving operational and financial management.

Maximize the earnings and cash flow from our assets and businesses and sell those that do not meet our goals. We are doing everything we can to improve productivity and maximize earnings from our current assets. But we also want to make sure that we pare off assets that are no longer a strategic fit with Exelon.

Prioritize acquisition opportunities based upon synergies and value creation potential, balance sheet integrity, and consistency with our model for serving customers and meeting regulatory obligations. Our joint investment with British Energy (AmerGen) has created substantial value. Our New England generating investments appear marginal in view of more recent power market conditions. Exelon Enterprises, our unregulated business unit, is being sold off, and some of our other generation investments are not performing as planned. We must learn from our failures as well as from our successes. We have instituted review programs and have built teams to do just that.

Return cash generated by the company to investors when higher returns are not available from other investment opportunities. Every investment opportunity must be measured against the option to return the money to shareholders. If we cannot find investment opportunities that create more value than investors can create on their own, we will return that money to investors. We are seeking to build a company that consistently adds value—year after year.

Exelon recently added this third component to our vision. I want each and every Exelon employee to know and be reminded daily how important financial discipline is to our success.

As the Vision Statement makes clear, we are driven by the value of our shareholders' investment. We believe we can become the best electric utility in America. We can do this by extending throughout our company the benchmarking and continuous improvement practices that have worked so well in our nuclear operations, by coordinating the operation of our diverse portfolio of assets to add value for both customers and shareholders, and by using our power marketing and hedging expertise to improve both the quality and the predictability of our earnings.

While other companies created huge wholesale trading organizations, built new generating stations or made investments outside of the United States, Exelon has stayed at home and stuck to our knitting. We may even look overly conservative to some of the go-go marketers of a couple years ago, but our goal is to be consistently profitable and slowly grow the business. We will not be satisfied until we are the best (and possibly the biggest) electricity and gas company in the United States.

The way we manage is by focusing on the basics; managing our costs, managing our service, and managing our relationships with our governing entities. We are not yet in a place where our problems are behind us, but we are dealing with them squarely. We try to report disappointing news up front, rather than surprise our shareholders and the investment community.

We are focused on implementing The Exelon Way, introduced this year to our shareholders and the financial community. The Exelon Way will transform how we do business by focusing on operational excellence, simplifying procedures and standardizing processes. Through consolidation and integration we will capture efficiencies, synergies and economies of scale. It will enable Exelon to consistently meet our commitments and achieve world-class performance levels, and to improve cash flow by $300-$600 million in cash savings annually.

We must improve to remain competitive and find more efficient ways of operating. Our competition comes from many sources, and our industry is facing the challenges of fixed retail prices, low wholesale electric prices, low growth rates in the current economy, and escalating costs. The Exelon Way will improve the quality of our earnings. It will increase our cash flow and strengthen the quality of the earnings we achieve.

The Exelon Way will centralize and integrate key functions, consolidate and align key business areas, and adopt a single business model for all business units. We will standardize and simplify key processes and use a single approach for all of our operating processes. The Exelon Way will benchmark our operations against other companies, both inside and outside our industry, utilizing skilled employees working on cross-functional teams. Our goal is to transform how we work, which will result in a centralized, fully integrated organization.

REALITY AND INTEGRITY

Over my extensive career, I have constantly endeavored to "be of some use," just like Dr. Wilbur says in the book, *The Cider House Rules*. We have made competition work in Illinois and Pennsylvania while reducing rates, and we continue to work for a clearer national vision. The Exelon Way will help us achieve even greater financial growth. Exelon's service delivery has greatly improved, both in the reduction of outages and the length of them. As we have trimmed our staff, we have used voluntary severance plans and generous severance pay to ease the transition. And we have turned two medium-sized weak utilities into what *Forbes* now calls "Best of Breed." We believe we are of much use and can be ever more effective.

John W. Rowe

CHAIRMAN AND CHIEF EXECUTIVE OFFICER
EXELON CORPORATION

John W. Rowe is the chairman and chief executive officer of Exelon Corporation, one of the nation's five largest electric utilities. Rowe has led electric utilities since 1984, consecutively serving as chief executive officer of Central Maine Power Company, the New England Electric System, and Unicom Corporation (one of Exelon's predecessors). Rowe is a lawyer, and was general counsel of Consolidated Rail Corporation and a partner in the firm of Isham, Lincoln and Beale.

Rowe is a member of the boards of Unum Provident Corporation and the Northern Trust Company. His civic and professional commitments include serving as vice chairman of the Chicago Historical Society and as a member of the boards of the Chicago Urban League, Field Museum, Art Institute of Chicago, Northwestern University, Edison Electric Chicago Club and the visiting committees of the Oriental Institute and the University of Pennsylvania Museum. He has previously been chairman of the Edison Electric Institute, president of the USS Constitution Museum, and chairman of the Massachusetts Business Roundtable.

Rowe holds B.S. and J.D. degrees from the University of Wisconsin and its law school, where he was elected to Phi Beta Kappa and the Order of the Coif and is the founder of the Rowe Professorship in Byzantine history. He is a board member of the Wisconsin Alumni Research Foundation and has received the university's Distinguished Alumni Award.

He holds honorary doctorates from Illinois Institute of Technology, Bryant College, Drexel University, and the University of Massachusetts-Dartmouth. He received the City Club of Chicago's Citizen of the Year award in 2002, the Corporate Leadership Award from the Spanish Coalition for Jobs in 2002 and the Anti-Defamation League's World of Difference Award in 2000.

EXELON CORPORATION

Exelon Corporation, parent of PECO and ComEd, is one of the nation's largest electric utilities with approximately 5 million customers and more than $15 billion in annual revenues. The company has one of the industry's largest portfolios of electricity generation capacity, with a nationwide reach and strong positions in the Midwest and Mid-Atlantic. Exelon distributes electricity to approximately 5 million customers in Illinois and Pennsylvania and gas to more than 440,000 customers in the Philadelphia area.

In order to achieve its goals, Exelon has created three business units: Exelon Energy Delivery, Exelon Generation, and Exelon Enterprises.

Exelon Engergy Delivery serves more than 3.4 million electricity customers in Northern Illinois through EcomEd and about 1.5 million electricity and 430,000 natural gas customers in Southeastern Pennsylvania through PECO Energy.

Exelon Generation is one of the world's largest power producers and wholesale marketers, with access to more than 48,000 megawatts of electricity. It has broken several performance records and established itself as a proven reliable power provider. Three operating groups comprise the business unit: Exelon Nuclear, Exelon Power, and Exelon PowerTeam.

Exelon Enterprises is a variety of businesses that compete nationwide in the areas of energy supply, infrastructure services, integrated communications, thermal technologies, energy-efficient offerings, turnkey solutions and capital funding.

Exelon is headquartered in Chicago, Illinois.

For more information, visit: www.exeloncorp.com.
Stock Symbol: EXC

Dr. Henning Kagermann

CHAIRMAN OF THE EXECUTIVE BOARD AND CHIEF EXECUTIVE OFFICER
SAP AG

"Only through continual investigation of the potential benefits of new technologies and processes can SAP remain on the cutting-edge…"
– Dr. Henning Kagermann

TRUSTED INNOVATION

These days, nearly everyone talks about trust and innovation, though usually not in the same breath. So why am I putting them together here?

I believe if you want to manage your business for tomorrow and create sustainable business value, especially in the digital age, when success or failure is just a click away, you can't have one without the other.

At SAP we understand firsthand that economic success starts with our ability to innovate. We also know that in order to sell our innovations we need to earn the trust of everyone we do business with.

In fact, we believe in this concept so strongly we recently created our first SAP Innovation Report, which is an innovation itself in the IT industry, to demonstrate what software can do and where we are investing resources to improve IT and create value for our customers. More than 100 pages long, the information in the report is geared toward everyone interested in SAP, whether they are already a customer, interested in becoming one, or are a partner, investor, or member of the general public.

Why did we do it? Simply put, we want to be known as the trusted innovator. And in an economic climate such as the one we're in, where cases of corporate malfeasance shout at us from the headlines, and too often companies communicate in an opaque rather than transparent fashion, we thought we'd take the lead in openly and honestly sharing our thoughts and practices about innovation.

If you will, allow me to take this opportunity to share some of those same thoughts and practices with you.

According to the Austrian economist Joseph Alois Schumpeter, invention is the creation of a new idea or concept. Innovation is taking that idea, reducing it to practice, and making it a commercial success.

These words indeed reflect the core of SAP's basic business philosophy: We want to make innovation happen. And we want to make it happen in a way that makes sense economically and technologically. We are focused on turning new concepts and ideas into real business benefits for our customers. In fact, the entire SAP organization is built around this credo. Its goals are not dissimilar to the principles articulated by Arthur W. Page.

TRUSTED INNOVATION

Innovation has been an important part of our culture since SAP was founded. Building on the groundbreaking idea of standard enterprise software, we have become the leading provider of complete business solutions and a trusted innovator and adviser to our customers. Every employee and process in our organization is focused on the complex challenge of driving and shaping innovation. As experts in their respective fields, our employees continually mine and analyze new ideas, whether from customers, the market, research institutions, or other employees. Only through continual investigation of the potential benefits of new technologies and processes can SAP remain on the cutting edge and help our customers get the most out of their investment.

We have learned over the years that technology, when combined with proven or innovative business practices, can indeed create competitive advantage and sustainable growth. The transformation toward an information-driven economy is in full swing. We have created a foundation with today's information systems, but many new ideas remain to be realized. This is why talk of the commoditization of IT is exaggerated. IT does matter and will continue to do so.

Beyond hype, IT is changing the way we do business. There are many ways of examining this. From a shareholder perspective, we are seeing a shift from an economy based on tangible assets to an economy based on intangible assets. In the industrial age, energy was abundant, while factories and equipment were the limiting factors. In the digital age, information is abundant, but only the right processes, people, and relationships can turn it into economic value. These intangibles turn out to be critical resources for success in today's economy.

Since it was founded, SAP has been on the forefront of this digital transformation and focused on helping to shape this transition in a meaningful way to create customer value. Indeed, many of our customers, such as Rolls-Royce, recognize their SAP solutions as strategic assets and include them in their annual reports.

JUMPING ON THE BANDWAGON IS NOT THE WAY TO GO

For SAP, added value begins with the development of high-quality, standard business applications that can find a broad range of uses. That means we are not innovating for innovation's sake or jumping on the bandwagon for every new idea that appears. This is important because our customers expect us not only to deliver reliable software, but also to maintain this software throughout the entire software life cycle. The timeframe for this can be five years for one release and up to 15 to 20 years for the life cycle of one product.

Our recipe for innovation begins by creating a robust extendable platform to support the accelerated adoption of innovation. Any product we deliver is a balance of reliability and renewal. Our solutions combine recognized best business practices on a stable, reliable core such as mySAP Business Suite, with the latest in leading-edge next practices such as SAP xApps. This reflects the varying needs of our customers. Some are interested only in stable, tried-and-true technology, while others are what we call "early adopters." These companies are willing to use technology that may not be completely bug free, but for them, fast adoption is everything. Of course, we constantly evaluate if and when these latest technologies will become part of the standard package.

To translate new ways of doing business into affordable business solutions requires the optimal combination of the latest technology with a sound understanding of customers' business requirements. As new technologies appear, we carefully evaluate their use and impact on our customers. This approach certainly proved itself during the dot-com era, when companies scrambled to be on the Internet with new businesses that were not necessarily sustainable. That didn't seem to matter, as being "on the Web" was all the rage. Throughout this fad, many software companies lost focus on the core of doing business, creating value for customers, sustaining a viable company with a leading-edge corporate culture, and being a socially responsible corporate citizen.

We do need to recognize, though, that not everything was lost when the dot-com bubble burst. With the Internet came many new inexpensive, open standards, which SAP has committed to using. With it also came an infrastructure that has tremendously lowered costs for computer-based communications. These shifts create new possibilities that will have an enormous impact on our economy. Indeed, e-business is not an empty promise. Still, unlocking its potential is not a matter of euphoria; it is a matter of thoroughly exploring the possibilities and shaping solutions that lead to a new level of business excellence.

PARTNERSHIPS ARE KEY

Whenever a company implements an SAP solution, it needs the entire "stack" around the software. This includes hardware, operating systems, databases, middleware, and complementary applications. It also includes consultants who can help a company make the most of their business-application investment.

Partnerships are vital for SAP. Only in close cooperation with our partners is it possible to unlock the full potential of our solutions—and to drive sustainable innovation.

Take the question of standards. With no common technical standards, the Internet would not exist. Today, we know that the full potential of collaboration can only be unlocked with additional semantic standards. More than ever, these standards are not a matter of a single provider alone. They can only be achieved by close coordination with other industry players.

Another example of the importance of partnerships is in the question of quality. The quality of a project and of a solution indeed depends on many partners. Only a joint commitment can make sure that the customer has the best possible solution. This aspect again shows that innovation takes much more than new features and possibilities. As IT increasingly plays a mission-critical role for the enterprise, new levels of quality and reliability are mandatory—and these require new ways of partner cooperation.

Yet another example is Total Cost of Ownership (TCO). It takes more than one company to make sure that innovation stays affordable. The whole ecosystem has to deploy the right creativity to make sure costs stay under control. The best innovation is of no practical value if it is too expensive.

Standard software by definition cannot include every function every company or industry needs. That is why we have made extendability an important part of our philosophy. Since the beginning of SAP, our solutions have been delivered to our customers with a development environment, which they can use to make changes in the software as needed. Our partners also develop flexible extensions to map additional customer needs to our software. Through extendability our customers can gain competitive advantage and have access to a cost-efficient mix of standard functionality and custom development.

We recognized the importance of partnerships early on and have grown an extended partner network over the years. We do have global partnerships, but we also want to consider local needs. That is why our partner network includes both global and regional companies. Today, our partners include such global players as Accenture, Hewlett-Packard, IBM, and Microsoft, but also more local companies in all regions and many industries.

INNOVATION NETWORK

Staying on the leading edge of information technology requires dedicated research resources. SAP Corporate Research is a worldwide organization responsible for researching, understanding, and developing new technologies and processes that may affect the future of SAP business applications. This group determines the business value of new technologies and then transfers them to SAP development groups for integration into new or existing product lines.

In addition, we have an SAP Innovation Syndicate, which is an internal network connecting all groups concerned with innovation at SAP. Our external network of researchers and universities is organized through our SAP University Alliances program, the highlight of which is the yearly SAP Innovation Congress.

INNOVATIVE DEVELOPMENT

When developing business software, two different life cycles must be aligned. On one hand, there is the customer engagement life cycle. Customers first need to explore the software and create a business case, which we can help them develop, before they make the final decision, particularly in today's difficult economy. They then need to implement, operate, and upgrade their systems. At the other end of the spectrum is the product innovation life cycle. Requirements must be evaluated, software must be designed, source code must be developed, and a solution production process must guarantee the quality and integrity of the individual solution. Finally, production systems must be maintained.

The strength of the SAP organization is to harmonize these two cycles and to make sure that we best serve our customers while maintaining efficiency. In our experience, only this balance can generate sustainable innovation.

Now, this balance is not static. It depends on circumstances and on the maturity of the different solutions. Today, we continue to focus on what we view as critical for successful software development. This includes ensuring our software has an industry focus, leveraging experience both within SAP and from our partners, working with pilot customers to test-drive new developments, and even looking to experts in their respective fields for insight.

In the past, the traditional core development process at SAP involved four distinct phases: specification, design, development/testing, and verification. These four phases are still important, but today we view them from a different angle, as a spiral instead of a straight line from beginning to end. Development processes have become more interactive and fluid, and actual development more incremental and evolving. With a new model of increased prototyping and customer feedback and continuous improvement, we can more easily redirect development, identify gaps, simplify reuse of software building blocks, and above all ensure flexible development. This incremental approach means a gradual increase in the breadth of functionality and allows us to deliver new in-depth functions quickly and solidly at any point in the cycle. At the end of each phase, results are reviewed and decisions are made on how to proceed. Concrete results are produced and verified during each phase and can not only be demonstrated to customers, but also reused in other projects as needed.

Reuse is crucial to our new development model and to our customers for a number of reasons. It underscores our commitment to delivering standard software for broad usage. By reusing common parts, we can speed up development through consistent reuse, reduce redundancies and improve solution homogeneity, more quickly identify and correct bugs, reduce development costs, and ultimately raise the overall quality of our solutions. For our customers, reuse means learning once and using multiple times because they have a more intuitive understanding of our software. Use of user interface patterns, for example, drives a faster learning curve and ultimately means higher quality.

CUSTOMER FOCUS

Just as our approach to development has evolved, so has our approach to involving customers in development. While we have always made sure we understand our customers' needs before writing code, we now take this to a new level with a strategic look at their business.

This results in open brainstorming. Country- and industry-specific advisory councils, such as Americas' SAP Users' Group (ASUG) and the German SAP Users' Group (DSAG), consider not just which functions may be needed, but where we can help companies identify how software can change and increase the value of their business. This means making sure the software we develop covers the maximum range of business processes and new business opportunities. With strategic development projects in conjunction with specific customers, we can help these companies quickly develop and implement new functions on the fly.

Thanks to this new development paradigm, customers have faster access to innovations they themselves helped drive. They can also be guaranteed that each innovation has been carefully evaluated, shaped, and verified for use in their heterogeneous IT landscape.

Over the past 30 years, software, information technology, and computers have significantly changed the way business is run. As a trusted innovator for our customers, SAP is a facilitator of this change, quickly turning ideas into reality and creating tangible business value. By ideas, we mean new technologies and new business practices that align with our experiences, because software applications are more than just the technology they are built on. They must combine technology and business practice to provide sustainable benefits for our customers. The road from recognizing the vision to building a solution with real benefits may at times be long, but I can truly say, "SAP makes innovation happen."

Dr. Henning Kagermann
CHAIRMAN AND CEO
SAP AG

Prof. Dr. Henning Kagermann is chairman of the Executive Board and CEO of SAP AG. From 1998 to 2003, he was co-chairman of the SAP Executive Board and CEO together with Hasso Plattner, co-founder of SAP. Following Plattner's election as chairman of the SAP Supervisory Board in May 2003, Kagermann became sole chairman of the Executive Board of SAP AG and CEO.

Kagermann has overall responsibility for SAP's strategy and business development, marketing, and global communications as well as for consulting and customer development. In addition, he leads the field management board and the product technology board. He is head of the Business Solution Group (BSG) Financial & Public Services, which includes the development organizations for financial services, insurance industries and public services as well as the human capital management, financials and enterprise resource planning development teams.

Kagermann joined SAP in 1982 and was initially responsible for product development in the areas of cost accounting and controlling. Later, he oversaw the development of all administrative solutions, including human resources and industry-specific development for banking, insurance, public sector and health care. His duties also included finance and administration in addition to the management of all regions of SAP. Kagermann has been a member of the SAP Executive Board since 1991.

A physicist and mathematician, Kagermann taught physics and computer science at the Technical University of Braunschweig and the University of Mannheim in Germany from 1982–1992 while at SAP. He is also a trustee of the Technical University of Munich.

Kagermann is currently a member of the supervisory boards of Deutsche Bank AG, DaimlerChrysler Services AG, and Münchener Rückversicherungs-Gesellschaft AG (Munich Re).

SAP AG

Founded in 1972 and headquartered in Walldorf, Germany, SAP is the world's leading provider of collaborative business solutions. It is the world's largest inter-enterprise software company, and the world's third-largest independent software supplier. SAP employs more than 28,900 people in more than 50 countries. Today, more than 21,600 customers in over 120 countries run more than 69,700 installations of SAP® software.

Through mySAP™ Business Suite, people in businesses around the globe are improving relationships with customers and partners, streamlining operations, and achieving significant efficiencies throughout their supply chains. The unique core processes of various industries, from Aerospace to Utilities, are supported effectively by more than 25 industry-specific SAP solution portfolios.

In 1997, SAP debuted on the New York Stock Exchange. Today, with subsidiaries in over 50 countries, the company is listed on several exchanges, including the Frankfurt stock exchange.

For more information, visit: www.sap.com.
Stock Symbol: SAP

BUILDING TRUST

A COMPANY'S TRUE CHARACTER IS EXPRESSED BY ITS PEOPLE

"What really characterizes the UPS culture [is]—not rules or procedures—but—[the] fierce determination to do the right thing for the customer."

– Michael L. Eskew

" Our word has to be as good as or better than any contract we've ever written."

– J. Wayne Leonard

"Allstate people hold the success and reputation of the company in their hands."

– Edward M. Liddy

"Who they (employees) are becomes what we are… —seeking not success—but significance."

– William C. Weldon

Michael L. Eskew

CHAIRMAN AND CHIEF EXECUTIVE OFFICER

UPS

*"At UPS, the culture is the brand, and the brand is the culture…
a culture that values efficiency, discipline and integrity."*

– Michael L. Eskew

DELIVERING ON THE PROMISE

If someone were to ask me to describe the business of UPS, I might answer that we deliver more than 13 million packages a day to businesses and consumers around the world. Or, I could say that we synchronize commerce for customers by uniting the flow of goods, information and funds—all on a global scale.

Both these answers are correct, but the real business of UPS is integrity: Integrity that is based on a corporate culture founded almost 100 years ago.

At UPS, the culture is the brand, and the brand is the culture.

We were founded in 1907 by Jim Casey, a man who put his personal stamp on a strong culture that still guides our 360,000 employees around the world.

Casey coined the slogan "Lowest Rates, Best Service" early on, and he set about putting policies and organizations in place to make sure this promise was fulfilled.

What he helped instill was a culture that values efficiency, discipline and integrity.

We manifest these core values through a set of principles and work methods that govern everything we do at UPS.

Before a driver takes over a route, he or she has to master what we call the "340 Methods."

The 340 Methods are based on very scientific time-and-motion studies, and prescribe very specifically how drivers are to perform each step of the work process—and in what order.

For instance, we know the average number of steps it should take for the driver to get from the package car to the delivery counter.

And drivers are taught the optimal way to hand over the handheld tracking computer to the customer for a signature.

Now, you might snicker at this kind of discipline, but let me tell you that there's a reason behind each of the 340 Methods.

Because the average driver can make more than 150 stops a day and handle more than 250 packages, every additional fraction of a second taken up by inefficient procedures can add hours to a daily work shift.

When you consider that we employ about 88,000 drivers and deliver a total of 13 million packages every day, you can quickly see the multiplied impact of the slightest inefficiency.

But more importantly, delays and bungled shipments can disappoint our customers. And that's really the point behind all our procedures — serving and satisfying the customer.

That's what really characterizes the UPS culture — not rules or procedures, but a fierce determination to do the right thing for the customer.

How exactly do you go about making sure your company culture is centered around fulfilling the brand promise to customers? At UPS, we achieve this by following three key "people" principles:

1. Be the boss.
2. Walk a mile in the customer's shoes.
3. Spread your loyalties.

Let me say that these three people principles don't just work at UPS. They're applicable for any company looking to better align its people with its brand promise. I believe, as Arthur Page did, that developing a good reputation begins with the quality of a company's employees.

Let's start with "Be the boss." What I'm talking about here is fostering a sense of ownership among employees. At UPS, we do that by giving our people equal parts authority and accountability.

If you're the cynical type, I suppose you could call this "giving them enough rope to hang themselves."

But what this really means is designing jobs so that employees have reasonable freedom to make decisions on their own.

And then making them accountable for the consequences of those decisions — good or bad.

For example, UPS customer-service reps are authorized to cut a check for damages to a customer shipment without going through standard procedures if the representative deems it necessary to retain a customer's good will.

Today, our drivers are empowered to set up new customer accounts and to spend an additional half-hour a week talking to customers about their business needs.

In effect, by doling out both authority and accountability, employees can become owners of their own specialized area of the company.

And, like owners, they begin to see a direct link between performance and rewards.

At UPS, that means we reward employees strictly on performance. It also means that we promote people from within, and provide them with very flexible career paths that leverage their personal strengths and don't necessarily follow a straight line.

That's why you can walk the halls of UPS and find marketing professionals who used to be engineers, HR people who used to be in operations, and finance folks who once were in marketing.

The senior management team I work with directly every day all started their careers on the front lines of the company — many of them as drivers.

Another important way we foster a sense of ownership is by giving employees a financial stake in the company.

In fact, until 1999's Initial Public Offering (IPO) of our stock, UPS was owned entirely by employees, retirees and heirs.

Any UPS employee can own shares in UPS. Today—even after the IPO—the majority of the company is owned by that employee base.

Give someone a financial stake and a voice in the business, combine that with a sense of trust and autonomy, and extraordinary things can happen to an organization.

It's a formula that I believe is probably our company's single greatest competitive advantage.

The second people principle, "Walk a mile in the customer's shoes," is also a natural outgrowth of a culture of ownership. Actually, in the case of our drivers, it's more like 1,000 miles, because that's the average distance some of them walk each year.

We ask our people to do more than just think like a customer.

We want to embed ourselves in our customers' business. In essence, we're asking our employees "to be the customer."

It's a mindset that leads employees to organize their jobs and their work processes around the stated and unstated needs of the customer.

You can't think like a customer until you know what the customer's thinking.

That means putting in place formal and informal means of assessing customer needs and their level of satisfaction with your service.

At the informal level, UPS drivers serve as excellent conduits of communication between UPS and our customers.

We've also established a series of more formal ways of keeping our ear to the marketplace.

Chief among them is our quarterly CSI—or Customer Satisfaction Index.

The CSI is an ongoing, comprehensive survey conducted by a third party of customers in every UPS region and district.

Customers and prospects are asked to comment on everything from our product line and pricing to billing, tracking, claims handling—even company image.

The CSI gives us a series of snapshots of the changing marketplace—what's important to customers, and what we should work on to satisfy their needs.

A section of the CSI asks customers about their satisfaction with our package-car drivers. I'm proud that our drivers consistently average the highest scores in the industry.

They rate high on qualities like professionalism and courtesy, being knowledgeable and responsive, showing concern for customers, maintaining good relationships and knowing a customer's business.

Since the UPS driver is the most visible aspect of our culture, and one of the chief stewards of the brand, it's critical they make a positive impression on our customers.

Embedding yourself in your customer's businesses extends beyond just listening to them. It also means earning their loyalty.

And that leads us to principle number three: spreading your loyalties. Spreading your loyalties means companies need to earn loyalty from their employees and, in turn, expect employees to earn the loyalty of their customers.

Imagine a workplace where employees feel the same sense of loyalty to their customers as they do to their employer.

A study of nearly 3,000 workers by the Hudson Institute and Walker Information revealed that American companies aren't doing a very good job of fostering employee loyalty.

Only 24 percent of employees say they are "truly loyal" to their employers and plan to stay with them for at least two years.

Survey respondents didn't point to obvious issues like pay and job satisfaction. Instead, they said employers are failing on the softer issues like concern, fairness and trust.

Fifty-six percent of employees surveyed said their employers fail to show concern for them; 45 percent said their companies fail to treat them fairly.

We as business leaders have to do a better job of earning the loyalty of our employees. Only then can we reasonably expect that our employees will extend that same kind of loyalty to our customers.

I'm not suggesting we have all the answers at UPS when it comes to employee loyalty. But we have been very fortunate over the years in retaining an extremely low turnover rate among full-time employees.

In fact, it's about four percent, which definitely runs counter to most trends today.

I've already outlined some of the reasons we've been successful here—giving people ownership, autonomy and flexibility.

But there's another important element working to our advantage, and that is our Employee Relations Index (ERI). This is a twice-annual survey of employee attitudes, feelings and perceptions. It includes all aspects of work, including relationships with peers, managers, and customers—and even viewpoints on senior management's abilities.

It's all voluntary and, of course, anonymous. Every year, over 300,000 UPS employees take part in the survey.

As you can imagine, the results not only give you an enlightening and intimate pulse on the company, but they also provide a platform for creating meaningful change.

Often the findings are put to use in the forms of new initiatives, processes and policies that have direct bearing on working at UPS.

It was through the ERI, for instance, that we found out that drivers wanted to spend more time with customers, to better explain to them the services we can provide to help their businesses grow.

We, in turn, developed an initiative, which I touched on earlier, that gives our drivers the freedom to do just that.

Happy employees make happy customers, right? Well, most of the time. But not always. In fact, when it comes to customer loyalty, many companies, I believe, are asking the wrong question.

They ask: "How do I make customers loyal to my company?"

What they should be asking is: "How do I make the company loyal to my customers?"

A flipping of nouns makes all the difference.

If we're worried about making our customers loyal to us, we tend to implement policies that are well intentioned but rather short-term and superficial.

For instance, we might institute frequent-user programs. Or include a discount to land a long-term contract. Or invite customers to golf resorts for thinly veiled business conferences.

On the other hand, if we're more concerned with how our company can demonstrate loyalty to our customers, we're more inclined to make fundamental changes in our business processes to accommodate our customers.

Changes like making our information systems readily available to our customers. And letting our customers control the flow of the supply chain.

We're also more inclined to care whether our customers are truly satisfied or not.

I can tell you from personal experience that if you follow these three people principles:

Letting your employees be the boss, walking a mile in the customer's shoes, and spreading your loyalties, then your customers will usually go out of their way to demonstrate their loyalty to you.

Every week, I get letters from customers praising UPS employees who have gone the extra mile to provide exceptional service—or occasionally even save a life.

Some of the letters make you smile. Some of them make you choke up. But all of them make you appreciate the true impact of people living out the company culture and the company brand.

Like Donald Rawls, a UPS driver of 17 years in Beaumont, Texas, who's been known to go into work on his Saturday day off just to retrieve a special package for one of his grateful business customers in downtown Beaumont.

He routinely gets invited to several company Christmas parties, because the businesses on his route think of him as one of their own employees.

But let me tell you, Donald Rawls is pure UPS!

And then there's Rene D'Augustino, a UPS driver whose route includes the Aberdeen Proving Ground in Maryland.

A few years ago, right before Christmas, Rene demonstrated the "Do the Right Thing" culture we emphasize so much at UPS.

She was on her rounds at Aberdeen, which was fairly empty because most personnel were on Christmas break, when she noticed an overnight letter with nothing but a name on the label.

There was no specific address, which meant she had no idea where the soldier was located on the sprawling base.

She asked around as to whether anyone recognized the name on the label, but people just shook their heads.

Not to be stymied, Rene called her UPS supervisor to ask if she could open the letter to look for some more clues as to the recipient's whereabouts.

To her surprise, all she saw inside was a handwritten yellow note and a money order.

The note read: "Make me happy. Come home for Christmas. Love, Mom."

Realizing that the money order was intended to pay for the soldier's trip home, Rene knew she had to keep trying.

She drove to the home of one of the Marine captains and asked him if he recognized the name.

He didn't, but he agreed to open up his office and check on his computer.

Sure enough, he located the young Marine's assigned barracks.

Accompanied by a Sergeant-at-Arms, she entered the barracks, but she couldn't locate the Marine. Another soldier told her that the Marine had gone to the Rec Center.

Rene proceeded quickly to the Rec Center and asked around until she was directed to the Marine.

The young military man was sitting on a couch, surrounded by a big pile of movie rentals.

He apparently was getting ready to start a movie marathon to get him through a lonely Christmas.

Rene yelled out, "I've got something for you!" and handed the opened package to the surprised Marine.

He read the note, saw the money order, grinned and jumped off the couch to hug his UPS driver.

He started running out the door to leave, letter in hand, when he turned back to Rene and asked her one more favor.

Could she return all those movies to the Rec Center rental counter for him?

You don't even need a face-to-face encounter with one of our people to feel it.

When you see one of our vehicles rolling along the streets of your town, or our shield on a Web site, or one of our brown-tailed planes at an airport, you feel connected to our company, and through us you feel a meaningful connection to the world.

That's what a great brand does.

In the days following September 11, 2001, folks said it was a great comfort to see those brown trucks rolling once again down the streets of lower Manhattan.

After days of shock and disbelief, the world was working again. Ordinary people were doing their jobs. Life was going on.

Those deliveries were resumed under great duress, to serve an area that was for all intents and purposes a war zone.

They were supervised by the UPS district manager for Manhattan whose actions on the morning of September 11 revealed our culture and brand at is very best.

When he learned of the attacks on the World Trade Center, he made two instinctive decisions right away.

He ordered an immediate accounting of every UPS employee's whereabouts.

And he ordered everyone in the facility to go through all the packages in the building and on our vehicles and find all the ones addressed to hospitals, doctors or pharmacies so they could be delivered right away.

Are our employees safe? How can we help our customers?

Those were the UPS manager's sole concerns.

It's in the culture. It's in the brand.

Living out the brand promise doesn't come solely from mission statements.

Or product differentiation.

Or lower prices.

Or snappy logos.

It flows from the intersection of culture and people.

It flows from the living, breathing brand.

The events of recent years have caused all of us in business to take a much closer look at what we do, how we do it, and why we do it.

I consider myself fortunate to have learned the ropes of business from some extremely principled managers at UPS.

As our company approaches its second century, we have to balance a new set of business realities with our time-honored values and principles.

I'm confident those timeless values are as relevant in today's time-scarce world as they were when Jim Casey was first shaped by them.

Actually, I know it in my heart. Because, deep down I, too, believe I am a better person for having worked at UPS.

———

Michael L. Eskew
CHAIRMAN AND CHIEF EXECUTIVE OFFICER
UPS

Mike Eskew serves as chairman and chief executive officer of UPS. Under Eskew's direction, UPS is expanding its capabilities into new lines of business that complement the company's global package delivery operations.

A native of Vincennes, Indiana, Eskew graduated from Purdue University with a bachelor's degree in industrial engineering. He also completed the Advanced Management Program at the Wharton School of Business. Eskew began his UPS career in 1972 as an industrial engineering manager in Indiana. His advancement continued in various positions of increasing responsibility, including time with UPS operations in Germany and with UPS Airlines.

In 1994, Eskew was named corporate vice president for industrial engineering. Two years later he became group vice president for engineering. Eskew has served as a member of the UPS board of directors since 1998.

In 1999, he was named executive vice president and a year later was given the additional title of vice chairman. Eskew held this position prior to assuming his current role on January 1, 2002.

In addition to his corporate responsibilities, Eskew is a trustee of The UPS Foundation and The Annie E. Casey Foundation, which is the country's largest foundation dedicated to disadvantaged youth. In 2003, Eskew was appointed to the President's Export Council. He also serves on the board of directors of the 3M Corporation and is a member of The Business Roundtable.

UPS

UPS is the world's largest package delivery company and a global leader in supply chain services, offering an extensive range of options for synchronizing the movement of goods, information and funds. Every day, UPS serves more than 200 countries and territories worldwide. In 2002, UPS delivered approximately 3.4 billion packages and documents. Approximately 360,000 employees worldwide serve 7.9 million customers daily.

UPS was founded in 1907 by 19-year-old James E. ("Jim") Casey, who borrowed $100 from a friend to establish the American Messenger Company in Seattle, Washington. UPS has grown into a $30 billion corporation by focusing on the goal of enabling commerce around the world. Today, UPS is a global company with one of the most recognized and admired brands in the world.

The company has won many recent awards, including the inaugural American Business Award for Most Innovative Company for the technical advancements of its Worldport global air hub in Louisville, Kentucky. In February 2003, *Fortune* magazine named UPS the World's Most Admired company in its industry. It was the fifth consecutive year that UPS has achieved this distinction. In March 2003, the Native American Business Alliance named UPS "Corporation of the Year," citing the company's strong commitment to supplier diversity and support of Native American business initiatives. UPS is headquartered in Atlanta, Georgia.

For more information, visit: www.ups.com.
Stock Symbol: UPS

J. Wayne Leonard

CHIEF EXECUTIVE OFFICER
ENTERGY CORPORATION

"[Create] an environment where every employee feels respected, appreciated, and that they truly make a difference."

– J. Wayne Leonard

IMAGINE

"No man can wear one face to himself, and another to the multitude, without finally getting bewildered as to which may be true."
— *Nathaniel Hawthorne*

When I became the chief executive officer of Entergy Corporation in 1998, I asked employees to imagine our then-troubled company as a winner. But first, I had to redefine what winning was. Financial success? Yes, of course, but that was only part of the answer.

We had to imagine winning not based on the bottom line alone and not built on strict adherence to rules.

We had to imagine success built every day on a culture that placed our most basic values (e.g., safety above all else) over short-term financial results or expediency in resolving problems; a culture built on principles and values that respected all stakeholders, including all forms of life.

It had to be an environment where every employee felt respected, appreciated and that they truly made a difference. It meant eliminating bullying and moral cowardice and creating an environment more perfect, more just, than you ever find in the outside world.

And while many were skeptical, most took the challenge. While we didn't change the world overnight, five years later our employee survey results show the progress we have made. Employee job satisfaction is up 50 percent and twice as many employees believe we are providing quality customer service.

American business faces new regulations and extreme scrutiny in the wake of the accounting scandals that brought the unprecedented fall of WorldCom and Enron, among others. The public has grown frustrated and cynical about business. In many circles, CEO is a pejorative term.

The electricity industry was not immune to these travails and has been the subject of numerous investigations and admissions of market manipulation and fraudulent conduct. Lives and careers destroyed, all in pursuit of short-term profits.

During this period, many companies saw their stock prices collapse, or even faced bankruptcy, as the pursuit of ever increasing profits lead to taking ever-increasing risks. At the same time, Entergy did more than survive—we prospered. Our stock price hit an all-time high in 2001, then again in 2002 and 2003. Why? I believe the answer is values. These values transcended mere words and guided our actions. They guided our commitment to shareholders, customers, employees and the world we live in.

When conventional wisdom said we should use our power as a corporation solely to promote our own economic self-interest, we embraced the idea that even legal entities like corporations must have both a conscience and a soul. We supported increased environmental protection, the highest levels of safety, transparent financial reporting and good governance, and aggressively defended those in our society least able to speak for themselves—like the nation's children and our low-income customers.

By rebuilding our company on values and giving it a "soul," we were able to do more than survive the perfect storm of economic pressures and increased scrutiny and regulations that beset our industry. Our soul, our imagination, our passion for doing what is right drove us to historic success.

I personally challenged my fellow employees to live lives worthy of the unlimited opportunities we have been given through the sacrifices of the generations that preceded us, and argued that, by extension, Entergy would be not just the best-performing company in our industry, but also the best company to work for. I then challenged myself to follow their example and be as good a CEO as I was capable of in order to make this a great company. My commitment was to do my very best to create not only a high-performing company, but also a just and compassionate work environment.

Happily, the employees continue to raise the bar on me. They continually make me stretch my own expectations of what's possible to stay ahead of their actual performance. They are not timid about pointing out inconsistencies between our practices and our policies, deviations from our core values, or ways we can do better by adjusting our point of view to today's realities, or eliminating bias, of which we may not even be aware. Together, I believe we've made Entergy the best company in our industry. And we've done it without cutting any ethical corners — financially, operationally, morally or ethically.

We've tried to ensure that everyone at Entergy knows that we must exhibit the highest possible standards when it comes to integrity in absolutely everything we do. Not just every financial statement that we distribute. Not just in complying with every law on the books. Not just in how we treat people. But everything we do.

Our word has to be as good as or better than any contract we've ever written. If our own employees don't have complete faith in the integrity of the leadership of the company, then our stock price — fueled upward by employees' improved spirits and personal ownership in our "commitments" — will fall apart.

Indulge me. I want to illustrate what I'm talking about with a story from my youth in Indiana. I ran cross-country track in high school. Cross-country is a lot tougher than sprinting. It's physically punishing and mentally demanding. Runners face difficult terrain and L-shaped corners, so you have to decelerate into the corner, then accelerate back out. It takes a lot of psychological determination and a lot of physical strength to run cross-country and be really good at it.

The home team puts out the flags that set the course. One day, we were putting out the flags before the other teams got there. As we were standing there looking, we could see some flags were not parallel with each other. The course was supposed to have two "L's," two 90-degree angles. But we had more of an oval shape because the flags had been improperly aligned. Being teenagers, when no one volunteered to backtrack the 200 yards to correct our mistake, we just left it. And then, as we moved on to put out the next few flags on the course, we started thinking how much easier the course was going to be without that sharp turn.

We began rounding all of the sharp turns off a couple of feet. We didn't change the course much. We just took some of the pain out of those corners. It didn't really matter, we told ourselves, because we were going to win anyway.

That day, I think everyone on the team ran about 45 seconds faster than we'd ever run before. Our coach couldn't quit talking about it. He spoke glowingly about how proud he was of every one of us. He'd never seen a team come together and improve like that. This was going to be the team that would win the state championship. Because this was the team that had more heart than any team he'd ever coached. He never was so proud of a bunch of kids in his life.

We all kind of had our heads down and I cracked. As he was talking, I just blurted out, "We moved the flags."

He said, "Why? What? Why did you…what did you do?"

I said, "Well, we moved some of the flags in on the corners, just a few feet. We rounded off the turns."

I never saw a person go through the five stages of grieving faster than this coach did. Denial: "No way!" Anger: "I'm going to kill you!" Depression: "I'm going to kill myself!" Bargaining: "I won't say anything if you won't do it again." To acceptance: "I'm going to tell the other team, and if we have to forfeit the season, we'll forfeit the season, and we'll just end it right here."

He spent a lot of time in anger and depression. He was so disappointed in what we did. We knew what we did wasn't right, but his fury and disappointment seemed over the top at the time. What was the point? Weren't we going to beat this team whether it was one mile, or three miles? It didn't make any difference.

I don't think our relationship with that coach was ever the same again. He was personally hurt. We had violated the trust that he had in all of us. And his point—which, again, I don't think we ever got while we were in high school—was that we weren't just cheating the other team, we were cheating ourselves, because we tried to take the easy way out. He could barely look at us. Not because we were cheats (which we were), but because he was a person of such integrity that he felt like a fraud himself. He was there not to make us great runners, but better people, to teach us the importance of integrity and the value of hard work and effort. And obviously he had failed.

I am sure over the years most of us have come to understand the importance of that day—that cutting corners never lasts; it never works. When the game is on the line, if you've spent your life cutting corners, then you're going to inevitably come up short, either physically or mentally. You live every day afraid you'll be found out for the fraud you are. And worse still, you know in your heart you cannot completely trust even yourself.

There is a new chapter to this story. Today, my three daughters run cross-country. Last year, one of them had a pre-season high school race. The contest was not sanctioned, just a practice run, so they could test their fitness level against other teams instead of each other.

My youngest daughter, who was 11 years old at the time, was planning to run cross-country for her middle school. I asked the coaches if it would be OK if she ran with my other daughters since she was going to be there anyway. The organizers were absolutely dead-set against it, but they really couldn't say no because it wasn't an official race.

Against the coaches' better judgment, I brought her along. She had run in AAU meets, and I knew she was pretty good. Since these coaches had tried so hard to dissuade me from allowing my 11-year-old from running with the older girls, I wanted more than anything to prove these guys wrong. It became personal to me.

It was a two-mile race. They came around at the mile, and she was third out of about 100. She was 25 yards behind the two lead girls, within catching distance of them. I screamed at her, "You've got to close it by a mile and a half, and then out-kick them!" I can't tell you how excited I was (she has a great finishing kick) at the very thought that she might win this race—coached by her Dad, I might add—and beat all these high school girls after the coaches had been so adamant that she didn't belong in this race.

When they came down the final stretch, nothing had changed. The two lead girls were still ahead. My daughter was still 25 yards behind them. She hadn't moved one yard in that final mile. And that's how she finished—third.

Everyone was in awe of her accomplishment. Everyone but me. I couldn't believe it. She didn't even try. As much as I coerced her and tried to coach her on how to win this race, there she was, still in the same place she had been. In my mind, of course, at that moment, the difference between third and winning was everything.

I didn't want a moral victory here! I wanted the bragging rights associated with winning this race! I was all over her. Why didn't you try? What were you thinking? Don't you even care? She kept trying to explain to me what went wrong, but I wasn't really listening. Finally, she got the story out. She "had" closed the gap. At a mile and a half, she was even with the older girls, but the coaches had told all the runners when they walked the course that they were not to go from this flag to that flag, but from this flag around a tree first. They weren't to cut between the flags, they were to go around the tree.

But when they got to that point, which was far removed from any spectator or official's sight, the two lead girls went from flag to flag, but she went around the tree because that's what the coaches had told her to do. It was more than 25 yards longer, and it cost her the race.

Her sister, who was running about 100 yards behind her, verified her story. Everyone else went around the tree from then on because they all remembered that was the course that they had laid out.

What do you say when she tells you that story after you've yelled at her? Good for you? You did the right thing? I'm proud of you? That's what I should have said. That's what I wish I had said. Instead, what I said was, basically, "That's no excuse for 'losing.'" But in tears, she reminded me of the story I'd told her about my old team, about how cutting corners or cheating never works and doesn't pay off.

It was like a knife through my heart.

Thirty-six years later I hadn't learned a thing from when I was in high school. It wasn't even a real race and, more importantly, it wasn't even about me. I was destroying the trust my own daughter had in me by arguing a point that I didn't even believe—that finishing "first" is all that matters.

That story, I think, is applicable to the credibility problem American business has been suffering. Regardless of how well-intentioned we might think we are, sometimes we're all still human. We're not immune. In a moment of weakness or thoughtlessness, we might make a call that could haunt us forever. It won't necessarily be a big thing. Big decisions usually get challenged and weighed. Big decisions are made by a lot of people in the bright lights. But character and integrity are defined by how we act when no one is watching; when we have no reason to believe we will be caught or found out.

When it comes to ethics, it doesn't make any difference whether it's a big decision or a small decision. It's either right or it's wrong. You can't cut corners. And people judge you by what's in your heart. Sometimes, even the smallest things reveal more about us than the big things, like it did about me that day.

Success breeds arrogance. Arrogance doesn't begin to describe my shameless behavior that day nor does the word "sorry" describe the regrets I have had since.

So when we in business—or in any human endeavor—talk about being the best, we'd better understand and keep in our mind the humility that it takes to accept the fact that being the best isn't always defined by leader boards, quarterly profits or personal wealth.

The United States is the richest, most powerful nation on earth. We are the last remaining superpower in the world. We are the only economic, political and military force on the face of the earth that can ensure that dark forces do not overcome our world. But the only, absolute only, real threat to our civilization, in my mind, isn't from those dark forces. It's the potential, slow self-destruction of the United States.

This country—and certainly its corporations and entrepreneurs—have achieved incredible, unimagined things over the last 200 years. We have unquestioned world leadership. But, as William James said, "As individuals, we typically live lives inferior to ourselves." We individually are capable of so much more, and collectively, we are capable of even greater achievements. And we have the responsibility to keep on doing it.

Our company, Entergy, has had extraordinary success the last five years. But it is clearly time for us — and for all of American business — to raise our expectations, both of ourselves and the world we inhabit. It is time to imagine something more.

Just imagine.

Imagine a world where confidence in American business is fully restored, where companies have a bond of trust with both their shareholders and customers. Imagine a safer workplace. So safe, accidents never happen. Imagine no need for customers to complain or regulators to watch over us. Imagine what it would be like if we had a workforce as diverse as the population we serve, and continuing education and training programs as good as those any university can provide. And imagine the reduction in stress if we had the most flexible work schedules possible, if we had job sharing, if we had on-site daycare, if we had work-at-home programs available for everyone — things we can not only imagine, but also make happen on our own.

But dream bigger. Imagine what it would be like if financial aid was widely available to those disadvantaged from ill health, age, or just simply from bad luck. Imagine if everyone had health insurance and access to quality healthcare. Imagine the world that we could create if every single year, we in the industrial sector lowered our pollution emissions. Imagine a society where good public education (equal to any private education money can buy) began during the most active stage of a child's development, when the intellectual potential, personality traits and social behavior skills are most affected — before the age of five. Imagine what would happen if kids started school not at six, but two years earlier. What if they started at four, when their brain is most able to develop?

Would good jobs be plentiful then? Would poverty be the exception? Would crime be reduced? Can you imagine that?

Imagine children all over growing up, wanting to join American companies not because they can turn a quick dollar but because here, you don't have to choose between being a good person and being a good employee.

Imagine the citizens; imagine the children, employees, shareowners having faith in American business as a genuine catalyst for societal change. Imagine knowing that companies can use the strength of their success not only to provide for investors, but also in the service of others, including future generations (who will be our customers and employees).

Imagine the real success that is at our fingertips if we all, as the Club of Budapest has proposed, lived in a way that others can also live, or did not act in a way that endangered the life of fellow human beings on earth.

Imagine that.

———

J. Wayne Leonard
CHIEF EXECUTIVE OFFICER
ENTERGY CORPORATION

J. Wayne Leonard became Entergy's chief executive officer on January 1, 1999. He joined Entergy in April 1998 as president and chief operating officer of the company's domestic business, and he assumed additional responsibility for international operations in August 1998. Under Leonard's leadership, Entergy created a new vision, strategy, organizational structure and corporate culture.

Leonard is a thought leader in the industry, having published articles on environmental issues and competitive market structure alternatives. Under his leadership, Entergy became the first U.S. utility to make a voluntary commitment to stabilize its power plant emissions of carbon dioxide. Entergy is a founding member of the Pew Center for Global Climate Change and a member of the Partnership for Climate Action. Leonard is also a champion of low-income customers, having initiated the first Low-Income Summit in 1999. In 2002, Leonard was given the Sister Pat Kelley Award for Achievement by the National Fuel Funds Network (NFFN).

Leonard began his utility career at PSI Energy, where he was senior vice president and chief financial officer from 1989 to 1994. Upon the merger to create Cinergy in 1994, he was named group vice president and chief financial officer. In 1996 he became president of Cinergy's Energy Commodities Strategic Business Unit and president of Cinergy Capital and Trading.

Leonard earned a Bachelor's accounting degree in 1973 from Ball State University and an MBA in 1987 from Indiana University. He is a member of the American Institute of Certified Public Accountants. He was the 2002 Ball State University College of Business Hall of Fame recipient.

ENTERGY CORPORATION

Entergy Corporation is an integrated energy company engaged primarily in electric power production, retail distribution operations, energy marketing and trading, and gas transportation. Entergy owns and operates power plants with about 30,000 megawatts of electric generating capacity. The company is the second-largest nuclear generator in the United States. Entergy delivers electricity to 2.6 million utility customers in Arkansas, Louisiana, Mississippi and Texas. Entergy has annual revenues exceeding $8 billion and more than 15,000 employees.

Through Entergy-Koch, LP, Entergy is also a leading provider of wholesale energy marketing and trading services, as well as an operator of natural gas pipeline and storage facilities.

Entergy's integrated strategy is to focus on customer service and reliability in its core utility business and to focus on its core capabilities—nuclear generation and wholesale energy service—in pursuit of growth. The company applies a simple set of values to its business operations: focus on customers, treat people with respect, and act with integrity. Its philanthropic vision is a natural outgrowth of those values: "Lighting the way for a brighter future by investing in our communities."

Some of Entergy's recent awards and distinctions include: listing on the Dow Jones Sustainability Index for 2003 and 2004; *Fortune* magazine's America's Most Admired Companies list (2003); an Edison Electric Institute Index Award (2003); a "Stevie" (2003) from American Business Awards for "Best Communications Team" for its work during hurricanes Isidore and Lili in 2002. Entergy's headquarters is in New Orleans, Louisiana.

For more information, visit: www.entergy.com.
Stock Symbol: ETR

Edward M. Liddy

CHAIRMAN, PRESIDENT AND CHIEF EXECUTIVE OFFICER
THE ALLSTATE CORPORATION

*"Open, honest, two-way communication is
the bedrock of ethical standards."*

– Edward M. Liddy

INVEST IN TRUTHFUL COMMUNICATION

Allstate is a company with two things at its core: people and capital. With the right people and sound stewardship of our financial resources, we deliver on a promise—to give our customers peace of mind by protecting their property and their lives, and to help them achieve financial security. Intrinsic to the promise that "You're in Good Hands With Allstate"® is an ethical foundation built on truthful communication with our customers, employees, agencies and shareholders.

The Principles at the core of the Arthur W. Page Society are all practiced at Allstate, as I expect they are at every well-run U.S. company. But for me, the Page Principle that stands out the most is the first one: Tell the truth. Let the public know what's happening and provide an accurate picture of the company's character, ideals and practices. We apply this principle as much internally as we do externally.

At Allstate, we invest in truthful communication in a multitude of ways, through our people and through our processes. The result is a culture in which people are free to express their opinions, challenge the status quo and help guide the company with a sound moral compass. It begins with setting expectations.

As CEO, I make it clear to my senior management team that integrity is a number-one priority. Ours is a business based on trust. Breaching that trust would jeopardize our very existence. Every day, in thousands of interactions with customers, Allstate people hold the success and reputation of the company in their hands. No one's looking over their shoulder; they decide to do the right thing. They do so because they're caring, compassionate and ethical people. They also know that doing the right thing is expected at Allstate. Throughout the company, leadership is charged with modeling ethical behavior and reinforcing that anything to the contrary will not be tolerated. Employees are encouraged to insist on ethical behavior from their peers, regardless of rank.

I believe that open, honest, two-way communication is the bedrock of ethical standards. How much time you invest in communication is equally important. An independent study showed that Allstate annually devotes an estimated two million man-hours to communication in all forms—face-to-face, electronic and print. These hours not only

INVEST IN TRUTHFUL COMMUNICATION

reflect corporate and departmental communications, but also local communication efforts throughout the company by individual units and offices that dedicate resources to communication.

Employees are introduced to our culture of communication from the start with something we call the Allstate Partnership *(see Appendix)*. Like most companies, Allstate has a code of ethics. On a yearly basis, employees are required to acknowledge that they've read and understand it. But as change increasingly became the norm in the business world, we knew employees wanted to know what was expected of them on a day-to-day basis; and, in turn, what they should expect of their company. So we created the Allstate Partnership.

All employees receive a copy of the Allstate Partnership when they're hired. The Partnership is a set of mutual expectations for success. Its goal is to create a high-performance, supportive work environment that will lead to company success and employees' personal and professional fulfillment. It covers topics such as skill development, learning opportunities, pay, career goals, personal responsibility, and the balance of work and personal life. Dialogue with leaders around the Partnership is part of every employee's formal evaluation. It helps set the tone for an employer-employee relationship built on honesty and mutual responsibility.

Access to leaders is especially critical during times of change. When I came to Allstate from Sears, Roebuck and Co. in 1994 as president and chief operating officer, it was a departure from Allstate culture to tap an "outsider" for senior leadership. (Today we often seek, when appropriate, the talents and experiences of business leaders outside the company.) So the chairman and I embarked on a round of visits to

Allstate offices across the country to introduce ourselves. Recently, we reorganized our two main business units, including naming new heads of each (both already Allstate senior executives). The two new leaders not only traveled the country to meet with as many of their employees as possible, they also established e-mail boxes solely for soliciting feedback, concerns and questions—personally replying to every inquiry.

The Allstate Partnership states that employees should expect the company to promote an environment that encourages open and constructive dialogue. We accomplish this in many ways, from encouraging an open-door policy for leadership to town-hall-style meetings that I conduct at office locations in and around our Chicago-area headquarters, as well as across the country. At these meetings, there is no agenda. There are no rules. Employees are free to ask me and other company managers in attendance about anything that's on their minds. And they do! They're not bashful about asking tough questions concerning jobs, company strategy or why certain decisions were made. I know that many of my peers adopt the same approach. The importance of meeting face to face with those at the front line of our business cannot be overestimated. Giving straight answers to straight questions reinforces for our people the value that we place on telling the truth.

Open and constructive dialogue is also critical with our Allstate agents. They operate as independent contractors and have been the cornerstone of our business for decades. They are the face and voice of Allstate in their communities. To further improve communication and our relationship with them, we recently established a National Advisory Board, made up of agents and other producers from around

INVEST IN TRUTHFUL COMMUNICATION

the country. The board was developed with agents to give them a greater voice and to improve planning and implementing of business decisions that affect them.

As CEO, I literally have dozens of planned communication opportunities with employees, Allstate agencies, analysts, community groups and other constituencies throughout the year. For example, I host quarterly employee communication meetings that are broadcast to Allstate offices around the country. At these meetings, timed to follow our earnings releases, our Chief Financial Officer reviews financial results in a way that gets behind the numbers, including key measures that help our employees understand the link between the results, their performance and company strategy. Other company initiatives also are discussed, and a detailed summary of the meeting is posted on the company intranet for those unable to view the meeting, and to reinforce key messages.

I believe that when employees are well-informed and understand the business and their roles, it shows in their performance—and in their commitment to the company and its standards.

While open communication is encouraged at all levels, we realize there are times when raising a particular issue with immediate management may be uncomfortable. For these occasions, employees have an alternative, confidential resolution process available to them. This process includes a telephone line that's staffed 24 hours a day, seven days a week. Called the Resolution Line, it can be used to report issues related to Allstate compliance with local, state and/or federal laws and regulations, and work-related concerns. In 2002, less than 1 percent of Allstate's approximately 40,000 employees called the Resolution Line—a clear indication of the comfort level in resolving issues with immediate management.

Compliance is a significant task in the heavily regulated business of insurance. We dedicate many resources and processes to compliance, and we also ask our employees to be vigilant in identifying and reporting possible noncompliance with laws and regulations that impact our company.

More and more, Allstate employees work in teams that cross departmental and functional lines. This approach brings together differing skills, styles and viewpoints that reflect the current business environment. People aren't afraid to say, "No, I don't agree with that. I have a better idea." This aspect of diversity helps drive our success. I believe that the free exchange of ideas and acceptance of alternate viewpoints is healthy for any business and helps promote candor and honesty that drive ethical behavior.

We expect that same honesty when it comes to measuring the effectiveness of leadership. In an ethical environment, leadership is a two-way street. Leaders must be held accountable by the people they lead. One of the ways we accomplish this is with a process called QLMS.

QLMS (Quality Leadership Measurement System) is a twice-yearly, company-wide survey that measures employee perceptions of the work environment, the effectiveness of leadership and behaviors that directly impact our business results. QLMS helps me—and all leadership—stay in touch with the work environment. It helps us identify opportunities for improvement.

Participation in QLMS is voluntary and confidential—results are reported on a "work group" basis. Participation rates historically have been above 90 percent. The results tell us that, overall, leadership is doing a good job in maintaining a supportive work environment.

INVEST IN TRUTHFUL COMMUNICATION

On a question specifically about ethics in the Spring 2003 survey, 95 percent of employees participating agreed that leadership has clearly communicated that unethical behavior will not be tolerated. While pleased with these results, we're always working to make them better.

Ethical standards—and telling the truth—took on a whole new dimension for Allstate when, after more than 60 years as a private company, we went public in June 1993. Countless new rules and regulations that govern public companies were now ours to learn, adapt to and follow. Employees were challenged to think like owners. They embraced their new role and have helped make our company more vital than ever. They helped drive change when we needed it most to remain competitive, all the while sticking to the highest ethical standards. At a time when some other companies lost their way, Allstate—led by a strong senior management team and independent board of directors—maintained its sound moral compass regarding ethics, accounting and corporate governance.

An extraordinary amount of attention has been focused on corporate governance, driven by recent high-profile corporate scandals. Lawmakers and regulators have raised the bar on corporate governance processes, including the independence standards to which corporate directors should be held. Allstate's board has undergone a strenuous review of its corporate governance to ensure that it continues to meet the highest standards of ethical corporate best practices, including the independence of its members and nominees. The board has established governance guidelines and reviews them regularly to ensure that they remain current and consistent with best practices.

That said, I believe that corporate governance is no one set of "check-the-box" criteria. It is the culture of ethics that the board sets, the moral tone of the organization. There is no one-size-fits-all corporate governance formula. A sound corporate governance program must include a certain amount of freedom for the board to make innovative decisions that an ethically sound business requires. That's what I feel we have at Allstate. "Nodding heads" have no place in The Allstate Corporation boardroom.

Communication is the engine that drives good corporate governance. Our governance processes are available to anyone—they're clearly detailed on our Web site (www.allstate.com). In addition, we go beyond accounting and SEC requirements to make our financial disclosures as timely, meaningful and transparent as possible, so investors and analysts alike get the most accurate picture of company performance. A recent redesign of our quarterly earnings statement and investor supplement drew praise from the tough analyst crowd. In fact, after a recent earnings conference call, several analysts said the release was so thorough that they didn't have any questions!

At a time when corporate governance practices are under intense scrutiny, Allstate is receiving high marks. In 2002, the Investor Responsibility Research Center, an independent research group, rated our board of directors among the top 10 most independent boards in its study of S&P "super" 1500 companies. This Washington, D.C. research firm based its findings on its own definition of independence, which is stricter than existing and proposed regulations. Our corporate governance practices also are reviewed by Institutional Shareholder

Services, which takes into account numerous objective factors relating to the company's overall governance processes. Its July 30, 2003, analysis rates Allstate as outperforming 96.9 percent of the companies in the S&P 500 index and 97.7 percent of its peer insurance industry group. That same month, another group, Governance Metrics International, ranked Allstate as one of only 17 firms worldwide with the highest possible governance score, using more than 600 pieces of data in seven categories.

The vast majority of U.S. corporations operate with high ethical standards. Unethical behavior is the exception. But it only takes a few high-profile incidents to cast a shadow over the entire American business landscape. For decades, Allstate has modeled ethical behavior in Corporate America. We've lived up to our promise that "You're In Good Hands" and have been rewarded with millions of loyal customers and a leadership position in our industry and society. Today it's my privilege to lead a company that helps set the tone for ethical behavior by investing in telling the truth through its people, its processes and its culture.

Edward M. Liddy
CHAIRMAN, PRESIDENT AND CHIEF EXECUTIVE OFFICER
THE ALLSTATE CORPORATION

Edward M. Liddy is chairman, president and chief executive officer of The Allstate Corporation and Allstate Insurance Company, the largest publicly held personal lines insurance company in the United States. Prior to becoming chairman on January 1, 1999, he served as president and chief operating officer.

Social responsibility and performance are a proud part of the Allstate culture. The Allstate Foundation, established in 1952, provides funding for organizations that focus on three core areas: building safe vital communities; fostering economic empowerment; and teaching tolerance, inclusion and diversity. In 2003, and 2004, The Allstate Foundation will provide more than $30 million to nonprofit organizations across the country.

Liddy serves on the board of directors of 3M Company, The Kroger Co. and The Goldman Sachs Group, Inc. He is active in industry affairs, serving as chairman of the Insurance Institute for Highway Safety and on the board of the Insurance Information Institute. He is also a member of the Financial Services Forum, The Business Roundtable, and Catalyst, the leading nonprofit organization working to advance women in business.

Liddy also is involved in charitable and civic endeavors. He is chairman of the Boys & Girls Clubs of America and serves on the board of Northwestern Memorial HealthCare. He is also a trustee of Northwestern University and Chicago's Museum of Science and Industry.

A native of New Brunswick, New Jersey, Liddy is a 1968 graduate of Catholic University of America and in 1972 earned a master's degree in business administration from George Washington University.

THE ALLSTATE CORPORATION

The Allstate Corporation is the nation's largest publicly held personal lines insurer. Widely known through its "You're In Good Hands With Allstate®" slogan, Allstate provides insurance products to more than 16 million households and has approximately 12,300 exclusive agents and financial specialists in the U.S. and Canada. Encompass℠ and Deerbrook® Insurance brand property and casualty products are sold exclusively through independent agents.

Allstate Financial Group includes the businesses that provide life and supplemental insurance, retirement, banking and investment products through distribution channels that include Allstate agents, independent agents, financial institutions and broker-dealers.

Social responsibility and performance are a proud part of the Allstate culture. The Allstate Foundation, established in 1952, provides funding for organizations that focus on three core areas: building safe and vital communities; fostering economic empowerment; and teaching tolerance, inclusion and diversity. In 2003 and 2004, The Allstate Foundation will provide more than $30 million to nonprofit organizations across the country.

Founded in 1931 as part of Sears, Roebuck and Co., Allstate became a publicly traded company in 1993. At the time, its initial public offering was the largest in U.S. history. In 1995, Allstate became a totally independent company. The company is headquartered in Northbrook, Illinois.

For more information, visit: www.allstate.com.
Stock Symbol: ALL

William C. Weldon

CHAIRMAN OF THE BOARD AND CHIEF EXECUTIVE OFFICER
JOHNSON & JOHNSON

"Ethical decision-making requires more than integrity."
– William C. Weldon

OUR CREDO: WHO WE ARE

The crisis of confidence in business today threatens the fortunes of all corporations, even those that have grown through principled action. Brought on by a just a handful of people, the crisis has rightly fueled calls for increased transparency.

Johnson & Johnson aims to be a leader in being open and honest about how we operate our business. As you continue to learn more about how we conduct ourselves, you may wonder if our commitment to do the right thing will deliver the kinds of returns you rightfully expect from the world's most broadly-based health care products company.

At some level, logical or emotional, you probably have been convinced that companies do well by doing good. If we've done our job right — and I think we have — you know Our Credo says our last responsibility is to shareholders.

Now, some will point out that at the time Our Credo was written, the only shareholder was its author, who respectfully subordinated his needs to the greater good. But no matter what the motivation, Johnson & Johnson has, over the years, used the order of constituencies as something of a moral compass. Our shareholders come after our customers, our employees and our communities. We'll invest in all of those areas and make decisions for their benefit, before we consider the impact to our share price. By operating in a way that builds deep, long-term trust, we deliver great value. I'm taking this opportunity to tell you more about how we do that.

This approach is built on the notion that if you do a good job in fulfilling responsibilities to customers, employees and the community, then the shareholder will come out all right. And over time, our strong Credo values have indeed charted a course that has proved successful. We've proven that we're "built to last," to borrow a term from author Jim Collins. We've delivered sales growth in each of 69 consecutive years, and 17 consecutive years of double-digit growth in sales and earnings. We've issued a dividend to our shareholders every quarter since 1944, with dividend increases for 41 years. For example, a shareholder who purchased one share of Johnson & Johnson stock on September 25, 1944, would now have 2,500 shares, worth about $127,125.

We focus on managing the company for the long term. That focus sustains our performance because it emphasizes investment for the future and the importance of true innovation. We make major enhancements and additions to our facilities and to our information technology infrastructure so as to accelerate our ability to bring new products to market—to deliver on the promise of technology.

We sustain our consistent performance through a culture that is based on a strong system of values. We expect the highest standards of ethical behavior throughout or global organization, achieved when each of us assumes responsibility for leadership and integrity.

This year, we are celebrating the 60th anniversary of Our Credo. It was born out of a drought of confidence in corporations in this country: the Great Depression. General Robert Wood Johnson, CEO at the time, wrote "Try Reality," a pamphlet that asked business to adopt a "new industrial philosophy." He said, "Industry only has the right to succeed where it performs a real economic service and is a true social asset." And he went on to specify and outline the responsibilities a company has to different stakeholders.

It was Johnson's view that if companies were going to be allowed by governments and society to operate in a free-market system, unencumbered by burdensome laws and regulations, then they were going to have to act in socially responsible and acceptable ways.

A few years later he expanded this view into a document we now call "Our Credo" *(see Appendix)*. In essence, it says that our first responsibility is to our customers: to give them high quality products at fair prices.

Our second responsibility is to our employees: to treat them with dignity and respect and pay them fairly. They must feel free to make suggestions—without fear of reprisal—and we must provide competent management whose actions are just and ethical.

Our third responsibility is to the communities in which we operate: to be good corporate citizens and to protect the environment.

And then it says our final responsibility is to our shareholders: to give them a fair return.

The Credo is not only our expression of managing the "triple bottom line"—evaluating what we do against economic, social and environmental parameters—but it also talks about our commitment to a fourth constituency: our employees. It's our framework for delivering value to all of our stakeholders. It expresses our values of responsibility, respect, humanity and sustainability. It is not prescriptive. Instead, it outlines fundamental principles that apply to not only our corporate behavior, but also our personal behavior.

Our Credo has proven over time to be a set of principles that appeal to the ethical aspirations of all kinds of people, from all spiritual and religious backgrounds. It gives permission for thousands of individual acts of responsibility. Together, these acts quilt together our overall record of performance.

We're often asked what we do to keep the Credo vital and relevant. At the most basic level, we reinforce that it is an integral part of our strategy for continued growth. We've identified four coordinated strategic principles: remaining broadly based in human health care, managing for the long-term, maintaining our decentralized structure and operating according to Credo values.

Together, these principles form the backbone of our approach to business and, inherently, our approach to our responsibilities. We work hard to make sure that values-based decisions and responsibility for our actions will never be the purview of a corporate program or

OUR CREDO: WHO WE ARE

department rather than our fundamental way of doing business. We consistently resist the bureaucratization of our values, and we do not want to vest ethical authority in any one person or group. Values are everyone's job.

We never underestimate the importance of repetition. I would go as far as to say that the Credo is mentioned in almost every management communication, from speeches to announcements of promotion. It is on display in every building in one of 36 languages and at most workstations. There's no question that it is a part of our daily lives as we make decisions and conduct business.

Importantly, we don't stop at the mere presentation of the Credo. Instead, we challenge our leaders and our employees to filter everything through the Credo.

We have attempted to define the responsibilities of the Credo for our employees in a policy of business conduct. It states, "Though the Credo does not always give specific direction, it tells us that, as a company, we should strive to be trustworthy, to respect all people, to be responsible to our constituents, fair in our dealings, caring of the people we affect and good citizens."

While we've always included Credo components in our executive development programs, we've recently gone a step further by publishing a handbook that details how to use the Credo to make everyday business decisions. Importantly, it shared the stage with four strategic imperatives at a recent meeting of the top tier of worldwide management. The handbook acknowledges that ethical decision-making requires more than integrity—like other business decisions, it requires analytical skills and strategies.

We track how we're doing. We invite employees every few years to complete a Credo survey, a quantitative tool that asks them to rate how well the company management is doing to meet its Credo responsibilities. We take the results very seriously. Every management team is expected to address issues that may be uncovered.

The bottom line is that the Credo is upheld by individuals and their actions. We absolutely must make sure that each of our people sees his or her job in the context of our values. The ethicist Michael Josephson has said of Johnson & Johnson's Credo: "The Credo is much more than an ethics code that tells employees what to do. It is a statement of the company's living heritage that tells employees who they are."

And just who are they? They are the researchers who believed that it was not only possible to prop open a defective heart valve, but to treat it with a pharmaceutical agent so that it would stay propped open. The result? A patient who thanks us because we've given her one more Mother's Day to enjoy her children and grandchildren. They are the technical representatives who sell and service blood typing equipment to hospitals all over the world, and preach the importance of blood donation to everyone who will listen. The result? A vital and vibrant mother, well after the horrifying transfusion of almost 200 units of blood, who would not be alive were it not for the personal sacrifice of many anonymous donors. They are the manufacturing supervisors who stop critical shipments because of the slightest concern over product quality. The result? Highest quality products reaching our customers, and plant workers who know it's not only OK—but critical—to voice concerns. They are the sales assistant who mistakenly received a competitor's bid by fax, and sent it back to the customer without using the information for competitive advantage. The result? An institutional customer who knows they can trust us.

So "who they are" becomes what we are — the world's most trusted healthcare company, seeking not success but significance. For financial success is fleeting, and notoriety even more so. But significance — a legacy that says we have made a difference — is enduring. And it is precisely endurance that delivers value.

I can't emphasize enough the importance of trust, both internally and externally. Inside the company, mutual trust between senior management and company directors makes decentralization possible. Trust binds us together in a way that strict policies and procedures never could; trust allows for the space to move freely and with confidence in the dynamic environment in which we operate. A foundation of trust provides the safety net for the risk taking so essential to innovation.

Externally, trust in our products is as important to our success as any key ingredient. A mother trusts our brand name and is therefore willing to try a high-tech (and, might I add, high margin) liquid bandage on her youngster. Our highly successful relationship with the world's largest retailer is built on the bridge of trust and values initially formed between their leaders and ours. We rely daily on a network of a few critical suppliers who trust us enough to share technological details and cost structures so that we can form the most productive long-term partnerships. We have a documented edge in attracting valuable third-party relationships because of our reputation as a trusted company; an underpinning of our 1999 merger with Centocor, Inc., was the consistency of values shared by our companies.

The net result is that Johnson & Johnson is no longer just a trademark—it is a "trustmark." It is our mission, and today our customers' expectation, that what we bring to the marketplace contributes to people living longer and healthier lives. And that is a huge asset in health care, an area fundamentally built on trust.

In his renowned book *The Fifth Discipline*, author Peter Senge uses something called a "trim tab" to explain certain theories of leverage within a system. In his example he asks, how do you get something really big—like an oil tanker ship—to turn? Well, you move the rudder, of course. But the rudder itself is so big that there's water pressure keeping it where it is. So there is this very small piece—a rudder for the rudder, if you will, called a trim tab, that compresses the water around the rudder to make it easier for the rudder to move through the water and change the direction of the ship. You don't see the trim tab—you probably never even knew it was there—but it makes an incredible difference to the navigation of the ship.

The trust we've earned and will continue to prioritize is like the trim tab for our success. It is that deep, sometimes invisible, point of leverage that makes a huge difference.

Our goal is to have a profound impact on health care. Does that mean relentlessly pursuing cures for the world's most devastating diseases like cancer, heart disease and tuberculosis? If we don't, who will? We recognize that the promise of technology is more than just the application of genius. It is also about cost effectiveness and real advances in the quality of health care and life itself. It's about responsibility and it's about caring and it's about being trustworthy. And these are three attributes I'm proud to see in such abundance at Johnson & Johnson. Our people have the courage to tackle the toughest problems, and they possess the skills and endurance to find solutions, sometimes against great odds. That's the character of the organization, and it is the strength of that character that sustains our success, now, and into the future.

———

William C. Weldon
CHAIRMAN OF THE BOARD AND CHIEF EXECUTIVE OFFICER
JOHNSON & JOHNSON

William C. Weldon is chairman of the board and chief executive officer of Johnson & Johnson. He assumed his current responsibilities in April 2002. Previously he served as a vice chairman of the board of directors and a member of its executive committee. He was elected to the board in February 2001.

Weldon joined Johnson & Johnson in 1971 in the sales and marketing department of McNeil Pharmaceutical. In 1982 he was named manager, ICOM Regional Development Center in Southeast Asia. Weldon was appointed executive vice president and managing director of Korea McNeil, Ltd., in 1984 and managing director of Ortho-Cilag Pharmaceutical, Ltd., in the U.K. in 1986. In 1989, he was named vice president of sales and marketing at Janssen Pharmaceutica in the U.S., and in 1992 he was appointed president of Ethicon Endo-Surgery.

In 1995, Weldon was named a company group chairman of Johnson & Johnson and worldwide franchise chairman of Ethicon Endo-Surgery. In 1998, Weldon was promoted to the executive committee and named worldwide chairman, pharmaceuticals group.

Weldon serves as a member of the board of trustees for Quinnipiac University. He serves on the board of directors and is an executive committee member of the Pharmaceutical Research and Manufacturers of America (PhRMA). He is a member of The Business Council. Weldon also serves on the Liberty Science Center Chairman's Advisory Council.

Weldon was born in Brooklyn, New York, and is a graduate of Quinnipiac University in Hamden, Connecticut. He and his wife are the parents of two children.

OUR CREDO: WHO WE ARE

JOHNSON & JOHNSON

Johnson & Johnson, with approximately 110,600 employees (more than 40,000 in the United States), is the world's most comprehensive and broadly based manufacturer of health care products, as well as a provider of related services, for the consumer, pharmaceutical, and medical devices and diagnostics markets. Johnson & Johnson has more than 200 operating companies in 54 countries around the world, selling products in more than 175 countries.

In 2003, an annual reputation poll conducted by Harris Interactive and published in the *Wall Street Journal* acknowledged Johnson & Johnson for having the best corporate reputation in American for the fourth consecutive year.

Johnson & Johnson's heritage includes a commitment to the community, which comes from a dedication to the principles defined 60 years ago by then Chairman of the Board General Robert Wood Johnson in Our Credo. This living document has been translated into dozens of languages and establishes the company's responsibilities to customers, employees, the communities in which the company operates and to its stockholders.

Johnson & Johnson was founded in 1886 in New Brunswick, New Jersey, by Robert Wood Johnson and two of his brothers, with 14 employees on the fourth floor of a building that once housed a wallpaper factory. New Brunswick remains home to the company's headquarters today. The company was family-owned until it became listed on the New York Stock Exchange in 1944.

For more information, visit: www.jnj.com.
Stock Symbol: JNJ

CODA

"Your role as a leader is to be a steward for future generations."

"The true value of a business leader cannot be judged until he or she has been gone at least ten years—only then can the world determine whether that person's leadership was sound."

"When you make a difficult decision, ask yourself if the decision you are about to make would show integrity, leadership, caring, and dreaming."

"Will the world say a company served as a positive link between the past and the future of their communities; that it added value, and helped society prosper?"

– Marilyn Carlson Nelson

Marilyn Carlson Nelson

**CHAIRMAN AND CHIEF EXECUTIVE OFFICER
CARLSON COMPANIES**

"In the end, doing the right thing will always triumph."
— Marilyn Carlson Nelson

THE LONG VIEW

To my children, grandchildren, nephews, nieces and family members to follow:

My purpose in writing this is to lay down for you what I believe are important truths about business and leadership.

Today we are emerging from a period in American business history in which an obsessive desire for gain led many people to commit acts of fraud, both overt (for which some may find themselves, deservedly, in jail) and moral (which perhaps not technically against the law, were certainly against the common good).

In this personal letter to future shareholders—her descendants—Marilyn Nelson lays out the family's principles of business.

You may someday find yourselves in similar times, and may be tempted to cut a corner or do something that may be legally acceptable but ethically wrong. It is for those times, should they come, that I write you this letter.

When you are hard-pressed to make a difficult decision, either in business or your personal life, I hope that you will always check it against that compass left to us by your ancestor (my father) Curt. He gave us the Carlson Credo precisely to help us make the right choices in difficult times:

THE CARLSON CREDO
Whatever you do, do with Integrity,
Wherever you go, go as a Leader,
Whomever you serve, serve with Caring,
Whenever you dream, Dream with your all,
And never, ever, give up.

When you're making a difficult decision, ask yourself if the decision you're about to make would show integrity, leadership, caring, and dreaming. And, if you make that particular decision, will you be giving up on something you should continue fighting for?

These are indeed hard guidelines to follow when others around you are ignoring the rules and seem to be besting you. But know this: Their win will only be temporary. In the end, doing the right thing will always triumph. It has always been so.

I urge you to always take this long view over one of expedience or convenience. This may seem like lofty and unrealistic advice, but it is what our company and our success have been built on for more than 60 years.

Never forget that your role as a leader is to be a steward for future generations.

Boppa (Curt) managed this company with the idea that it would exist well into future Carlson generations. And I have always considered it my duty to operate the company as if it were in trust for you.

I am, as you will someday be, a living link between the past and the future. The ultimate measure of my success as a leader will be whether or not our company continues to prosper and thrive long after I am gone. It has been written that, "The true value of a business leader cannot be judged until he or she has been gone at least ten years—only then can the world determine whether that person's leadership was sound."

This is the ultimate question which must be answered: Will the world say a company served as a positive link between the past and the future of their communities; that it added value, and helped society prosper?

All companies must be stewards of natural and human resources for subsequent generations around the world. The leader of a company who drives short-term results at the expense of the future is ignoring the judgment of history and the fact that the scorekeeping will continue well beyond the existing generation.

The long-term sustainability and success of any business, or society for that matter, has everything to do with the ability of its leadership to think and act beyond the horizon of the current generation.

Today businesses like ours wield great international influence that reaches beyond business. We find ourselves on center stage, whether we like it or not. Countries look toward American capitalism as either a promise for the future or, as happens all too often, a source of trouble.

I believe, as I hope you will, that it is the duty of those of us in this world who have been blessed with freedom to bring freedom of thought and enterprise to countries constrained by fear and terror.

If we are only seen as taking, and not giving back; if we allow depletion of a people's resources for our own or others' enrichment; and if we allow the destruction of hope in communities and countries in which we operate; we will find this is a short-term, destructive gain and a poisoning approach.

This approach always allows demagogues to take root and grow. It allows hate and discontent to ultimately result in the destruction of innocents, and the end of the destructive system itself.

There is a poem by Edwin Markham that captures what I believe you must always be about. I have always tried to live my life by it, and I hope you will too:

> *He drew a circle…that shut me out.*
> *Heretic, rebel, a thing to flout.*
> *But love and I had the wit to win—*
> *We drew a bigger circle, and drew him in.*

I hope you will see that your role, and the role of our company, is to be a torchbearer of hope for the future. There is no greater ambition or worthy endeavor.

Remember that the greatest philanthropy of all is giving a person a job. To do this, a company must make an honest profit. Never be ashamed of taking a profit for the value your efforts have added. But never let the pursuit of profit become a light that blinds you.

As you lead, be stewards of both financial and human capital. It is a balance of the two that creates success. Balance is the key. Consider the needs of all constituencies—shareholders, employees, customers and the communities in which you operate. An imbalance in favor of one will threaten the whole.

The world will always face problems. The questions I hope you will ask yourself are, "What might I do to be part of the solution? What actions must I take to promote understanding, be more inclusive, show more leadership?"

You must always remember that you are a link in the chain. You do not exist in a vacuum. The actions you take today will influence those who follow you, just as certainly as the actions Curt took to found our family's company in 1938 are influencing your life today.

Boppa, and many of us who followed, have always been very proud of our Swedish heritage. He loved the words of an unpublished poem by the great Swedish-American poet Carl Sandburg, which talks about the responsibility of being true to one's beliefs and values:

> *It has cost to build this nation.*
> *To do it took men willing to throw in all they had*
> *And we've got to let those who now are to shape the future*
> *Know what the present time came from*
> *And what it's worth as a heritage.*
> *For we know when a nation goes down,*
> *When a society or a civilization perishes,*
> *One condition may always be found.*
> *They forgot where they came from.*
> *And the struggles farther along.*

Never forget. Always be true to the timeless values, even in the face of adversity. This philosophy has never failed us, and it will never fail you.

Marilyn Carlson Nelson
CHAIRMAN AND CHIEF EXECUTIVE OFFICER
CARLSON COMPANIES

Marilyn Carlson Nelson is a member of the International Business Council of the World Economic Forum and has led that organization's discussion of the global travel and tourism industry since 1997. She currently serves on the boards of Exxon Mobil Corporation, the Mayo Clinic Foundation and the Singapore Tourism Council. In 2002, she was appointed by President George W. Bush to chair the National Women's Business Council.

Nelson holds the Woodrow Wilson Award for Corporate Citizenship from the Woodrow Wilson Center for International Scholars and the FIRST Award for Responsible Capitalism.

In July 2003, the Swedish American of the Year honor was bestowed upon Nelson by Their Majesties King Karl XVI Gustaf and Queen Silvia of Sweden at her ancestral home in Sweden. She was previously awarded the Swedish Royal Order of the North Star, and Finland's Order of the White Rose for her commitment to preserving and promoting Scandinavian heritage.

Nelson graduated from Smith College with a degree in international economics and attended the Sorbonne in Paris and the Institute des Hautes Etudes Economiques Politiques in Geneva, Switzerland.

CARLSON COMPANIES, INC.

Privately held Carlson Companies—parent of Radisson hotels, T.G.I. Friday's restaurants, Carlson Wagonlit Travel and other travel, hospitality and marketing brands—was founded in 1938 and is in its second generation of family ownership.

Ranked among the largest privately held corporations in the United States, Carlson Companies is based in Minneapolis, Minnesota. Carlson-related brands and services employ about 190,000 people in more than 140 countries. In 2000, 2002 and 2003, Carlson Companies was named to *Working Mother* magazine's list of "The 100 Best Companies for Working Mothers." The company made *Fortune* magazine's 2002 list of "The 100 Best Companies to Work For."

For more information, visit: www.carlson.com.

APPENDIX

Aetna

Allstate

American Standard

Eaton

EDS

General Motors

IBM

Johnson & Johnson

Verizon

BUILDING TRUST

APPENDIX

Aetna

Mission and Values

Our company's mission, values and goals are expressed through The Aetna Way. The Aetna Way, comprising the elements below, encompasses our shared sense of purpose and provides clarity as we pursue our operational and strategic goals:

- **Why We Exist: The Aetna Mission**
- **What We Believe In: Our Values**
- **What We're Trying to Achieve: Our Goals**
- **How We Run Our Business: Our Operating Principles**

Why We Exist: The Aetna Mission
Aetna is dedicated to helping people achieve health and financial security by providing easy access to safe, cost-effective, high-quality health care and protecting their finances against health-related risks. Building on our 150-year heritage, Aetna will be a leader cooperating with doctors and hospitals, employers, patients, public officials and others to build a stronger, more effective health care system.

What We Believe In: Our Values
At Aetna, we put the people who use our services at the center of everything we do and live by a core set of values:

- Integrity
- Quality Service and Value
- Excellence and Accountability
- Employee Engagement

APPENDIX

Aetna continued

What We're Trying to Achieve: Our Goals
We seek to achieve superior customer satisfaction through innovative products, comprehensive health and related benefits choices, effective service and easy-to-understand information.

Our goals are:
- To give individuals and families affordable coverage choices, helpful service and information so they get the financial protection and health care they need — from prevention through chronic and critical care.
- To respect and work effectively with doctors and hospitals by establishing efficient processes and providing prompt claims payments and useful information that helps them provide safe, cost-effective, high-quality health care.
- To provide employers advice, cost-effective benefits choices and programs that improve the health status and productivity of their work forces.
- To partner with brokers and consultants through responsive service, timely information and attractive commissions so they may effectively advise employers on their benefits choices.
- To offer employees an engaging and diverse work environment that permits them to satisfy their professional ambitions, take pride in their contributions and share in Aetna's success.
- To be a leading corporate citizen, improving the quality of life in communities where we live and work.
- To award shareholders a superior return on their investment in our company.

How We Run Our Business: Our Operating Principles
Based on our values, which guide our day-to-day activities, we adhere to specific business practices that help us fulfill our mission, reach our goals, and achieve profitable growth.

APPENDIX

- PLANS: We build and monitor business plans, taking corrective actions on negative variances.
- PRODUCTS: We develop and accurately price innovative products.
- NETWORKS: We develop and manage networks of doctors and hospitals to support multiple product and funding choices.
- ACCESS TO CARE: We provide our members access to cost-effective high-quality health care while accurately predicating and managing medical costs.
- CLAIMS AND BILLING: We achieve timely and accurate claims payments and premium billing and collection.
- PRODUCTIVITY: We pursue continuous productive and process improvement.
- SERVICE: We work together effectively cross the organization to give our customers quality service.
- INFORMATION: We provide objective information to help our members make informed decisions about heir financial and health care needs.
- INTEGRITY: Achieve financial and operational integrity through clear, prompt and reliable information that accurately reflects our financial and operational performance.
- REWARDS: We appreciate effort but we recognize and reward employees for achieving business results.
- SATISFACTION: We deliver superior customer satisfaction.

For more information, visit *www.aetna.com* > About Aetna > Corporate Governance > Code of Conduct

APPENDIX

The Allstate Partnership

Allstate expects you to:

1. **Perform at levels that significantly increase our ability to outperform the competition.**
   Our customers, shareholders and fellow employees deserve first-rate performance that is unequaled in the industry. To outperform the competition, each of us, regardless of job or position, must perform at the highest level possible – every day.

2. **Take on assignments critical to meeting business objectives.**
   Our business objectives are linked to where customer demands and a dynamic marketplace takes us. Based on your skills, experience, and career goals, Allstate expects you to take on assignments that will help our company meet its business objectives.

3. **Continually develop needed skills.**
   Imagine using only the skills of ten, or even five, years ago in today's rapidly changing business environment. We all share the responsibility of developing new skills that are applicable to today's – and tomorrow's – business requirements.

4. **Willingly listen to and act upon feedback.**
   Can you see yourself the way others see you? In a supportive environment, listening to and acting upon constructive feedback from peers, leaders, and customers can improve your performance and enhance your value to Allstate.

5. **Demonstrate a high level of commitment to achieving company goals.**
   Achieving company goals begins with taking the responsibility to understand the goals. Everything you do should align with company goals and contribute to achieving them.

6. **Exhibit no bias in interactions with colleagues and customers.**
   At Allstate, we foster an environment where no individual is placed at an advantage or disadvantage because of his or her background or perspective.

Allstate continued

7. **Behave consistently with Allstate's ethical standards.**
   We're in a business that's built on trust. Any violation of that trust impacts our image and our ability to do business. We expect you to adhere to Allstate's ethical standards and follow the law.

8. **Take personal responsibility for each transaction with our customers and for fostering their trust.**
   Our business is a transaction business, built one employee, one process, and one customer at a time. During any transaction, customers can decide to stay with us or leave us. We all have a personal responsibility to earn and repay the trust customer's place in us — every day.

9. **Continually improve processes to address customers' needs.**
   If we don't serve customers quickly, compassionately and fairly, they'll find some one who will. It's that simple. Each of us must always look for ways to improve our processes and serve the customer better.

You should expect Allstate to:

1. **Offer work that is meaningful and challenging.**
   Everyone should have a job that matters, a job that challenges you to grow and strive to do better. You should also see how your work ultimately touches and creates value for the bill-paying customer.

2. **Promote an environment that encourages open and constructive dialogue.**
   Change and innovation start with your thoughts. Allstate supports a work environment that encourages new perspectives and differing opinions expressed through constructive dialogue.

3. **Recognize you for your accomplishments.**
   Everyone wants to make a difference, and everyone deserves to be recognized when they do. Your accomplishments — whether in the

APPENDIX

area of business performance, professional development, or community service – are important to both Allstate's and your success.

4. **Provide competitive pay and rewards based on your performance.**
   We know other companies would value your services. Our compensation policy is designed to attract, motivate, and retain highly qualified employees with a pay-for-performance system that rewards excellence.

5. **Advise you on your performance through regular feedback.**
   You should always know how well you are meeting your performance standards. If you're not receiving feedback when you need it, feel free to ask for it.

6. **Create learning opportunities through education and job assignments.**
   Whether you need to enhance skills for your present job, or to move on to other jobs, we'll help you with the appropriate learning opportunities.

7. **Support you in defining career goals.**
   Doing what you do best is good for everyone. Allstate will support you in trying to match your skills and aspirations to career goals that are mutually beneficial to you and the company.

8. **Provide you with information and resources to perform successfully.**
   Allstate depends on your skills, ideas, and creativity. We'll make sure you have access to the tools and information necessary for achieving your performance goals.

9. **Promote an environment that is inclusive and free from bias.**
   As individuals, we're all unique. Your background and perspectives are important to Allstate's work environment and business decisions. We value our diversity, and need to continue to leverage the differences among us in both the workplace and the marketplace.

10. **Foster dignity and respect in all interactions.**
    Treating each other with dignity and respect, regardless of job level or relationship, is the standard at Allstate. Nothing less is acceptable.

APPENDIX

Allstate continued

11. **Establish an environment that promotes a balance of work and personal life.**
    We know there's more to life than work. In today's world, juggling work and personal life can be more challenging than ever. We also know that to run a successful business, we have to be there when our customers or business objectives require us to be. Allstate is committed to helping you balance your work and personal commitments.

A Shared Responsibility

The Allstate Partnership is about working together to create an environment in which you can do your best, so the company can do its best. We all share the responsibility to make it work. The company is responsible. Each employee is responsible. Leaders share a dual responsibility, both as employees and as drivers of positive change.

The Allstate Partnership acknowledges that we all have a stake in the success of the corporation, and in creating the high-performance, supportive work environment that will lead to achieving that success.

For more information, visit *www.allstate.com* > About Allstate > View of Corporation Governance Information > Code of Ethics

© Copyright Allstate Insurance Company 1997–00

APPENDIX

Our Mission

Be the best in the eyes of our customers, employees and shareowners.

Our Values

We Are Driven by Customers
We succeed by exceeding customer expectations. Our commitment to premier customer service begins with understanding customer needs. It is realized through the design, manufacture and delivery of quality products and services and the personal support we provide. Each contact with a customer is an opportunity to increase customer satisfaction and win new business.

We Recognize the Importance of Our People
Our people built this business and are the key to its future. We are committed to creating a workplace that is safe, a workplace where diversity is valued, and a workplace that thrives on teamwork and leadership. We are committed to a workplace where individuals are treated fairly and with respect, where all people have the opportunity to expand their skills and take advantage of new opportunities, and where accomplishments are recognized.

We Operate with Integrity
As a company and as individuals, we do the right things and never compromise our values. We honor our agreements and are honest in our communications. Our relationships with co-workers, customers, suppliers, partners and the investor community are based on openness and opportunities for mutual gain. Our sense of responsibility extends to leadership in protecting the environment and good citizenship in the communities where we work.

APPENDIX

American Standard Companies Inc. continued

We Strive for Excellence
No matter how good our products, services, processes and performance, we are dedicated to making them better. We strive for excellence in everything we do by being open to new ideas and better ways of working and not being afraid to take risks. We recognize that each of us can add real value to our business. By approaching our daily work with a passion for innovation and a desire to learn and share that learning with colleagues, we all can make a difference.

We Deliver on Our Promises
We set goals high because we know we can do great things. We treat these goals as promises to our customers, our shareowners and ourselves. Our continued success depends on keeping our promises. Success is measured by the results we produce in customer satisfaction, sales, profitability, investor value and the scope of opportunities we provide for our people.

Frederic M. Poses
CHAIRMAN AND CEO
on behalf of all of our employees around the world

The Values Statement has been translated in 22 languages including English.

For more information, visit *www.americanstandard.com* >> About Us > Our Company Values > Download Values Statement

APPENDIX

E·T·N

Eaton Corporation requires that all directors, officers and employees of Eaton, its subsidiaries and affiliates ("Eaton"), abide by the fundamental principles of ethical behavior listed here in performing their duties.

1. **Obeying the Law**
   We respect and obey the laws, rules and regulations applying to our businesses around the world.

2. **Integrity of Recording and Reporting our Financial Results**
   We properly maintain accurate and complete financial and other business records, and communicate full, fair, accurate, timely and understandable financial results. In addition, we recognize that various officers and employees of Eaton must meet these requirements for the content of reports to the U.S. Securities and Exchange Commission, or similar agencies in other countries, and for the content of other public communications made by Eaton.

3. **Respecting Human Rights**
   We respect human rights and require our suppliers to do the same.

4. **Delivering Quality**
   We are committed to producing quality products and services. Our business records and communications involving our products and services are truthful and accurate.

5. **Competing Ethically**
   We gain competitive advantage through superior performance. We do not engage in unethical or illegal trade practices.

6. **Respecting Diversity and Fair Employment Practices**
   Throughout the world we are committed to respecting a culturally diverse workforce through practices that provide equal access and fair treatment to all employees on the basis of merit. We do not tolerate harassment or discrimination in the workplace.

Eaton continued

7. **Avoiding Conflicts of Interest**
   We avoid relationships or conduct that might compromise judgment or create actual or apparent conflicts between our personal interests and our loyalty to Eaton. We do not use our position with Eaton to obtain improper benefits for others or ourselves. We do not compete with Eaton.

8. **Protecting Our Assets**
   We use Eaton property, information and opportunities for Eaton's business purposes and not for unauthorized use. We properly maintain the confidentiality of information entrusted to us by Eaton or others.

9. **Offering/Accepting Gifts, Entertainment, Bribes or Kickbacks**
   We do not offer or accept gifts or entertainment of substantial value. We do not offer or accept bribes or kickbacks.

10. **Selling to Governments**
    We comply with the special laws, rules and regulations that relate to government contracts and relationships with government personnel.

11. **Political Contributions**
    We do not make contributions on behalf of Eaton to political candidates or parties, even where lawful.

Reporting Ethical, Legal or Financial Integrity Concerns

Any person may openly or anonymously report any ethical concern or any potential or actual legal or financial violation, including any fraud, accounting, auditing, tax or record-keeping matter, to the Director – Global Ethics of Eaton. For reports that are not made anonymously, confidentiality will be maintained to the extent possible while permitting an appropriate investigation.

APPENDIX

The Eaton Values and Philosophy

Eaton's Values:
The Foundation for Continued Success
As a corporation owned by its shareholders, Eaton's fundamental purpose—the reason the company exists—is to operate profitably, provide an attractive return for those who have invested in us and increase shareholder value. Through our long history, we have come to understand that our ability to achieve these business goals depends on our adherence to Eaton's core values:

- Make our customers the focus of everything we do
- Recognize our people as our greatest asset
- Treat each other with respect
- Be fair, honest and open
- Be considerate of the environment and our communities
- Keep our commitments
- Strive for excellence

The Eaton Philosophy:
Excellence Through People
Eaton's success depends on the superior performance of each Eaton employee in support of our customers. Sustained high performance is most likely when employees commit themselves to the goals of the organization. This level of commitment does not just happen; it is created when employees, managers and the company all share certain key beliefs about their mutual responsibilities to one another. The Eaton Philosophy sets out these shared beliefs; it describes a culture in which employees can achieve their full potential to make exceptional contributions, confident that these will be welcomed and rewarded.

Eaton continued

The Eaton Philosophy Statements are to be pursued by every employee at every location. They are to be encouraged and promoted by managers. The company and its employees are jointly responsible for their implementation wherever we do business.

We expect the best of ourselves and each other.
We believe that employees want to do the right thing—for customers, for the company, for one another. Our workplace policies and decisions are based on that premise. By always doing our best, we constantly validate that belief through our actions.

We are committed to attracting, developing and keeping a diverse work force that reflects the nature of our global business.
Our business is global, diverse and highly competitive. Our success depends on our ability to draw the very best from the entire pool of available talent, unlimited by gender, race or any of the other characteristics that differentiate us. We are committed to having a work force that is diverse at all levels, reflecting the diversity of our customers and the varied environments in which we conduct business around the world.

Our communications with one another are open, honest and timely.
Eaton provides the regular, timely information necessary to enable employees to do their jobs effectively, to make decisions, and to achieve the company's goals; employees respond by giving the company their ideas and feedback. The result is an ongoing candid dialog about the business that is fundamental to continuous improvement.

We strive for the active involvement of every employee in our continued success and growth.
High performance comes from employees who are fully involved in their work: thinking, making decisions, sharing ideas. Eaton provides the environment, the tools, the information and the resources to encourage maximum involvement from every employee and team. Employees respond by taking responsibility for their work and their careers.

APPENDIX

We accept the challenge of lifelong learning.
As we face accelerating change in customer expectations, markets, competition and technology, we recognize that we must be lifelong learners to contribute to Eaton's business goals. This means learning skills that enable us to be effective in our assignments and that help us to be adaptable to changing demands. Eaton is committed to providing a learning atmosphere at work.

We do our work with a sense of urgency.
Global competition has quickened the pace of business everywhere. It is no longer enough just to do a quality job; the difference between success and failure is doing a quality job faster than our competitors. Eaton is committed to removing barriers to speed and timeliness throughout the organization. Employees accept the need to balance quality and safety with speed and responsiveness in all we do.

We are accountable for our commitments and expect that our performance will be measured.
Accountability is essential to high performance. Just as Eaton is accountable to investors, customers and employees, employees are accountable for their responsibilities: satisfying customers and contributing to the company's growth and success against world-class competitors. Accountability involves accepting goals that stretch our capabilities and welcoming candid and constructive feedback. Eaton's accountability to employees includes fair and accurate assessment of performance, recognition of achievements and appropriate career development guidance.

Compensation at Eaton is fair and competitive for performance that contributes to the success of the business.
It is essential that employees be rewarded both fairly and competitively for their contributions to Eaton's success. "Fair" means that compensation should reflect the extent of our contributions: the greater the contribution, the higher the reward. "Competitive" means that we will have the opportunity to earn at least as much at Eaton as we would in similar positions at other companies with which we compete.

APPENDIX

Eaton continued

We value employees' ideas, and we purposefully build an environment in which new ideas will flourish.
We grow—as a business and as individuals—when we think actively about our work and feel encouraged to contribute our ideas. This means welcoming and discussing all ideas, the "losers" as well as the "winners," and the ideas that challenge the status quo as much as those in the mainstream. When employees trust the company to value their thinking, we all gain access to a rich vein of creativity and innovation.

For more information, visit *www.eaton.com* > Who We Are > Our Company > Ethics and Governance > Ethical Business Conduct Statement

APPENDIX

EDS is committed to providing high-quality professional services and to conducting business ethically and with integrity. We have earned a reputation as an honest and ethical organization by setting and meeting consistently high standards with clients, employees, suppliers, shareholders and governments. Our solid corporate reputation for integrity is the result of our policy of strict compliance with law and the sum of the ethical decisions of the men and women of EDS. It is their hard work and diligence that engenders successful long-term relationships, open communication, a strong sense of the corporate "family" and a world-class work environment. In short, our corporate commitment to integrity is one of the core values that link each of us, regardless of location, work assignment, language or customs.

To protect our legacy, we must be diligent guardians of our hard earned reputation so that EDS will always be a company we are proud to support. Our commitment to legal compliance must be unwavering and we should accept nothing less than unrelenting honesty and integrity in everything we do.

The Code of Business Conduct reflects and illuminates our corporate standards and provides specific guidance that employees can use to guide their decisions. The standards in the Code of Business Conduct are written with the following decision points in mind; and in fact, the Ethics Quick Test is a good tool to guide every decision-making process:

Is the action legal?

How would it look in the newspaper?

Does it comply with EDS values?

Am I treating others the same way I would choose to be treated?

If I do it, will I feel bad?

APPENDIX

EDS continued

EDS employees should always act with integrity and honesty in every situation. Our corporate standard calls for nothing less than unrelenting honesty and integrity in everything we do and the Code of Business Conduct is written to help us attain that goal.

Though the Code of Business Conduct covers a variety of topics, other resources are available for specific guidance on a particular issue. Those resources include leaders, the Open Door practice, EDS Human Resources, EDS Legal Affairs, and the EDS Office of Ethics and Compliance. The EDS Office of Ethics and Compliance provides advice and counsel to EDS employees around the world. Contact with the Office of Ethics and Compliance can be anonymous.

For more information, visit *www.eds.com* > Investor > Corporate Governance > Code of Conduct

APPENDIX

SUMMARY INDEX

Winning with Integrity

Personal Integrity

Integrity In the Workplace
- Fair Treatment and Respect, Diversity, Health and Safety
- Conflicts of Interest
- Integrity of Our Information and Property

Integrity in the Marketplace
- Gifts, Entertainment and Gratuities
- Fair Competition
- Insider Trading

Integrity in Society and Our Communities
- Government Bribery and Foreign Corrupt Practices Act (FCPA)
- Export Controls
- Integrity Toward the Environment

For more information, visit *www.gm.com* > Investors > Investor Information > Corporate Governance > Winning with Integrity > Full Winning With Integrity Document

BUILDING TRUST

APPENDIX

IBM

IBM Values:

- **Dedication to every client's success.**
- **Innovation that matters – for our company and for the world.**
- **Trust and personal responsibility in all relationships.**

For more information, visit *www.ibm.com*

BUILDING TRUST

APPENDIX

Johnson & Johnson

Our Credo

We believe our first responsibility is to the doctors, nurses and patients,
to mothers and fathers and all others who use our products and services.
In meeting their needs everything we do must be of high quality.
We must constantly strive to reduce our costs
in order to maintain reasonable prices.
Customers' orders must be serviced promptly and accurately.
Our suppliers and distributors must have an opportunity
to make a fair profit.

We are responsible to our employees,
the men and women who work with us throughout the world.
Everyone must be considered as an individual.
We must respect their dignity and recognize their merit.
They must have a sense of security in their jobs.
Compensation must be fair and adequate,
and working conditions clean, orderly and safe.
We must be mindful of ways to help our employees fulfill
their family responsibilities.
Employees must feel free to make suggestions and complaints.
There must be equal opportunity for employment, development
and advancement for those qualified.
We must provide competent management,
and their actions must be just and ethical.

We are responsible to the communities in which we live and work
and to the world community as well.
We must be good citizens—support good works and charities
and bear our fair share of taxes.
We must encourage civic improvements and better health and education.
We must maintain in good order
the property we are privileged to use,
protecting the environment and natural resources.

Johnson & Johnson continued

Our final responsibility is to our stockholders.
Business must make a sound profit.
We must experiment with new ideas.
Research must be carried on, innovative programs developed
and mistakes paid for.
New equipment must be purchased, new facilities provided
and new products launched.
Reserves must be created to provide for adverse times.
When we operate according to these principles,
the stockholders should realize a fair return.

– Johnson & Johnson

For more information, visit *www.johnsonandjohnson.com* > View Our Credo

The Verizon Promise

Our Core Purpose:
We bring the benefits of communications to everybody

Our Core Values:

Veritas Values:
- Integrity
- Respect

Horizon Values:
- Imagination
- Passion

Service: Service is the value that bridges our past and future. It captures our reliability, quality and excellent performance for customers.

Our Core Goal: We will create the most respected brand in communications

Our Future: We will be a successful company when we make and keep our promises to:

- Our customers
- Our communities
- Our shareholders
- Our employees

Verizon continued

Why a Verizon Promise?

Creating a great company – and a great brand – boils down to two simple things:

- Making the right promises.
- Keeping them.

But notice something: the word "promise" is a lot more powerful than the words "strategy" and "performance." That's because strategy and performance are about *corporations*. Promises are about *people*. And that's why we aren't introducing the Verizon Strategy or the Verizon Performance Plan. It's the Verizon *Promise*. Because it's about *people*. It's the people who work for this company who are going to determine whether we keep our promises or not – and whether we win or lose. To understand the Verizon Promise, let's take it step by step, and start with its framework.

Built to Last
There are lots of ways to construct a vision and values platform. The framework used here is based on the bestselling book, *Built to Last*. The authors of this book spent years studying companies that not only had attained world class status – but sustained that level for decades. Companies like Sony and Merck – companies that other companies admire and study, and companies that are, literally, built to last.

Truly visionary companies have a Core Purpose that is a simple and lasting statement of what the company does and why people come to work . . . a set of Core Values that define behavior and attitude in employees . . . one or more Core Goals that really stretch the organization . . . and a vivid description of the Future.

APPENDIX

Our Core Purpose, Values, Goals and Future

The Core Purpose is meant to define the company at its most fundamental. Ours does just that: *We bring the benefits of communications to everybody.* There are several very important words in this statement:

- **"We"** means everyone who works for the Verizon brand.

- **"Benefits"** is a big one, and goes to the heart of why what we do matters. It isn't just the technology we bring. It's the benefits that result. Like connecting human beings to each other; enabling commerce; creating solutions that help families stay in touch and businesses grow. Which brings us to the next word:

- **"Everybody"** Why didn't we specify businesses or government or education or any other segment? Because no matter what communication you're talking about, at some level it's a human being interacting with another human being. If you're thinking, what about business-to-business? Isn't that the hot ticket these days? The companies that win in the B2B war are going to be the companies that understand it's really about /2/ — *Individual to Individual. The end customer is always — always — a human being.*

If this statement brings up images of "all things to all people," or that we intend to gain every human being as our customer, consider this: When the market leader invents the future, everybody benefits. Even those who aren't their customers (yet).

Our Core Values: To guide us day-to-day, the promise includes *Core Values*. The root names for Verizon are "veritas" and "horizon." The basic idea: *building upon our heritage to create the future.* The **"veritas"** values are those we bring with us from our heritage — the foundation upon which to build a new company. These values represent the best traditions of both GTE and Bell Atlantic:

Verizon continued

- **Integrity**: It's how we win the trust of stakeholders, and the primary value we need to deliver on our promises.
- **Respect**: It's how we treat everyone we touch and how we value a diverse world.

The "**horizon**" values represent the attributes we need to deliver the future.

- **Imagination**: It's more than innovation; it's creativity to find the right solution for customers and change the industry as a market leader;
- **Passion**: It's more than speed and determination; it's what fuels our vision, and drives us – and those around us – toward our goal. But there is one value that bridges both our past and our future:
- **Service**: It captures our reliability, quality focus and excellent customer performance as well as our heritage of community service. And it is as critical for the future as it is today.

The most important point about this two-tiered set of values is that we can't win without both. A company can be filled with passion and imagination – but if it can't *deliver* on its potential, keep its promises and *live up to its expectations*, so what?

Our Core Goals: For our Core Goals, we decided on just one: *To create the most respected brand in communications.* The word "brand" includes much more than effective advertising. It's the promise we make to all our stakeholders, and is the sum of millions of interactions we have each day with the people that touch our business. The word "respect" is really at the heart of our vision. Because respect must be *earned*. To do that, you make a promise and keep it: Make a promise and keep it – to all your stakeholders. That is the at the heart of successful brand building.

Our Future: To be a truly great company, all four of our stakeholder groups have to draw real value from Verizon. These four groups will ultimately decide whether or not Verizon becomes the most respected brand in communications. All in all, we are making several huge promises:

APPENDIX

- We're promising the world of communications that we will lead it.
- We're promising customers — and all our stakeholders — that they absolutely can rely on us.
- We're promising ourselves that we're going to settle for nothing less than greatness.

Our new company has the financial strength, the market positioning, the technology, the track record, the leadership, the strategy and — most of all — the people to live up to the Verizon Promise. We have what it takes to make this vision a reality. We can do it. Promise.

For more information, visit *www.verizon.com* > Investor Relations > Company Profile > The Verizon Promise